Samuel Holberry

Revolutionary Democrat
1814–42

Samuel Holberry
Revolutionary Democrat
1814–42

**JOHN BAXTER
and STEVEN KAY**

Copyright © John Baxter and 1889 Books 2025
The moral rights of the authors have been asserted.

The cover image of Samuel Holberry
has been generated digitally from
a photograph taken by 1889 Books of the bust.
Considerable work went into it,
in selecting the right photograph
and working on the image,
so copyright is asserted.

The title font is an enhanced version
of what is believed to be Holberry's signature,
requiring much time to perfect,
likewise copyright is asserted for that also.

www.1889books.co.uk
ISBN: 978-1-915045-44-7

The Six Points of the People's Charter:

- All men to have the vote (universal manhood suffrage).
- Voting should take place by secret ballot.
- Parliamentary elections every year, not once every five years.
- Constituencies should be of equal size.
- Members of Parliament should be paid.
- The property qualification for becoming a Member of Parliament should be abolished.

Contents

Sheffield Around the time of Samuel Holberry

Part One – A Life in Struggle

1. Introduction 1
2. Gamston 1814- 1832 3
3. Woolwich, Gosport, Weedon, Lichfield, Newcastle-under-Lyne, Warrington, Manchester (and Ireland?) 1832-1835 5
4. Sheffield 1835–1837 – first coming 9
5. London 1837-1838 12
6. Sheffield 1838–1840 – second coming 14
7. York. The Assizes March 1840 47
8. Northallerton – A Voice from the Hell-hole 49
9. York Castle September 1841 – June 1842 54

Part Two – The Spectre – Holberry Remembered

10. Sheffield – the Funeral 67
11. Britain – The Breaking Wave of Solidarity
12. Immediate Recognition June -October 1842 74
13. Collections for Mary Holberry Come to an End .. 84
14. Commemorations: the Gravestone, the Bust and Verse .. 85
15. Sheffield – Chartism's Passing 92
16. Holberry in Popular Memory 95
17. Holberry in the 20th Century to Today: Collective Memory and History from Below 97
18. Historians and Holberry 101

Primary Sources for the Study of Samuel Holberry 103

Acknowledgments 225

End Notes 226

Sheffield around the time of Samuel Holberry:

South East View of Sheffield from Park Hill, by William Ibbitt: Sheffield Local Studies Library, Picture Sheffield: w02071 (Date 1855, the Tontine is replaced by Norfolk Market Hall 1851)

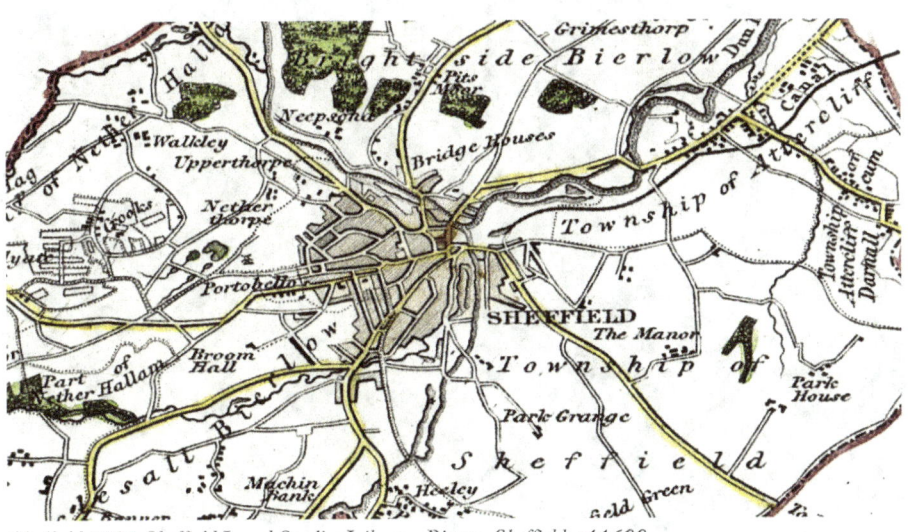

Sheffield 1835 Sheffield Local Studies Library, Picture Sheffield: y11699

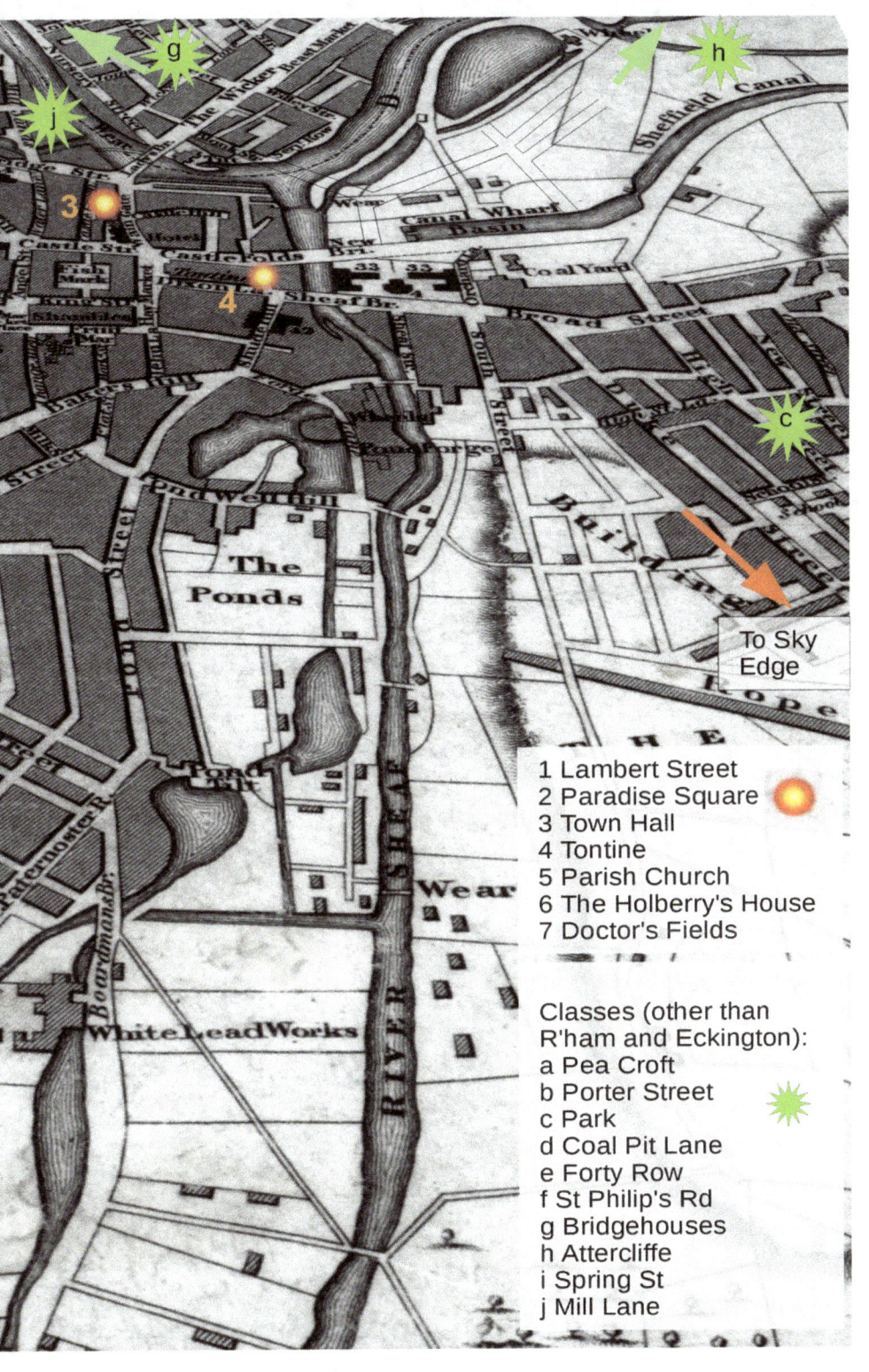

INTRODUCTION

This is more than a biography of a lone individual. The story of Samuel Holberry's life, death and memory invites us through the portal of time to view Sheffield's revolutionary past (and maybe its future). It is the story of a coming together of a exceptional man and a remarkable town. Sheffield was no ordinary Northern town in Holberry's time. He was the latest torch bearer in a long line of radicals and reformers going back at least as far as the time of the Jacobinism of the 1790s (in 1968, historian Gwyn A.Williams dubbed it "English faubourg Saint Antoine").

Due to its trades being organised into workshops run by "little mesters," its working people had long been independent, organised and relatively well educated. 2-2500 were enrolled in the principal reform association, the Constitutional Society – the earliest-formed and strongest anywhere in the land. Here they read the local newspaper, the *Sheffield Register*, owned and edited by reformers Joseph and Winifred Gales.[1] Copies of the Thomas Paine's *Rights of Man* were printed and circulated, of which it was said that every "cutler had a copy."

In 1792, fearing trouble, the Deputy Adjutant-General was sent by the Secretary of War to assess the disposition of the troops. Of Sheffield he said: "Here they read the most violent publications, and comment on them, as well as on their correspondence, not only with the dependent Societies in the towns and villages in the vicinity, but those... in other parts of the kingdom..."[2]

They held meetings attended by thousands to listen to speeches supporting democratic reforms, and signed mass petitions pleading reform. Joseph Gales and later James Montgomery were persecuted and silenced during Pitt's reign of terror and the town's radicals went underground, organising in the workplace.

The lead up to Holberry's time saw great upheaval. Sheffield, being central to the Industrial Revolution, was a magnet to immigrants bringing new ideas and energy. It had no resident aristocracy, the nearest living at Wentworth, and so class deference was uncommon and tensions with a legacy of residual feudalism and a parliament gripped by the propertied classes, never far from the surface.

Sheffield's economy suffered from a number of economic shocks, its workers being very dependent on trade and having next to no safety net in hard times, so dissatisfaction surfaced alongside crushing poverty. As elsewhere, there were protests and calls for reform in the recessionary period around the time of the 1819 Peterloo Massacre.

The "Great" Reform Act of 1832 was a disappointment and seen by many as a betrayal, with only around 4% of the town's population getting a vote. Protests over the election of a candidate who did not have the popular support led to five people being shot dead by the military.

An economic depression in the United States in the late 1830s hit Sheffield badly, dependent as it was on trade with an expanding America.

This was the Sheffield, in the grip of Chartism, into which Holberry arrived.

For those that followed, and are here today, Holberry always remained with us, a touchstone to inspire.

One of the Holberry cascades in Sheffield's Peace Gardens

PART 1 – A LIFE IN STRUGGLE

1. GAMSTON 1814 – 32

Samuel Holberry was born on the 18th November 1814 in the small village of Gamston in rural Nottinghamshire, seven months before the battle of Waterloo (June 18th 1815). He was the youngest of nine children (five sisters and four brothers) born to John and Martha Holberry who rented a cottage on the Tory Duke of Newcastle's estate which included the village. His father was a labourer on the Duke's estate and all the family worked on the land[3].

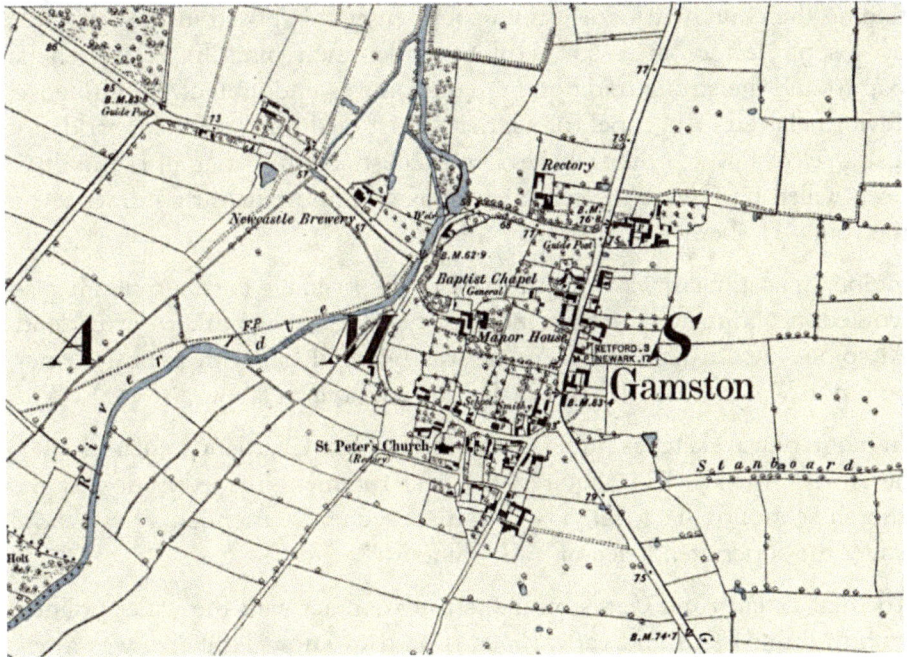

Gamston, where Holberry spent seventeen years, was described in a Nottinghamshire directory of 1832 as a "neat village" situated on the east bank of the River Idle that was 3.5 miles south of the small town of East Retford. At the time there were close to sixty individual houses, cottages and other premises. In the early 1830s there was a public house, significantly named the Newcastle Arms, two shops (a grocer/draper's and another unclassified shop), a shoemaker, a tailor, a blacksmith, a wheelwright and a converted corn mill now making cotton/linen textiles with bleaching grounds in the meadows by the river (firm of Haworth and Buckle). There were around eight "farmers" listed. Some had been listed in a directory as "cottagers" or smallholders and who may have been the survivors of an enclosure of local common land six years before his birth. Others were, in all likelihood, tenants of the Duke of Newcastle. The population had shifted downwards from an estimated 383 to 306 inhabitants between 1821–31. This might reflect the "forced migration" that enclosure could initiate but may have just reflected economic stagnation in the area. The village had an Anglican church, St Peter's. Its rector in the late 1820s early 30s was the Reverend Joshua Brook.[4]

Another key religious group in the village were the General Baptists who had a meeting room in the village. When the Reverend Dan Taylor, founder of the General Baptist New Connexion tired of the Wesleyans, he travelled to Boston where he knew there was General Baptist church but, finding the church at Gamston en route, he was baptised in the river Idle by Joseph Jeffery in 1763.[5] Holberry identified himself as a General Baptist and the strong tradition in Gamston was undoubtedly an influence. Taylor believed in a gospel for all: that Christ died for the whole world, not just a select few. He didn't believe in predestination – that all events have been willed by God. This can be seen as an important early influence on the young Holberry's philosophy on life.[6]

Holberry, as a child, was sent to work in the riverside cotton mill. He also worked, no doubt with family members as a seasonal worker on the land. At some stage in his early teens he was boarded out with a local farmer, Solomon Waterhouse of nearby Clayworth as a farm labourer.

In biographical sketches published in the English Chartist Circular in 1843, he is said to have had acquired the first rudiments of education at the church school of his local village, and subsequently attended a day school under the superintendence of a Mr Blincorn."

To what extent rural Gamston had strong contact with the wider political world of the 1820s and early 1830s is hard to know. Holberry was a few months old when Waterloo took place and five years old when Peterloo happened. The country experienced agrarian depression in the decade after Waterloo (1815). Radical politics, after the repression of two waves of popular radical agitation taking place between 1816–20, were still promoted in the 1820s and early 1830s in the guerrilla warfare waged by printing presses and unstamped paper sellers in defiance of the Stamp Act.[7]

Everyday political corruption, the buying of votes and other forms of electoral bribery promoted by landed oligarchs like the Duke of Newcastle continued on the political surface of the world he inhabited. Spectacularly this blew up into a national scandal highlighted in the power struggle to control the local East Retford parliamentary seats, with the Duke of Newcastle battling the Fitzwilliam family interest in 1827–8. Exposure of bribery meant East Retford faced losing its parliamentary representation.[8]

From his later life events, it is doubtful that Holberry was getting a radical political education in his birthplace though events occurred there he might have gone back to draw lessons from. Rural poverty was rife in the agricultural depression in the 1820s. The local enclosure and its effect might have added to the burdens of everyday survival.

The downward shift in Gamston's population in the 1820s possibly reflected the enclosure's impact on the numbers of small holders and this was probably manifested in the population drift to nearby towns with more promise of work. Holberry's parents were waged land workers on an aristocratic estate. Some of his male relatives showed there were other routes out of Gamston. The biographical sketch of Holberry offers clues claiming that: "the monotony of a farm labourer's existence had no attractions for the subject of this sketch; of an ardent temperament, he was anxious to see the world." One of Holberry's elder brothers had joined the army and six of his uncles (from both sides of the family) had been soldiers. Tall tales of military exploits and distant lands and a sense of patriotism seem to have stirred his mind. He later observed in the context of his joining the army, "that all my relations are Conservatives." Aged 16, he attempted to join the Army in 1831. This attempt failed but a year later on 24th March 1832, still under age, at 17, he was signed up on for the 33rd Regiment of Foot, receiving the sum of £2 10s. The record states that he was still only 5'6". His army career was perhaps to see the making of the man in more than one sense.[9]

2. ARMY SERVICE 1832–35

Holberry, private 746's military career has been previously constructed by speculation but now, using information from General Muster Books and Pay Lists and the military magazine *United Services Journal* which posted the locations of regiments in the British army on a quarterly basis, it is a little clearer.[10] In mid-1832 Holberry's, intended regiment had just returned from a tour in Jamaica. He marched with other new recruits to Coventry and on to Fort Cumberland in Portsmouth where he joined with the 33rd regiment in early May. In July the regiment transferred to Weedon barracks in Northamptonshire. Weedon's Royal Military Depot established from 1803, with its strategic canal connections, housed industrial scale arms and ordnance stores.

The 1832 Reform Act created some new urban constituencies with a restricted urban franchise that excluded the majority of workers. This exclusion and the perceived deception of the political classes caused widespread disillusionment which boiled over at some of the hustings., Sheffield included, where 5 were shot dead by the military. Holberry's regiment appears to have remained on standby at Weedon, but a detachment of the 33rd Foot was, for example involved in the election riots at Walsall.[11] On 14th August Holberry was detached to Dudley, so he may have been involved.

He returned to Weedon in January 1833, and spent 5 days in hospital, then went on detachment to Northampton where he remained until April 1834. Northampton (population of 15,351) was the centre of the leather processing and shoemaking industries. The shoemakers had a union that covered the towns and villages in the area. It is suggested by the 1843 biographical sketch that Holberry experienced political awakening at a Northampton night school. The National Union of the Working Classes, a national radical political body committed to democratic political reform that had sprung up in the Reform bill crisis years 1830–32 was backed by shoemakers and organised meetings in the local area during 1833. Holberry possibly came into contact with radical workers at night school or in local taverns. He also may have witnessed in his official duties forms of radical political activity in the small towns and villages of the area.

Northampton was the location for a rally against the Irish Coercion bill in March 1833 and a July protest against the police brutality exhibited in the breaking up of a NUWC meeting in London's Cold Bath Fields ('Calthorpe Street affair') in May. The town had four identified sellers of the radical unstamped press who operated in defiance of the law. This period and into 1834 witnessed industrial unrest in the central and eastern Midlands associated with Owenite-influenced syndicalist unionism (trying to create one big union covering all trades) through the newly formed Grand National Consolidated Trades Union. The Northampton and Daventry shoemakers worked to make links with the GNCTU and showed solidarity with the GNCTU's fight for unionisation that climaxed in the Derby employers lockout (1833–4) of GNCTU members. Holberry may have possibly policed meetings and he will have been aware of what role the army generally played. In a recollection of him and his behaviour given in 1840 one testifier suggested he had confronted people who had taken "promises" instead of oaths to promote their cause. This is suggestive of action against trade unionists aware of and taking heed of the basis of the Tolpuddle labourers' prosecutions in Dorset that year.[12]

Weedon Barracks

There is some indication that Holberry was for quite some time in his army life still locked into the family mindset of his upbringing, and relatives who were soldiers. He had been sworn in to the Orange Lodge by some of his barracks mates.[13] This swearing in was in defiance of two sets of army general orders issued in the 1820s prohibiting this. The Lodge was a civilian loyalist ultra-Protestant body that had taken root in the British Army despite official disapproval. Seen through an early 19th century lens, and outwith its Irish roots, the Orange Society's principles of loyalty to the king and defending the English Constitution and the gains of the Glorious Revolution of 1688 from foreign interference from Rome may go part way to explain its appeal to young Holberry.

But, by the early 1830s rumours were surfacing suggesting that the Lodge's head, the Duke of Cumberland, had with his deputy, Colonel Fairman, been plotting a coup to depose William IV and also his potential heir, Princess Victoria. There were claims the Orange Lodge had 500,000 armed supporters primed for action in Britain. Joseph Hume and other radical MPs were able to further expose this through a parliamentary inquiry in 1835.[14] This successful investigation originated in the public challenges to the Duke of Cumberland by a Sheffield Orange lodge master in Sheffield. It was this affair that caused Holberry to resign from the Orange Society.

The ECC biographical sketch says he was briefly in Ireland which has led to speculation on how he may have viewed his Orangeism in the light of suppression of Irish nationalism. The other evidence does not support this, though the regiment was sent to Ireland in the summer of 1835 after Holberry was discharged. However, an intriguing report in *The Liverpool Standard* of October 14th 1834 gives details of a company of the 33rd lending assistance at a warehouse fire: fortuitously they were "passing through the town."[15]

We are told, somewhat cryptically, that at his Northampton night school he acquired "really useful knowledge" and that:"As his mind improved, he began to see through the false glare of military glory which had so much enchanted him when a boy." There certainly was a change of heart and the swirl of events being played out around him locally and wider afield was part of it.

Nationally, the Whig government had pulled up the electoral drawbridge after their 1832 franchise reforms left the millions without a vote. They were repressing radical 'unstamped' newspaper sellers. The Whigs had earlier passed the notorious Anatomy Act (paupers' bodies given to medical schools for dissection) in 1832. The Coercion Act introducing martial law for Ireland in 1833 was followed by the enacting of a heartless poor law reform introducing a workhouse-only basis for poor relief for England in 1834. In early 1834, as the Owenite-led Derby strike was being defeated, the government had transported six Dorset farm labourers (the "Tolpuddle Martyrs") who had sworn oaths in joining a union linked to the GNCTU. The 1797 Mutiny Act, that supposedly was directed at members of the armed forces taking secret oaths, was used to banish farm workers to the other side of the world.[16]

April 1834 found Holberry on detachment in Stafford, then to Nantwich in July, then to Oldham and Eccles. He was furloughed during November and December of that year and in 1835 was on detachment at Chester.

The records also tell us that his duties twice included escorting deserters alongside one of the corporals of the regiment, marches that took many days.

A posting to Ireland loomed.[17] Holberry's regiment was indeed deployed to Ireland, but perhaps significantly he decided not to go there. It can only be conjecture what stories he had heard about things like the Tithe Wars from other soldiers.

Ahead of this expected posting, Holberry had come to a decision that was probably informed by the acquisition of a mature radical viewpoint. He then borrowed money from family and with £20 bought himself out of the army (this loan he paid back over the following three years). He was given an honourable discharge with testimony to his character in April 1835 after three years and twenty five days service.[18] The regiment shortly after sailed to Ireland and was in Dublin in June and then was sent to Newry in August 1835.[19]

On a visit to Gamston, Holberry burned all the letters he had written home from his army postings – evidence of his new "disgust for the life of a soldier." His political awakening, in all likelihood involved embrace of radical reform politics, views on the emancipation of oppressed communities and his disavowal of Orangeism. Within a few weeks he set off for a new life in the cutlery metropolis (just under 100,000 inhabitants) of Sheffield, forty miles to the north-west. His wife told the sketch writer in 1843 that Holberry was radicalised before she met him and that could only mean while in the army. It may connect with what he had been asked to do and what he heard others in his army circle had done. It also probably involved reading political literature.[20]

3. SHEFFIELD 1835–37 – first coming

Things appeared more promising for Holberry arriving in Sheffield in the late spring of 1835. The town had at least 100,000 inhabitants and was growing rapidly A trade boom was in full swing. He found lodgings and then found work at Abraham Howe's cooperage (premises in Eyre Lane 1833 and at 66 Charles Street in 1836). He worked for Howe for over a year and then in the autumn of 1836 moved on to John Baines, Spirit Merchant who had premises at 11 Howard Street. His trade was mentioned as "rectifying distiller" which in effect meant mixing and bottling of spirits and cordials. He was with Baines in regular work till the winter of 1837 when commercial problems left his employer reluctantly letting him go.[21]

A shock to the local economy, however, hit in 1836 when bank speculation and failures in North America hit trade in Britain. Sheffield sold a third of its cutlery ware to America and the commercial crisis started to bite. Holberry worked as skilled worker in the more secure drink trade and his wages were steady for a while at 25 shillings – 30 shillings a week. This in the wage hierarchy of the town was in the middle range.[22]

Holberry was courting. He had met Mary Cooper from Oakes Green in Attercliffe, two years his junior, at nineteen.[23] John Cooper, her father, was a maltster/labourer, or her brothers, may have been Chartist activists, later on; however, we don't have evidence that the Cooper family or young Holberry were directly involved in radical politics at the time of his arrival. What is certain is that they were living through politically heightened times, a prelude to Chartism. Events further gave encouragement to engage in political practices.

Oakes Green, Attercliffe, Sheffield Local Studies Library, Picture Sheffield: s11672

The local political scene was heavily over-shadowed by the events following the Reform Bill, passed in June 1832, and protests over the result of the first election which led to a horrific bloodbath in Sheffield on the 14th December when the front rank (20 men and a corporal) of two troops of the 18th Irish Foot fired a fusillade into the protesting crowd in Waingate with five killed on the spot.[24] Afterwards, local veterans of 1790s Jacobinism (Painites and supporters of the principles of the French Revolution) together with post war (1815–20) radical veterans came to the fore again locally. They were supported by democracy-minded trade union leaders who had established a trades council which, as the Trades General Union in 1832, had taken on a political role, financially supporting the popular (and unsuccessful pro-further reform) local candidate in the 1832 general election.[25]

Sheffield contained a nucleus of a few hundred surviving earlier generation radicals. This included, William Lee, back from transportation.

He served in Portsmouth's naval hulks for being a member of a secretive United Britons revolutionary group connected to Colonel Despard's 1802 plan for a coup starting in London.[26] Several members of the Wolstenholme family linked to Scotland Street Methodist New Connexion chapel were similarly "Despard's men" and connected to the two preceding radical "generations." These activists intersected with some of the town's leading trade unionists whose later testimonials at commemorative gatherings in the 1840s reveal they had organised workers to join the massive 5000-strong Peterloo protest in the Brocco (a large sloping open space with distinct brown earth on north western edge of town) in late October 1819.[27]

In the 1830s there were claimed to be 8,000 paid-up union members in thirty plus trade unions. There had been some links with the Owenite GNCTU in 1833–34 and local lodges formed. The unions campaigned to have the six Tolpuddle transportees returned with a large indoor rally on the 9th April 1834 and made contributions to national petitioning activity. Industrial solidarity extended outwards. The "United Trades of Sheffield" raised funds for Staffordshire Potteries' strikers in 1836–7.[28] Where organised labour didn't intercede, the angry masses, sometimes with strong moral justification, took things into their own hands, as with the 1835 physical attacks on the Charles Street Medical School premises where paupers' bodies from the poorhouse were unrestrictedly given to be dissected as specimens.[29]

In the 1830s, Sheffield seemed slow to establish a Radical Association as nearby Barnsley had done. A network of these was created during the mid-1830s tours of Irish- born, London based ex-MP and lawyer, Feargus O' Connor who later recalled his hostile public reception by some in Sheffield in 1835.[30] There may have been a local RA in place but such a proto-Chartist group was not reported till the brief parliamentary campaign of London radical journalist John Bell in an 1836 local parliamentary by-election when the sitting MP, lawyer John Parker (son of veteran local magistrate, Woodthorpe country house owner, significant landowner and banker, Hugh Parker), had to temporarily resign and seek re-election on obtaining government office. Parker won again with most of the 3500 electors behind him, but Bell's candidacy and the political pantomime of election hustings served some politicising purpose.[31] The following year, strikes in the file and building trades in 1837 saw the strength of organised labour in the town further displayed.[32]

Other popular campaigns commenced. Radical minded veterans like James Wolstenholme (detained with his father William under Habeas Corpus for six months in Winchester jail in 1817 for insurrectionary activity) and his "next generation" 34-year-old son, also James, with other local radical nonconformists and trade unionists, commenced campaigning against the harsh New Poor Law workhouses. The Whig government appointed travelling commissioners to bring these to the region and the wider North.[33] Did Holberry attend any meetings or meet some of these people that he would interact with later in a second Sheffield coming in 1838–39? We have no evidence but there is every chance he and Mary were faces in the Sheffield election crowds gathered at the hustings in the mid-1830s parliamentary elections.

Holberry was informed he would be soon laid off in mid-autumn of 1837[34] at the very time the Sheffield Working Men's Association (first local Chartist organisation) was emerging with its leadership dominated in the first instance by a mix of small master employers (like iron founder and poet Ebenezer Elliot) and skilled elite artisan tradesmen and workmen (such as Michael Beale, a watchmaker, and William Gill, a bone scale cutter).[35] Holberry's political sensibilities had doubtless picked up the growing potential for a new political movement. He may have been on the streets sensing popular mood during the sullen, working class cold-shouldering of the official celebrations of Queen Victoria's Coronation months earlier in June 1837.[36] There was a groundswell for a new movement to tap into. The SWMA held its first official activity in October which Holberry may have witnessed.[37] However, by now, his employer had provided sound references and advice on the best London employers to approach. With some confidence Holberry left for the capital.

4. LONDON 1837–8

In London late in 1837 Holberry soon found employment on the banks of the Thames in the heart of the City. We know where he was working but not exactly who his employer was. He may have worked at a large riverside brewing and distilling enterprise run as

Calvert's Hourglass Brewery at 89 Upper Thames Street or some smaller distilling enterprise in that street.³⁸

Holberry was in London for at least ten months and he told a prison inspector in 1840 that it was in London he joined the Chartists.³⁹ We could speculate that he gained a heady dose of radical politics in the company of a young George Julian Harney and his circle of veteran Spencean revolutionaries (involved in attempts at insurrection in 1816–17 and 1820, including the 1820 Cato Street plot) in a branch of the London Democratic Association close to his lodgings. In correspondence between Harney and Holberry five years later in 1842 and evidenced later, there is, however, no suggestion on either side of any previous familiarity.

The fact is that all we have concerning London is Holberry said he joined the Chartists there and it is more likely he met up with one of the more militant rapidly growing LDA groups such as City, Tower Hamlets and Southwark branches than the staid respectable craft artisans and lower professionals in a branch of the much smaller London Working Men's Association fronted by William Lovett or among the older district based Radical Associations in the City.⁴⁰ Being in London and in its heart with Westminster (and the Palace Yard meeting space used by radicals) around a mile and a half away, brought Holberry close to the national political cockpit. We have no evidence of his actual activity but he claimed his Chartism began in London.

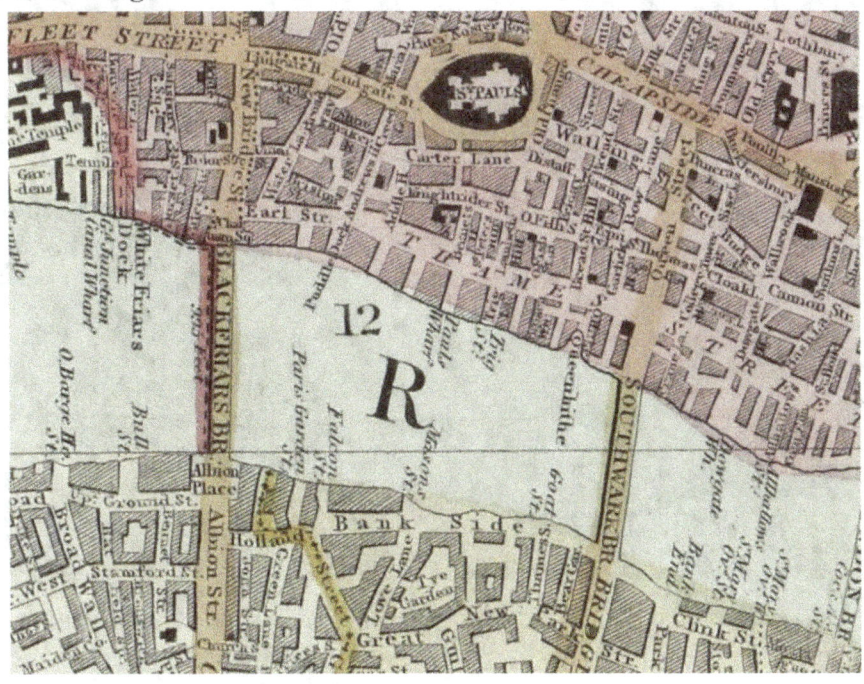

5. SHEFFIELD 1838–1840 – SECOND COMING

In the autumn of 1838 Holberry received a letter from Baines, his former Sheffield employer. It was a job offer and he returned to Sheffield. He renewed his relationship with Mary and they married on 23rd October 1838 at the Parish Church.[41]

Mary's address on the marriage certificate is given as St George's Terrace (it can be reasonably safely assumed she was, at the time, in service there). Samuel's address was Eyre Street, and they subsequently moved to Eyre Lane, which was in one of the slightly better parts of town, according to the 1848 *Report on the Sanitary Condition of the Borough of Sheffield*.[42]

Eyre Lane: Sheffield Local Studies Library, Picture Sheffield: s15510

Cottages on Eyre Lane: Sheffield Local Studies Library, Picture Sheffield: s15509

How quickly Holberry re-engaged with the Chartist movement, we don't know. His wife's account cited in 1843 testifies to his joining the Sheffield Working Men's Association, then established in George Street, before the year was out.[43] The earliest evidence of any leadership role were in the accounts of fellow activists reflecting on the churchyard protests in the autumn of 1839.

Sheffield Chartism had been slow to progress beyond small scale indoor meetings in rooms rented from the Mechanics Institute and in back street public houses that led eventually to a move in 1839 to a new headquarters in an old schoolroom in Fig Tree Lane at a 10 shillings a week rent.[44] The 1st May 1838 had seen national Chartist figurehead, Feargus O'Connor speaking at the Town Hall. The first large rally was held in September 1838 in open fields off Penistone Road on the northern edge of town. Roscoe fields were in the vicinity of an old foundry, Roscoe Place. Any number from 4,000–40,000 attended but probably close to 20,000. The weakness in the local movement was seen in borrowed banners from Manchester and the need to have speakers shipped in from established centres of moderate Chartism like Birmingham as well as Manchester. The lack of preparedness was instanced by a wooden platform that physically collapsed.[45]

The Sheffield Chartists had elected William Gill as Convention (Chartist assembly/alternative parliament) delegate at Roscoe Fields. His attendance at the London Convention from February 1839, fund raising (National Rent) and the collecting of signatures for the national petition produced more activity in Sheffield, its out-villages, and eastwards into the wider Don valley and nearby parts of Lincolnshire, Nottinghamshire and Derbyshire.[46]

The local Chartist membership grew with local area meetings in public houses and on street corners as winter turned to spring. Collections of signatures for the national petition(to call for universal suffrage, annual parliaments, ending property qualifications for MPs and paying them, equalisation of voter numbers in constituencies and a secret ballot) and collection of funds as "national rent" were a feature of organised street level activities.[47]

Paradise Square today. The first floor doorway in the left of the picture originally had steps leading up to it from where the speaker could address the crowd, the square's acoustics allowing everyone to hear

The next big open air rally took place at Whitsun 1839. Part of a national plan for "simultaneous meetings", a rapidly filling Paradise Square basked in sunshine on Monday 20th May. Chartist contingents, after parading through parts of the town, marched into the square. Estimates vary from 3,000–20,000. It makes sense that Holberry and Mary would be there. The meeting was poised to see the national impact of the presentation to Parliament of the 1.2 million signatures contained in the Chartist national petition.[48]

The lead in chairing was taken by a 34-year-old filemaker, James Wolstenholme (the younger). James and his father James (detained with his own father William and his brother Thomas under the suspension of Habeas Corpus Act in Winchester gaol for six months in 1817 for planning an insurrection) had become recently anti-Poor Law supporters of the Reverend Joseph Rayner Stephens, a renegade Methodist with his own chapel in Ashton-under-Lyne. Stephens had joined with factory reformer Richard Oastler to found a national anti-Poor Law campaign responding to the introduction of the Poor Law Amendment Act of 1834.

It was a crowd buzzing with expectation. Two of the foremost national Chartist leaders were billed to speak. However, Feargus O'Connor (double-booked and attending the vast West Riding meeting that day) and John Frost from Newport in Wales (delayed trying to gain the youthful militant Henry Vincent's release from recent arrest) and others sent last minute apologies. The local "platform" rose to the challenge.

The meeting was a success. The *Sheffield Independent* newspaper cryptically noted something that hinted at what was effectively a left wing shift in Sheffield Chartism. Apart from the "next generation" firebrand, James Wolstenholme jnr, chairing, the paper noted of the platform that day was characterised, "with a change of personnel… a total change of speakers." This was a direct reference to the absence of the small employers, skilled craftsmen and respectable trade unionist leaders of the local Chartist movement in 1838. Such people had promoted Gill's candidacy for Convention delegate. Gill was present and reported on his largely effective missionary work in South Yorkshire and the North East Midlands. The *Independent* referred by implication to the contributions of Wolstenholme, to Peter Foden, a radical Christian from the Independents, a baker by trade, and William Barker, the outspoken radical-minded leader of the town's bricklayers union.

In late May and early June, moves to present the national petition and the frustrations caused by national governmental upheaval which delayed it, provoked popular anger that itself invited the increasingly repressive interventions by the state against leading figures and the Chartist Convention itself. The defeat of Lord Melbourne's government on the constitution of Jamaica bill and would be Tory successor as Prime

Minister, Robert Peel's, subsequent clash in May 1839 with the Palace over the political associations of "bed chamber ladies" delayed the national petition's presentation till June. The Whigs regrouped and were invited back into power. The Chartist national petition was rejected in early June by the House of Commons, and the forty nine member National Convention began planning a series of escalating counter measures or "ulterior measures." These were designed to escalate from boycotting taxed goods like alcohol, removing savings from savings banks, exclusive dealing to penalise anti-Chartist business people, to general strikes and defensive armed preparations to add to the pressure for reform. The general strike was originally planned to be a month-long stoppage "the sacred month" but the National Convention fell to disagreeing about its chances of success and was at the last minute reduced to a day's action, followed by protests for three days.[49]

Larger meetings soon resumed with Sheffield seeing Feargus O'Connor's visit on the evening of 27th June to Paradise Square, again chaired by "Young" Wolstenholme. The chair challenged the legitimacy of the action of Lord John Russell (Home Secretary) encouraging middle class anti-Chartist Armed Associations and evoked the necessity of armed defensive preparations. In support, O'Connor saw the "Higher Authority" derived from the masses justifying counter force, warning: "the first shot that was fired on them… would be the signal of general revolt."[50]

In the face of repression the Chartist national Convention moved from London to what it believed to be a more friendly environment in Birmingham in early July. This was undermined when the Birmingham authorities sent for a detachment of London Metropolitan police who brutally attacked the crowds of Convention supporters (the "Bull Ring riots") and arrested some key delegates who challenged their action.[51]

In Sheffield, meetings and street and neighbourhood campaigning increased consequent on the events in Birmingham. On Monday 15th July another meeting, chaired by a young cutlery worker James Birks, was held in Paradise Square where 'Young' Wolstenholme was chosen to go to London as a replacement Convention delegate for the weary, financially impoverished and disillusioned Gill.[52] Some visiting speakers, like another recently returned political transportee from Van Dieman's land, Barnsley linen weavers trade union leader and Irishman, William Ashton, articulated a belief that repression required the people to be armed to defend themselves from physical attack. Local leaders, Peter Foden and William Barker (highly articulate bricklayers union leader), also seemed to accept that government repression was taking people to the brink of violent confrontation. Wolstenholme led the several thousand hearers through the list of the Convention's recommended "ulterior measure" tactics for public acclamation one by one. The political temperature was rising.

Local Chartists anticipated local restriction on meetings in public places by switching to innovative semi-religious campaigning led by Foden (an Independent chapel lay preacher and, by trade, a successful baker) who started "street preachings" on Tuesday 16th July. The following day two public meetings were held, an early evening Paradise Square meeting moved down to the New Haymarket later in the evening.

The next night,[53] on Thursday 18th, the Sheffield Chartists began the "ulterior measures" tactic of encouraging exclusive dealing or boycotting anti-reform shopkeepers. James Duffy, the Irish community's leader and a strong O'Connellite, but who now moved towards Chartism's call for democracy and Irish freedom, presided at a quarter full Paradise Square. Foden read out the names of forty-six businesses to boycott.[54] On Friday night the supporters of the movement gathered again in Paradise Square to hear Wolstenholme's letter from London detailing events at the Convention.[55]

The town authorities could take this surge of militant public display no more. On Saturday 20th a warning letter was circulated about the town from the Town Clerk, Albert Smith, declaring future meetings in Paradise Square illegal. The Chartists gathered a couple of hundred yards away in the Haymarket as a response later that day.[56] Sunday saw a further response with a defiant Foden organising street preaching in three public spaces. In the morning in Barker's Pool in the town centre, close to West Bar and the old workhouse site in the afternoon and at the south end of town on Sheffield Moor, at the Old Sugar House, a deserted industrial site in the early evening.[57]

The following week, on Monday 22nd July, Paradise Square was defiantly three quarters occupied, with James Birks and Peter Foden the main players. The following night another local activist spoke: the soon to be proven revolutionary, James McKetterick, another Irishman, brushmaker by trade and active in the Brushmakers' Society. The meeting heard extracts from a sent by Wolstenholme in London, saying they were on the edge of revolution and that he had been dining with revolution-minded delegates from the Convention like Dr Taylor and a London based Polish exile, Major Beniowski. He also recommended arming. The meetings continued nightly in Haymarket and the street preaching continued on Sunday.[58]

V. R.
ILLEGAL MEETINGS.

It having appeared on the OATH of several Inhabitants before the Magistrates, THIS DAY, that the Meetings of the Parties calling themselves CHARTISTS, which have lately been frequently held in this Town, have occasioned considerable alarm and fear, and been productive of GREAT and ILLEGAL EXCITEMENT, the Magistrates feel it their duty TO PREVENT THE HOLDING OF ANY FUTURE MEETING of a like nature: and

Hereby give Notice,

That in case any such Meeting be again assembled, efficient means will be resorted to for dispersing the same, and the Magistrates request all Masters and Parents to *keep their Servants and Families at home.*

BY ORDER OF THE MAGISTRATES,

Town-Hall, Sheffield, Tuesday, 13th Aug. 1839, Five o'Clock. **ALBERT SMITH.**

RIDGE, PRINTER, MERCURY-OFFICE, KING-STREET, SHEFFIELD.

More meetings continued the following week as the month of August neared. Some were smaller scale street meetings with an aim of recruiting and promoting exclusive dealing. A Monday rally was postponed for a week waiting on Convention decisions. This was eventually held on 5th August and was defiantly located in Paradise Square and addressed by a leading West Riding Chartist, William Thornton. Another two of Holberry's future local collaborators in revolution, a painter called Thomas Bradwell and James Boardman, an Irish bricklayer, spoke at this meeting. Wolstenholme, back from London at this meeting highlighted the repressive nature of the police and army and reminding his fellow citizens of the brutal shootings of the 14th December 1832 after the contested general election and the cover up by the coroner. "That job would not have been wrapped up if the persons killed had been middle class men," was his verdict.[59]

The local authorities in Sheffield now started acting to curb public meetings. Things came to a head in mid-August when nationally the Chartist Convention called for one of the harder sanctions from the ulterior measure menu to be carried out. The Convention was struggling to get unanimity and the original "sacred month" national strike that had been planned was watered down to three days of action' involving strikes on 12th, 13th and 14th August 1839.

Monday 12th August proved to be a very dramatic day for Chartism in the town. A few thousand gathered with Foden and visitors Thornton and Clark in Paradise Square at 9 a.m. As more people arrived, they heard Wolstenholme promoting sending a Memorial to the Queen challenging state repression and, significantly, supporting Irish freedom, calling for repeal of the Act of Union of 1801. He was supported by another young activist, Charles Fox, a cabinet maker from Heeley. Fox, as did Foden later in the day, made reference to being armed and acquiring powder and shot. He used euphemisms like "biscuits" for muskets and "bags of flour" for powder. This was going to catch up with him. The meeting called for an adjournment and for reconvening at 4 p.m, but sections of the crowd went on an impromptu procession with their banners and held another meeting outside the Corn Exchange where a collection was made for a band

Wiley's shop: old no.12 Haymarket

for the afternoon's procession. Outside the premises of Thomas Wylie on Haymarket they stopped to boo – his views hadn't endeared him to the Chartists. Wylie's was a tavern, wine merchant and newsagents. It was in the window of this shop that printed news from outside the town was first posted on arrival at the coach office, so it was a bit of a Sheffield

Institution. During the 1832 protests the shop front got damaged by the murderous rifle volleys of the Irish Foot across the street at the Tontine.

Later in the afternoon, led by Peter Foden and James Birks, they marched around the town in procession with banners flying and the band playing. Passing the Town Hall in Waingate they were challenged from the steps by Hugh Parker, a senior magistrate, who told them their activity was illegal. They held a meeting nearby, outside the Corn Exchange, in a large space about 200 yards from the Hall.

The Old Town Hall in its current state of decay - thanks to modern-day tyrants!

Later crowds re-assembled with up to 12,000 defiant in Paradise Square between 5–6 p.m.[60]

The following day Fox and Foden were arrested in their homes at midday.[61] At 5 p.m. the town's magistrates placarded the town with a declaration against any more "Illegal Meetings" signed by their clerk, Albert Smith. Chartist crowds defiantly gathered at the Corn Exchange not far from the Town Hall. James Birks chaired the meeting and Wolstenholme read out the magistrates' address. The meeting decided to postpone an evening meeting planned till Thursday. This did not end things for the day. Somebody fired a pistol as if giving a signal and a group backed away from the gathering and occupied the Town Hall steps chanting "All in a Mind" and "All of a Mind." There is a strong possibility this was Holberry who used his ex-army horse pistol. It could be speculated Holberry was already the leader of a small direct action group or as it is later analysed as a "circle." Whoever was involved in this activity, they were mindful of the past. These specific words were cries heard in militant street protests in Sheffield's past in 1812, 1816 and 1820. They were associated with the street leadership of the twice-imprisoned, Spencean, radical tailor, John Blackwell, known locally as "Jacky Blacker, the King of the gallery" but now in 1839 an old man who had languished for months in the workhouse and recently died.[62]

The evening saw street fighting which largely ended with the 8 p.m. arrival of the Dragoons from the barracks, but a section of the crowd stayed longer, hurling stones, and were only dispersed by determined effort made by local police and soldiers from a recruiting party. The *Independent* report noted the significant numbers of "youth, boys, women and girls active in the crowd." Over seventy arrests were made but Holberry was not among them.[63]

In archival sources related arising from the later court case there are explicit references to Holberry's emergence as a leading figure.[64] This connects to the sequence of events that followed the Sheffield Chartist "National Holiday " of 12/13th August 1839. In order to find a way to defy the authorities and assert their right to meet freely they switched to the tactic of "churchgoings." This had been a previously recommended tactic for Chartists at a regional delegate gathering in Stockport some weeks earlier.[65]

The Sheffield Chartists sent a note to the Vicar of Sheffield telling him they were attending the parish church on Sunday 18th August and provided him with a biblical text to preach from.[66] Chartists assembled in Paradise Square ostensibly to join together and attend church as one body. Many processed to the church singing hymns and others filled the churchyard to overflowing. The following Sunday 25th August this was repeated with three Independent chapel ministers (showing solidarity with Foden) who ministered to an even larger churchyard overspill.[67]

Holberry was at the centre of this activity. The following Sunday (1st September) the crowds found the police in occupation of Paradise Square's entrance but they still assembled and packed the church and churchyard. In anticipation of more frustration on 8th September

Holberry, drawing on his military experience and growing reputation as a street fighting tactician and joined by young Irish born itinerant Bradford radical shoemaker William Martin, gathered a group of young militants in Daisy Walk out on the edge of the fields half a mile away to the north west. Some carried sticks (the euphemism "sticks to cross drains" was used to make reference to being armed with wooden staves). At six feet two (and possibly taller – see later) and with an erect military bearing, Holberry would have been able to communicate authority and command loyalty. Martin was a lively character with a sharp political brain previously hired as a campaigner by radical Whigs. His clever use of more euphemisms to describe the sticks and shillelaghs their supporters were encouraged to march with showed his sharp political wit. The two were an ideal foil for each other. Their group drew others who marched, some singing Chartist hymns, to church and determinedly took over its gallery without challenge.[68]

The Chartist local leadership was active on other fronts in the first two weeks of September. Wolstenholme circularised the thirty plus local trade unions seeking open declarations of support. The local Committee of Trades, meeting in their regular headquarters, West Bar's London Prentice public house, were split and voted 20 to 12 to avoid direct collective involvement as a body in Chartist activity.[69] The elite trades like sawmakers were the most aloof, in contrast with lower end bricklayers, table-knife makers, cordwainers and spring-knife trade. The town was a cradle for trade unionism but there were inwardly-facing 'aristocratic' unions and outwardly-facing 'democratic' unions. The vote did not prevent individual trades continuing with their support but it added to Convention delegate, and de facto, pivotal local leader James Wolstenholme's frustration.

The start of the month, more positively, found some local trade unions and sick clubs involved in the boycott of anti-Chartist shopkeepers and in the withdrawal of bank holdings and savings. There was a claim that £7000 taken from the town's savings bank by trades unions and sick clubs.[70]

James Wolstenholme was shuttling between a world of local success mixed with some frustrations and the less inspiring world of the capital with the squabbling remnant section of the London Convention. In London, the revolutionary fringe at the Convention was starting to think about the earlier April case for a rising made by national leader, Henry Vincent, in Wales, and the possible need to shape a national insurrection as a final resort when the more peaceable ulterior measures became played out.[71]

Back at the level of the Sheffield streets, Holberry and his militant associates carried on attempting to defy the authorities and meet in public places. On Monday 9th September some Chartists started "silent meeting" protests in Paradise Square. Between 3–5,000 met in the Square, including a several hundred strong group from the nearby nail-making village of Ecclesfield armed with "walking sticks" that the authorities feared pike heads could be screwed into. They stayed there defiantly then marched to West Bar Green, a nearby open space close to the old workhouse site. They booed to signify their hatred of the poor law and cheered to signal their fighting spirit.

They repeated this for two nights resulting in the arrest of Holberry's close associate, William Martin.[72]

Thursday night's repeat saw the Dragoons sent to Paradise Square, and a running fight traversed the church yard and ended up as a stand off between a thousand activists, presumably led by Holberry and his circle, and the police and military. This was located three quarters of a mile away at the south end of town in "Doctor's Field" – a rough open land near disused industrial premises, not far from where the Lord Nelson pub is now (bottom of Earl St).[73] When they eventually dispersed, the police and troops followed a few of them and made further arrests involving the confiscation of weapons. Some escaped into people's houses and exited the scene but then returned next day to pick up weapons left there.[74]

The following night the militants reconvened at Doctor's Field with no challenge. The following Sunday (15th September) the Chartists again tried churchgoing but were met by police issued with cutlasses lined up behind barricaded church gates. The most determined insurgents then crossed the town and headed a mile east in the direction of the rocky outcrops in the Park area, that provided the stone for recently constructed St John's church. A religious type meeting was held in a quarry during the afternoon and was repeated in the early evening.[75]

At this juncture Wolstenholme and several local leaders, including the Sheffield WMA's current secretary George Chatterton, in frustration with some local union leaders and unnerved by the vindictiveness of the authorities (perhaps compounded in Wolstenholme's case by his being so drawn into the secret national planning for an uprising that he doubted would succeed), made moves to leave Sheffield by emigrating. They headed for Liverpool and a ship that on 26th September took many of them to a new life in Westport, Connecticut in the USA.[76]

Holberry, who in prison in 1840 said he wished for a new life in America, could not consider leaving. He was drawn to a "Liberty or Death," do-or-die insurrectionism.[77] The situation was dire. Unemployment was rapidly rising. Harsh poverty characterised most districts in the town. He was about to be laid off by his employer who had got into business difficulty.[78] Nevertheless, his political stock was rising as his charisma enthused young workers and some older ones with similar military experience who could make a firm connection with him.[79] However all this was happening in the face of a further intensification of repressive actions by the local representatives of the state.

The Sheffield Chartists defiantly continued meeting through other religious under the cover of religious gatherings the next few weeks through the device of "camp meetings" that the Primitive Methodists had used to evangelise. There were three camp meetings held over a space of three weeks (Hood Hill near Wentworth, Loxley and Attercliffe).[80] Theses were largely attended by moderates: "moral force" chartists and supporters of the principles, but the Sheffield Chartist branch hard core militants stayed largely indoors planning in their Fig Tree Lane room for the next six weeks up to the Newport (Welsh) Rising (4th November).

HYMNS, TO BE SUNG

AT THE

SHEFFIELD AND BARNSLEY
CHARTIST CAMP-MEETING,

On Sunday, Sep. 22nd, 1839.

HYMN I.

The following beautiful Composition was written expressly for this occasion, by that Philanthropic Friend of the People,

E. ELLIOTT ESQ.

When Stewart reign'd, God's people fled,
Chased like the helpless hunted hare;
But kneeling on the mountain's head,
There sought the Lord, and found him there.

Lord! we, too, suffer; we, too, pray,
That thou wilt guide our steps aright;
And bless *this day*, tir'd labour's day!
And fill our souls with heavenly light.

For failing food, six days in seven,
We till the black town's dust and gloom;
But *here* we drink the breath of heaven;
And here, to pray the poor have room.

We seek the dewy, daisied plain,
Or climb thy hills, to touch thy feet;
There, far from splendor's heartless fane,
Thy weary sons and daughters meet.

Where, wheeling wide, the plover flies
O'er field, and flood, and rock and tree;
Beneath the silence of thy skies,
Is it a crime to worship thee?

"We waited long, and sought thee Lord"
Content to toil, but not to pine;
And with the weapons of thy word,
Alone assail'd, our foes and thine.

Thy truth and thee, we bade them fear;
They spurn thy truth, and mock our moan!
"Thy counsels, Lord, they will not hear,
And thou hast left them to their own." *

* See the hymn of Rebecca, in Scott's Ivanhoe.

HYMN II.

Sad oppression now compels,
Working men to join themselves;
Ye sufferers don't no more delay,
Work with might while it is day.
CHORUS.
I a Chartist now will be,
And contend for liberty.

The Charter springs from Zion's hill,
Though opposed, go on it will;
Will you serve its sacred cause,
And receive its equal laws.
CHORUS.
Union is our Captain's name,
By just laws he'll rule the main;
Before his face he'll make to flee,
All bad laws of tyranny.
CHORUS.
Brothers and sisters now unite,
And contend for your just rights;
Then soon the poor will happy be,
Glorious times we all shall see.
And the Chartist's song shall be,
My country and sweet liberty.

HYMN III.

Lord of all Lords, even Lord of they
Who claim us as their lawful prey;
Who puff'd up high with lordly pride,
Thy poor despise, thy law deride.

Yea there are men in higher spheres,
Who mock our prayers, insult our tears;
Great God, convince their haughty clay,
Thou made us men the same as they.

Teach them that we have hearts and arms,
Hearts—that the voice of friendship warms;
Arms—that no nobler pleasures know,
Than to embrace a friend, or curb a foe.

Lord let them know that us oppose,
We wish to mend, not break the laws;
Yet we can not from murmuring cease,
Till justice shall have purchas'd peace.

O let each manly bosom feel,
The glow of patriotic zeal;
Strengthen'd with knowledge, arm'd with might,
To know and to assert our right.

The malice of our foes defeat,
Drive bigots from the judgement seat;
And give us power to rend in twain
Each hateful link in slavery's chain.
A. S. G.

HYMN IV.

"When Adam delved and Eve span,
Who was then the gentleman?"
  Wretched is the infant's lot,
  Born within the poor man's cot;
Be he generous, wise, or brave,
He must only be a slave,
Long, long labour, little rest,
Still to toil to be oppressed;
Drained by taxes of his store,
Punished next for being poor;
This is the poor wretch's lot,
Born within the poor man's cot.
While the peasant works, to sleep—
What the peasant sows, to reap—
On the couch of ease to lie,
Rioting in revelry;
Be he villain, be he fool,
Still to hold despotic rule;
  Trampling on his slaves with scorn!
  This is to be nobly born.
"When Adam delved and Eve span,
Who was then the gentleman?"
R. SOUTHEY ESQ.

O Lord our God arise,
Scatter our enemies,
  And make them fall;
Confound their politics,
Frustrate their knavish tricks,
On thee our hopes we fix,
  God save us all.

E. SMITH, PRINTER, FARGATE.

They held respectable "front" meetings. They advertised regular speakers and on Monday 20th October, the women's wing, the Female Radical Association, held a tea-drinking "soiree" attended by 300 members. Speakers included a Mrs Barker, who made remarks on the necessity of admitting women into the political sphere, and James Boardman. The apparent respectability barely concealed an identification with armed struggle. Around the walls were paper banners with the inscribed names of "patriots," including the names of Henry Hunt, Feargus O'Connor and Jeremy Bentham. These were counterbalanced by other banners highlighting internationalists and others associated with armed resistance and revolution, including Watt Tyler, William Tell, Robert Emmett, Edward Fitzgerald and George Washington.[81]

The Chartists had adopted "class" meetings in members' homes several weeks previously.[82] In some of these political cells, there were between 10–12 persons and some were significantly larger. Here, knowledge about an impending national rising starting in Wales was shared. Sheffield had contacts with the North-East Tynesiders as well as London and Birmingham. Links with London and Birmingham effectively meant South Wales as well.[83] Holberry, with his recent practical military experience in the Army, was a pivotal leader. In his circle he had a Waterloo veteran, others who fought in the Napoleonic Wars, one was at the burning of Washington in the War of 1812 and another was a sailor fighting at the battle of Navarino with the Greeks for their independence from the Ottomans in the 1820s. He also had a group of impressionable young men, cutlery workers, building workers, craft-based non-cutlery artisans and a warehouse clerk. Several key players had Irish roots.[84]

The Holberry circle now running the Sheffield WMA held a defiant "hit and run" Paradise Square meeting on Monday 11th November, a week after the Newport rising in South Wales. The group used the square despite the Master Cutler (a leading office-holder in the town) turning down their application for a meeting: there was a requirement for a forty-freeholder signed requisition to be presented to the Master Cutler for permission to hold a meeting. It started 15 minutes after midday.[85] Holberry (the press was so unfamiliar with him they incorrectly spelt his name "Holbein") chaired the meeting. Around 400 were there. The superficial aim of the meeting was claimed to begin a local petition to memorialise the Queen concerning the fate of the leading Welsh prisoners including John Frost. One of Holberry's out-of-town allies, Joshua Mitchell, an Irish edge tool maker from Eckington, 8 miles away in Derbyshire, made a veiled threat, stating: "the peace of the kingdom was not safe so long as the Chartists were confined to prison… they were memorialising now but a day would come when they should want the men of Sheffield to support them with something else!)

"Aye lad, thou't right," people responded, according to the newspaper.

James Birks and an Irish bricklayer named Boardman raised the issue of rising poverty in the town. Boardman cited his aged father "compelled to toil for a shilling a day, and working 16 hours, while her Majesty, who had done nothing for her country, in comparison, had her thousands." (probably a reference to military experience in the Napoleonic Wars). Both stressed the failure of petitioning. Boardman reflected on the middle class use of force to engineer reform in 1830–32. He declared: "What has the Reform Bill done for working people? Nothing. The oligarchy and the shopocracy now told those they formerly flattered that they would be willing to give all the people the franchise, if they had knowledge enough to exercise it."

The final speaker for the circle, Thomas Bradwell, a painter, delivered their bottom line: "So exasperated were the people of Wales at the conduct of the aristocracy; that they determined to resort to physical force. But they acted wrong, they were premature and not united or determined, or they might have done it. Now I tell you, do not rush madly into the field but be prepared to do it effectively when you do. The laws of the country allow you to get arms. A man has been taken into custody {*on 13th August*} for using in this square the word "biscuit" I will not be at the trouble of using such an epithet. I tell you it is your duty and it is your privilege to get muskets (loud cheering)."

The meeting dispersed quickly. It was as if the starting gun for a Chartist uprising was fired.

Over the next few weeks Holberry and his supporters were involved in procuring weapons like daggers, pikes, caltrops (spiked balls) pistols and muskets. They engaged in arms manufacture with shells and grenades. They used some of the technical information on manufacturing combustibles provided in updated re-prints of Francis Macerone's 1832 pamphlet "Defensive Instructions for the People" that was widely available in many bookshops.[86]

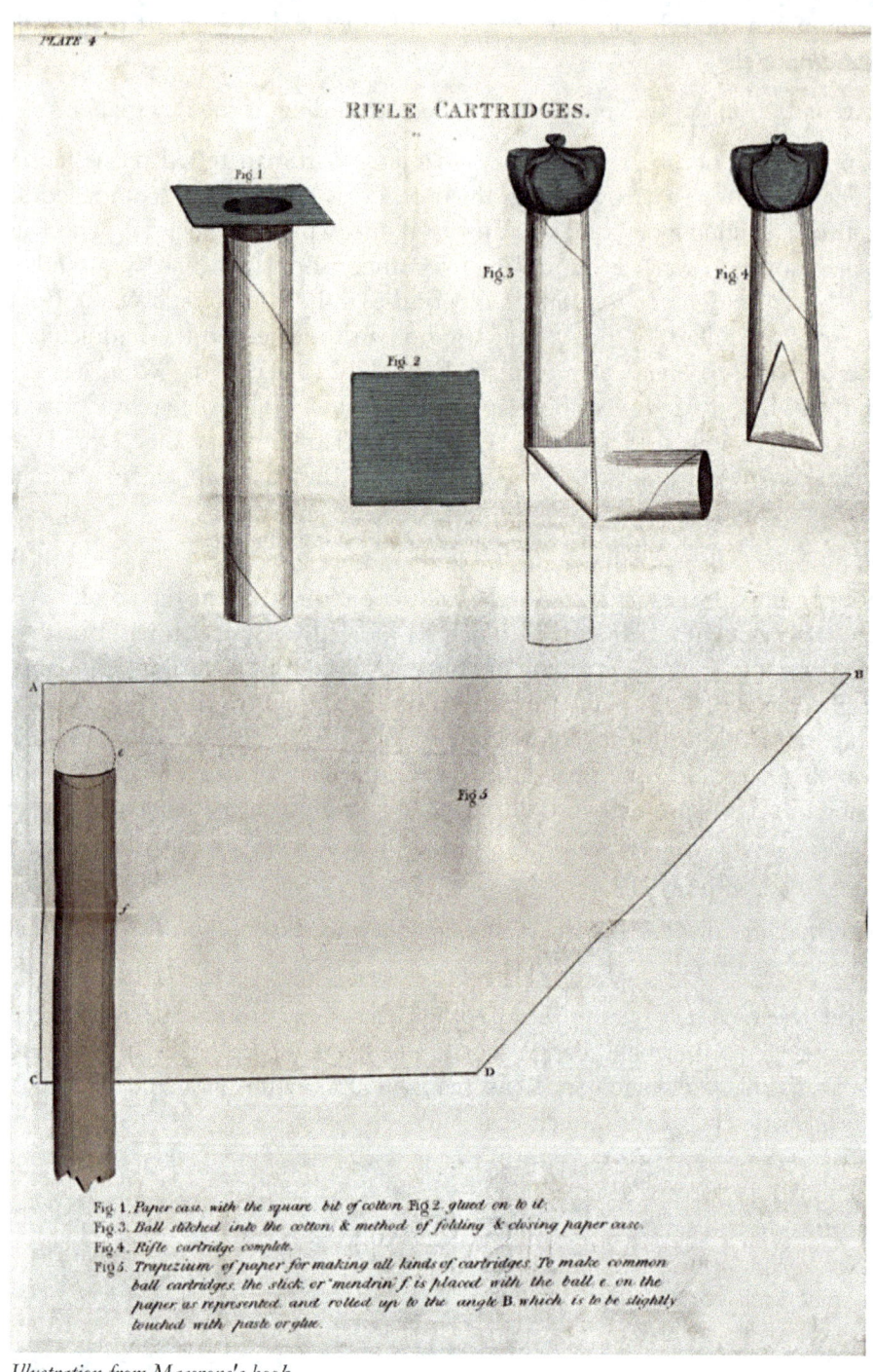

Illustration from Macerone's book

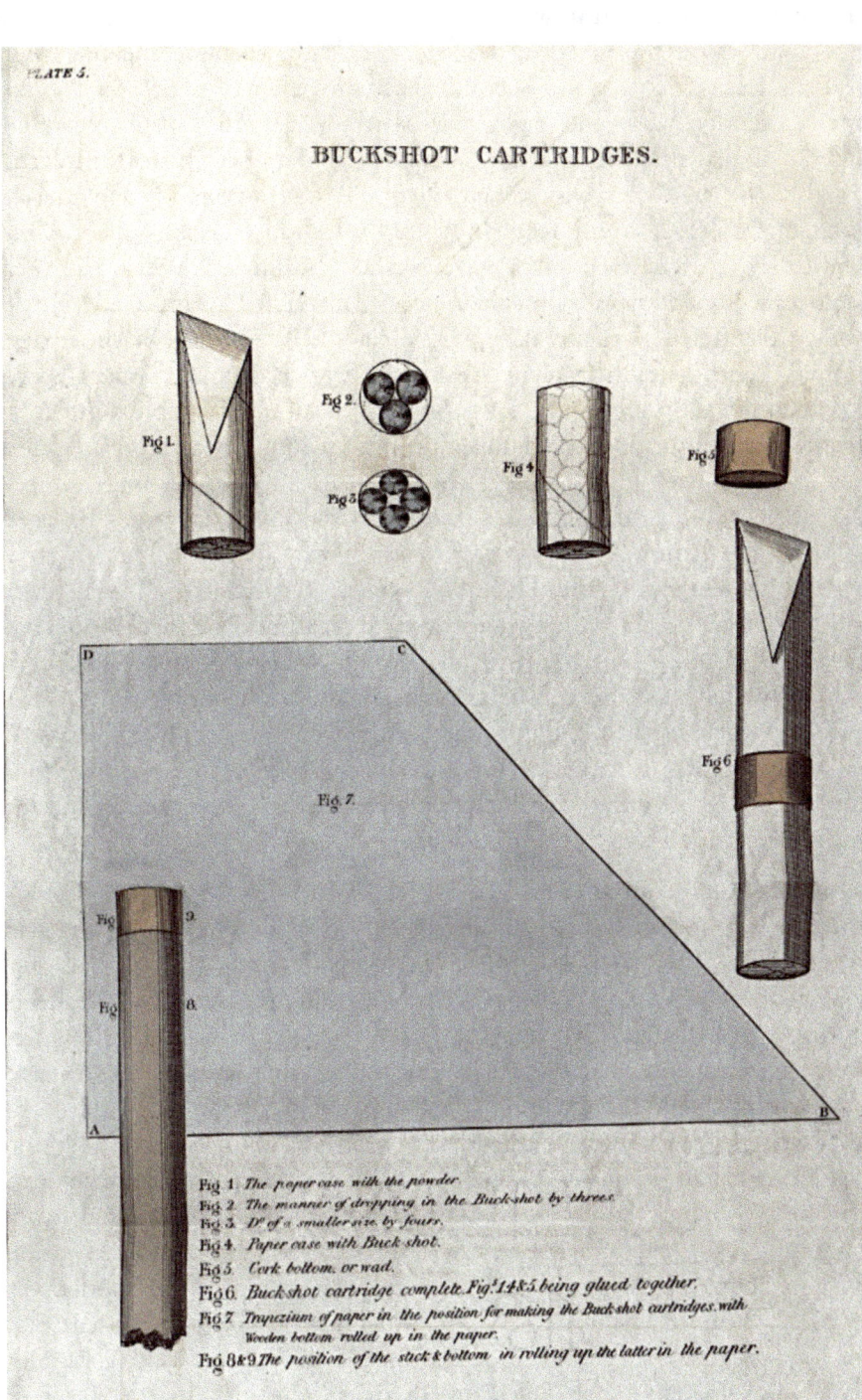

Illustration from Macerone's book

The Chartist association now contained two levels and a "new" association grew apart from the confines of the "old." Respectable meetings with speakers were followed by second meetings when "tilers" or "tellers" vetted attendees for the right password. Passwords were constantly altered.[87] On one occasion at least, Holberry had a horse pistol with him – probably the one that was seized when he was arrested.[88] He met his lieutenants there. A young teenage factory warehouse clerk, William Wells, became a trusted messenger. Wells was stealing daggers from his employer's warehouse. Other lieutenants included "class leaders" like James McKetterick, brushmaker, whose class cell was held in shoemaker, Thomas Penthorpe's, house in West Bar. Engine Tenter, Samuel Powell Thompson's group met in the Park district, John Clayton, table knife cutler became leader after Daniel Hands, another Irishman, was stood down as class leader due to his deafness. They met already in Clayton's home in Porter Street. John Marshall led a group in Coal Pit Lane. James Birks led the Mill Lane group, Boardman was in St Philip's Road and Duffy's group probably met in Pea Croft. There was a class in Forty Row whose leader remains unknown but where there was a radical family called Birkinshaw. There was another class in Bridgehouses, possibly led by Joshua Jervis. Joshua Mitchell who the census said was living in Newbould in 1841 was the Eckington and north Derbyshire leader. The mostly likely candidate for the Attercliffe leader was John Cooper, Mary's brother, though her brothers might have had some role. James Allen, a stove grate fitter and beer house keeper, was Rotherham's leader.[89]

Holberry's inner organisation was involved in money raising for the Frost Defence Fund and some money was potentially diverted to arms procurement. Pawning possessions, claims made later of foreigners with money and donations from well wishers including the "out on bail and on the run" Peter Foden, who was rumoured to have £500 savings from his successful career as a master baker, were possible sources of money.[90] Travelling along the secretive network lines of Chartism was the idea of a Northern/Midlands rising, helped by a Welsh attack on Brecon leading to a wider national fight to rescue the Welsh prisoners, with the army weakened by being drawn into multiple engagements in industrial towns. In practical moves, the Sheffielders tested their explosive devices in various locations above the town to the east including "Edge Bottom" underneath Sky Edge. A church, St Mary's (a "Million" church built in 1820s with state grants to contain the working class) in Bramall Lane, had a window broken by fireballs, that failed to detonate, on the night of 25–26 November.[91] That same night a meeting was called in the Fig Tree Lane Chartist room by handbill to elect a local delegate to a "convention" of

N Derbys Class
Leader: Joshua Mitchell, 50, sickle maker, in Newbould, Chesterfld in 1841

Spring St Class
@ Thos Penthorpe's, aged 33, **shoemaker**
Leader: Jas McKetterick, 23. brushmaker, of Pinstone St (in 1841)
40 members

Bridgehouses Class
Leader: Joshua Jervis, 35, beer house keeper?

Attercliffe Class
Leader: Wm/John Cooper? Labourer, ~25, Oakes Green?

St Philip's Road Class
Leader: Jas Boardman, bricklayer/shoemaker, 34, of Wilkinson's Yd, St Philips,
50 members

Coal Pit Lane Class
Leader: John Marshall, 42, table knife hafter,
42 members

Rotherham Class
Leader: James Allen, publican/ stove grate maker, Station Hotel, R'ham

Samuel Holberry, 25, rectifying distiller, of 19 Eyre Lane

Park Class (met at Bentley's house/ V. Bennison's pub
Leader: Samuel Powell Thompson, engine tenter,
50 members

Mill Lane Class
Leader: James Birks, cutlery worker, 25,
20 members

Wm Wells 18, clerk
Morton
Saml Bentley, cutler
Simpson
V Bennison
Joseph Bennison, table knife cutler

Porter St Class
@John Clayton's of no.87, aged 32, table knife hafter,
Leader: Dan'l Hands, 39, Labourer, of Gibraltar St. Ct.
32 members

PeaCroft Class
Leader: Jas Duffy, 40, beerhouse keeper/pedlar, of 87 Spring St
64 members

Forty Row Class
Leader: Wm Burkinshaw, 49, of Forty Row

Francis Rose
Saml Foxhall, file cutter
Wm England
Thos Bradwell, painter/ builder
Geo Swallow
Thos Booker, 55. table knife cutler.
Wm Booker, 20, table knife cutler, of Bennet Lane
Peter Foden, 30, confectioner/baker

Others mentioned: Benjamin Glossop, McCarthy, Geo Morton, Mooney, Peacock, Wm Saunders, publican of the Reuben's Head, Lambert St,

● Object: to take the Town Hall

● Object: to take the Tontine

Sheffield's Chartist class organisation, so far as is known

northern delegates in Newcastle. The police raided the meeting three times and discovered 40–50 men and youths.[92] The Chartists evaded further interference by issuing a new handbill for the evening of the 26th and a meeting "to consider the case of Mr Frost" was held in a hillside field to the east of town just below Sky Edge.[93] The meeting was attended by several hundred supporters, some carrying burning ropes as improvised torches. Two police, who were sent out as scouts and who hid in the grounds of the Shrewsbury Hospital a couple of hundred years away, estimated 17 torches and around four hundred people there. They heard clapping and cheering. The meeting was revealed later to have selected James Boardman as delegate to Newcastle.

Boardman went to Newcastle and stayed there between 2nd and 4th December. He met Welsh and West Riding representatives and a host of Tyneside and Wearside activists, many with similar Irish roots, enthusiastic about a future rising. In respect of Sheffield's dynamism and an earlier offer from the Sheffield Chartist leaders to hold a convention style gathering in the absence of the former London Convention which had broken up, Boardman was asked to chair three of the four day long sessions. In that capacity he signed a public declaration headed: "Address to the people of Great Britain," that outlined key demands. The "District and Border Convention" closed with agreement to reconvene the national convention in London by the start of the New Year and gave some impression that it backed organised moves involving an armed intervention to save Frost as the clock ticked towards the start of a special commission assembling in Newport to examine prisoners from 10 December.[94]

Back in Sheffield the Holberry "circle" tightened security with new signs and passwords to prevent penetration. "Promises" (to avoid illegal "oaths") were extracted from members to keep their secrets.[95] In a further development, Sheffield was inducted into the inner sanctum of West Riding, militant Chartism by sending representatives to the council of delegate meetings regularly held in Dewsbury. Sheffield had never before linked itself to the West Yorkshire-focussed, powerful militant Great Northern Union. Now Sheffield was seen as stepping up to the mark. This body approved Dewsbury and Bradford-based delegates to attend the new London gathering. At a public meeting on the 16th December in Sheffield, James Boardman was selected to attend the London Convention. Holberry would appear to have gone to London also and met Beniowski. Boardman also renewed links with Birmingham militants with the appearance of Edward Brown in Sheffield on 15th – 16th December.[96]

Boardman attended the Convention when it started on Thursday 26th December. He had stopped off in Birmingham on his way to urge an election of a delegate. Brown was chosen there on the 31st, at a meeting where Porter was publicly indiscrete about a rising: this indiscretion was picked up in London and provincial press Boardman stayed at the Convention for a few days then around the 2nd went to Manchester to ask for another delegate (Dewhirst from Bolton was already there). Returning from there via Birmingham he'd found Brown indisposed and went back to London, and spent very little more of frustrating early January time at the Convention. Brown still did not arrive. This may partly explain Boardman being called home by the West Riding leadership to organise closer to home. Law then went down to tell them the West Riding leadership thought it was time to rise for the 11/12th.[97]

The last weeks of the year saw further evidence of the severe worsening of local employment conditions. A local observer noted that "manufactures were closing, others were working 2–3 days a week… two thousand workmen had been thrown out of work."[98] This pauperisation extended to the would-be insurrectionists. Holberry was pawning furniture to keep his rent paid. Additional money for arms was obtained from an unknown source, possibly a well-to-do Sheffielder.[99]

Holberry was on the road a lot at that time. He was in Dewsbury on 28th December at the Wellington Inn, headquarters of the West Riding regional committee of the GNU, and went to Nottingham in the New Year.[100]

Frost's treason trial began on the last day of 1839. Time was ticking to save him. Holberry was in Sheffield again on 4th January possibly having met up with the returning Boardman.[101] Holberry had been expected, all that Saturday, back from Dewsbury. Anxious Sheffield activists tried to get a pony and trap to go and fetch him. He turned up in the early hours of Sunday before they set off. Francis Law, a hatter from Spinkhill in West Yorkshire, was with him. On Sunday 5th, after breakfast at Bentley's house in the Park district, Law was seen off later on the London-bound coach from Sheffield, probably carrying the West Riding's instructions to the Convention concerning the rise.[102]

Sheffield was also continuing communication with Birmingham where the recipient, John Porter, seemed to be a security risk. The rising had been put off from the 4th to the 11th.[103]

Fig Tree Lane Chartists worked on, with what they believed to be adequate security. On Wednesday 8th January, Holberry was away on his second mission into old Luddite heartlands. He appears to have travelled to several East Midland towns, Nottingham, Sutton in Ashfield, Mansfield, Leicester and Loughborough.[104] He shared news of the London Convention and decisions made to act in Sheffield and the West Riding to signal the need for supportive local risings across the country. One of Holberry's most trusted followers, "Old Booker," a Waterloo veteran, usually seen wearing a trademark long white greatcoat, was also sent to Eckington, Chesterfield and nearby Brampton under the guise of "family business" to alert north Derbyshire activists of the impeding action in Sheffield.[105]

On the 9th Holberry was back and meeting Francis Law returning from London in Thomas Kirk's pub, the Rock Tavern, in Dixon Lane. Law mentioned that Wales was with them. Accompanying Law was William Ashton, the veteran Barnsley activist, who, after being singled out for arrest earlier in the autumn of 1839 for making speeches advocating arming, was lying low,[106] Ashton was off to Barnsley to await the outcome of the now agreed 11/12th January Sheffield triggered rising where groups would seize and fortify the Town Hall and across the road seize and similarly barricade the Tontine coaching inn. Mail coaches leaving in both northern and southern directions would be stopped. Their non-arrival would trigger further risings in the West Riding and North Midlands.

The Tontine

Friday evening the 10th was the scene of a last minute "new branch" gathering.[107] They were now aware of the verdict in Frost's trial. Along with the familiar faces of the Holberry circle, was a newer recruit to insurrectionist Chartism, James Duffy. This Irishman had a history as an Irish community leader in Leeds in the early 1830s, then had turned professional political canvasser for established radical Whig politicians. He had settled in Sheffield later in the 1830s, ran a beerhouse in the Crofts area and became through the Hibernian Society a pivotal figure in the Irish community. He had publicly questioned Sheffield parliamentary candidates on the hustings in the later 1830s general election. Now, he commanded an armed Irish class. He was asked to chair this gathering. He was anxious before the meeting started and asked for a new password to be used. Sitting around him were Holberry, Bradwell, Birks, John Marshall, Boardman and McKetterick. At least two and possibly three of the named group he met with were Irish or had Irish roots, as was Peter Foden, still on bail.

Some said that also there was an unnamed Frenchman who inspected their weapons. He was said to have been in the French Revolution, a possible reference to 1830 when the Orleanists came to power with the aid of street barricades thrown up by the Parisian masses, or later failed Parisian risings of the early 1830. He was possibly the French-speaking exiled Pole from London who had deserted the Russian army where he served as a surgeon and went over to the Polish patriots in the 1830–31 year of revolutions: Major Beniowski. Based in London and connected to the LDA, he had travelled around the country and had visited Wales. James Wolstenholme had met him months before in London. Holberry and others in their statements, confessions and prison reports suggested the presence of an "outsider," a Frenchman, some called him "Hartley" though that might have been a corruption of "Otley" a moderate Sheffield Chartist's name to put the authorities off the scent whoever the visitor was.[108] At the meeting's climax, Holberry stood up on a wooden form and, pistol in hand, dramatically issued some last minute instructions and some threats if members failed to turn up at the class mobilisations.[109]

The final order given that night was that all class members were to be at their class meeting places by 10 p.m. on Saturday 11th. The rising and seizure of buildings was to be preceded at 2 a.m. on Sunday morning, 12th January, with the firing of the barracks at Upperthorpe, followed by attacks on the police office, the Town Clerk's house and the homes of isolated magistrates outside of the town. Any magistrates driving towards the town before the attack groups moved on their homes were to be assassinated on the road. Holberry and eight of his most trusted followers were to complete this task.[110]

Regarding the town centre area, action was planned which was to involve the seizure of the two key buildings, classes being assigned to each target. Selected town centre gun shops were to be broken into and looted and the contents taken to the occupied "forts": the Town Hall and the Tontine coaching inn. These two buildings were to be defended, the Town Hall from the roof with grenades and home-made shells. Marksmen were to pick off the soldiers and police. Spiked balls, "night cats" (to cripple horses) were to be scattered on the approach roads for cavalry coming from the Shalesmoor Barracks.

The key was stopping the mail coaches leaving the Tontine to signal to the West Riding and other towns in the Midlands that the rising had begun. The gates of the inn were to be barred by wagons and it was to be similarly defended. It was intended to communicate with the East Midland towns by similar coach non-arrivals.[111] Dewsbury and Bradford were to rise up and send out further signals. Similarly, Barnsley was to be occupied. Dewsbury Chartists, did in fact, as part of the plan, go on to occupy their town for a few hours, co-ordinating their arrival using a signal balloon and firing fusillades in the centre of the town.[112]

Holberry was the pivotal figure on Saturday afternoon's meeting of key players in the upstairs room (usually used by an Oddfellows branch) of William Saunders' (an apparent sympathiser) Reuben's Head public house in Lambert Street. Some of the class leaders were present, including Rotherham's leader, James Allen and someone of the name of Cooper, from Attercliffe. This could have been Mary's father, John or perhaps one of her brothers. However, a mystery figure (the outsider, possibly confirming the promised second Welsh rising – a diversionary attack on Brecon and then a retreat to the safety of the hills which would pull army units in the North and Midlands out of position and facilitate the risings triggered by Sheffield's actions) was not in attendance. According to Holberry's statement to the prison inspector, Sheffield was left out of the message loop to stand down, because Wales was not ready. Dewsbury's Wellington Inn leadership knew, he said. (Though this does not tie up entirely with the fact that an aborted rising did start in Dewsbury on the same night.) The plan in Sheffield seemed to be proceeding, involving preparations for class assemblages over the next few hours.

O'Connor and the *Northern Star* at the turn of the year

In a letter published in the *Star* on 3rd May 1845, reproduced from *The National Reformer*, William Ashton said that after the December 19th London Convention a deputation went to see Feargus O'Connor to secure his support and he was purported to have said he would: "place himself at the head of the people of England, and have a bloody revolution to save Frost." When William Ashton stopped at Sheffield on the 11th on his way to Barnsley for the rising, he said they were all in high hopes on account of O'Connor's promise.

But in reality O'Connor was using his newspaper to try prevent any "emeutes," as he called them.

On the 4th January the leader included the following: "We hear of secret meetings; but we know not whether such have been holden. If there have, we are satisfied that very few of the people have been thus seduced, and we say to those few beware! For you are all sold; and a worse fate that that of Frost awaits you of you are not careful."

The on the 11th, the very morning that the Sheffield classes were making their final plans, they will have read this: "Let the people now then be every where on the alert. Let strong memorials, firmly, but respectfully worded, pour into the Home Office, from all quarters, like hail. Let every effort that can be made be made instantly; BUT LET ALL BE DONE PEACABLY; NOTHING WILL BE GOT BY VIOLENCE." Ashton said that it was expected that the Star would appear printed in "letters of blood. But, lo, and behold! it appeared with a denunciation of the whole plan! This struck dismay into tens of thousands; the whole affair was blown to atoms by that cursed paper."

Finally, the week after the attempted rising the *Star* comments: "With the most inexpressible pain, we chronicle in another part of our paper, the stark-staring mad proceedings of a small knot of fools at Sheffield!"

Later in the evening of the 11th, some of Duffy's large Irish contingent were at his home in Pea Croft arguing with him regarding his apparent sudden cold feet. Holberry was carrying the ultimate burden. Why was there no message arriving from Wales about action that Francis Law was so sure of days earlier? Numbers of active members met in the Fig Tree Lane room at 7 p.m.[113] Then the members dispersed to class meeting places in the town with the groups from outside (Rotherham and Attercliffe from the North and Eckington from the South) knowing the timings and locations to arrive to make their contribution.

Possibly still unknown to Holberry, the Rotherham leader had been "turned" by the authorities a few weeks earlier. According to the accounts written in 1864, James Allen, in a final act of betrayal, left the Reuben's Head and headed off to Rotherham to inform the police of the rising's start. By early evening a leading magistrate, Henry Howard (Lord), was riding at breakneck speed to rouse Sheffield magistrates and to alert the 1st Royal Dragoons and their commander, Colonel Marten, in the Upperthorpe barracks, to the impending attack.[114] The Dragoons and the police were mobilised to pre-empt the Chartists moves on the key buildings. Holberry also mentioned to the prison inspector that the non-arrival of the the Frenchman, "Hartley," made them "all awry and decided us not to go on, but it was too late to prevent some from going out."

A Wostenholm knife with ivory handle and silver-tipped Morocco sheath as was found on Holberry

Later 19th century folklore, stoked by the 1864 public lecture which brought ex-moderate Chartist, Richard Otley, into a public debate, had it that several leaders were forewarned of the plan's betrayal and instead of them joining in, they dispersed their classes at their assembly points. Otley, who claimed Allen tried to involve Gill (the first Convention delegate) in the rising, decades later claimed he was instrumental in warning other people off and "saving them."[115]

Police and Dragoons closed in on Holberry's home in Eyre Lane around 10 p.m. Some accounts say it was closer to midnight. Holberry's wife was downstairs, with a small girl (according to one report but denied in others). The police first asked at the door for "Hartley." Mary responded by saying perhaps they meant "Otley." They then entered and Mary was forced to indicate her husband in the room above. He was dressed and lying on a bed. Holberry was confronted with claims he was about to lead a rising. He was dispossessed of a dagger in his breast pocket.

All this is very unsatisfactory for the historian. Was Holberry still intending to head out in a short while to meet the other eight who were supposed to be going with him to fire the barracks (we have no idea who these men were). If so, was he resting, or thinking, before the long night ahead? Why else would he be lying in bed, clothed, with a dagger in his jacket? If this were the case then he must have told the prison inspector a story to detract from his own involvement. It would not be in his interests for a potential pardon or leniency to admit to being a ringleader: it was really the Frenchman who was to be the Field Marshall, and he wasn't actually going to do anything himself. And why would he give the authorities the satisfaction of knowing the truth? The prison inspector does after all say in his report that Holberry's "mention of the Frenchman I conceive to be an invention to blind the true source from whence the money was obtained." It is fair to assume that W. J. Williams was no fool and had enough experience of interviewing people to reasonably judge veracity, even if he represented an establishment view. If the Frenchman not turning up was so crucial, then the events that followed do not make much sense. More effort could have been made to call it all off: and the knowledge of this "no-show" would not have been exclusive to Holberry.

Another hypothesis would be that, either due to seeing the heavy troop presence, or realising they were betrayed, Holberry decided not to go ahead, could only do so much to try to warn the others and ran out of time. Being resigned to his fate, he chose his own Gethsemane moment, rather than trying to evade capture.

The James Allen story told over two decades later, also does not make sense. All the authorities were concerned with, we are told, was the names of the ringleaders. James Allen was involved in the planning all that week. He knew on the Friday that the rising was to take place on the Sunday morning at 2 a.m. Yet we are told he rushed to Rotherham on the Saturday and that *chivalrous* Lord Howard galloped over to Sheffield to warn the authorities there. But, why then did they then turned up at Holberry's house asking for "Hartley" not "Holberry." They could have made Holberry's arrest earlier if they had genuinely suspected him. Going by earlier behaviours of the magistrates they did not hesitate in waiting for evidence of a guilty "act" before making arrests; they just hauled people in and made the evidence fit, as they did with William Martin. Is there something in the speculation by some that the Government actually wanted evidence of violent conduct to subdue the seemingly irrepressible calls for reform? So it was in their interests for minor insurrection to take place, that they could then inflate in the public eye? Were they complicit through *agents provocateurs*? It was later proven that the Bradford Chartists of 1840 were committed on the evidence of a Whig government-paid *agent provocateur*, James Harrison, who had actively encouraged insurrection. Was Allen also being paid? His association with soon-to-be Whig member of parliament, Henry Howard, not coincidental? So long as they could make an example of Chartists leaders; it mattered little whether they were the key antagonists or not: metaphorical heads on stakes was the main thing.[116]

At Holberry's house, at the top was a garret where they found home-made shells, grenades, powder, and fireballs. His horse pistol was found upstairs, also. He said little, though some of what he was claimed to have said featured in the hearings and subsequent trial.[117]

His arrest had circumvented the key part of the plan with his attack plan for the barracks, police office, Town Clerk's home and some magistrates homes in the northern out-townships. He and his wife, joined by some found on the streets or in their homes, were taken for what turned out to be overnight questioning till 4 a.m. His recently pregnant wife was thrown into a cell with a female drunk. Mary refused to give any information even though the magistrates were telling her she had committed treason.[118] Holberry, while refusing to talk about others' roles, commented on his own role, stressing that warning of betrayal had led him to countermand the whole operation.[119]

This was probably true, but it hadn't wholly succeeded. Several of the 10–12 "attack groups" were activated in the early hours and proceeded towards their objectives. Members of the groups led by Birks, Boardman, Hands and Thompson and numbers of Duffy's Irishmen were on the streets in various parts of the town. The leaders could see the Dragoons, police and special constables at several street junctions. Forty Row and Bridgehouses classes did not appear to be on the streets. An order, claimed to be given by Holberry as a fall back position: to "Moscow the town" by burning some of their own homes, was not heeded, although the Reuben's Head publican, Saunders, was keen for this to happen even at this late stage.[120]

The rising attempt descended into a tragi-comedy of "cat and mouse" as in the darkness knots of armed Chartists tried to reconvene in new assembly points and when this failed discarded their weapons and returned home. Some groups were larger than others. A group of fifty with pikes glinting in the moonlight was seen on Glossop Road a mile and a half from the town centre. In the end this group too discarded weapons near the Crookesmoor reservoir as some headed out of the town towards Crookes via Steel Bank.[121] In gathering daylight, other caches of discarded weapons were also found in the northern edge of the town in St Philips Road and some others to the west a mile and a half outside the town near the new Botanical Gardens.[122]

Holberry was taken to the Town Hall for interrogation and some other participants were steadily picked up. Some, like Boardman, escaped from the town, passing a picket of expectant Barnsley Chartists as he headed north.[123] Wells was not picked up for a few days and visited Barnsley to see what the state of affairs was there.[124] Bradwell, Birks and McKetterick also went temporarily missing. Foden hid in the town then escaped to Wales.[125] Five others were taken with Holberry.[126] Others were to follow, being taken into custody within days.

Holberry, his wife, Old Booker (Thomas) and his son William, Samuel Foxhall and Samuel Thompson senior were all interrogated into the early hours of Monday morning. Charges of treason were laid by prosecutor Luke Palfreyman before the magistrates at a Town Hall hearing on Monday morning, as the preliminary examination (committal hearing) began. The bench was comprised: Lord Henry Howard, who was responsible for the the agent-provocateur, Allen, William John Bagshawe, owner of the Oakes estate at Norton, Hugh Parker of Woodthorpe Hall and father of the Sheffield M.P. John Parker, Rev William Anderson of Aston, Rev George Chandler of Treeton Rectory and Charles Brownell, lawyer. Accounts vary but others mentioned include: Henry Walker of Clifton House, Colonel Marten of the Dragoons and "several other officers."

There was no legal representation for the accused. Holberry asked for a pen and paper seemingly prepared to manage his own defence. Defendants back then knew nothing of the prosecution's evidence to prepare their defence.

Holberry was able to play little part in the public interrogations of witnesses over the next two days. He managed to make a point that witnesses were giving testimony while other would-be witnesses were in the court, thus evidence was being corrupted by collusion. There was a huge amount of detailing the actions and consequences but very little threw light on Holberry's thoughts and statements. Police constable Wild recounted what he claimed had been dialogue at the time of the arrest.

> Mr Wild asked him: "Are you one of the people called Chartists?
> Holberry replied: "I am"
> Wild: " Are you a moral or physical force man?"
> Holberry: " I am a physical force man"
> Wild: "Surely you would not take a life?"
> Holberry: "But I would, in defence of Liberty, and in obtaining the Charter. Mind… I am no thief and no robber… I will fight for the Charter, and I will not rest until I have got the Charter; to that I have made up my mind."
> Wild: "Surely you would not shoot me?"
> Holberry: "Oh yes I would, or anyone else to obtain the Charter. We fight for Liberty and the Charter." (Cheers in gallery).[127]

There may have been an element of fabrication, but there could be an element of Holberry's direct style. Holberry did accuse the police of fabrication when he appeared at the preliminary hearing, as reported in the press accounts of the time.[128]

The Times had an agenda of demonisation of Holberry:

> "The reckless conspirator, Holberry, committed for high treason, who, on his apprehension and examination, boasted of his intended outrages to obtain the charter, is a cadaverous-looking man, with long black hair. He is between 25 and 30 years of age. He was originally a sort of porter and clerk to a wine and spirit merchant, and has since served four years in the army. Most of the situations he has filled have been lost by him through his violent conduct as a politician. Like many others, in the absence of honest industry, he has lived upon the fruits of agitation, viz, upon the hard-earned peace of his dupes."[129]

Who'd have thought the press would make things up to fit their own agenda! The *Sheffield Independent*, more balanced perhaps, described him as "very tall, well formed and muscular young man, with much the appearance and manner of an itinerant showman."[130]

Among the principal witnesses, interspersed by members of the public witnessing events, watchmen, army personnel etc, the principal witnesses heard on the first two days of the week were turncoats: Thompson and Foxhall.

Samuel Powell Thompson was a class leader. His father was in the dock alongside the Holberrys and the Bookers. Weapons had been found at Thompson senior's house, but there was little other evidence against him. It was barely disguised that he was in the dock solely a means of ensuring his son gave evidence. Indeed, as soon as that evidence was completed in the committal, the prosecutor said that the case he had opened against the elder Thompson was a weak one and he now submitted that that he might be discharged.[131] Thompson junior, had been kept in a cell with Foxhall; they seem to have colluded. Both sold their comrades for immunity. Thompson was trusted and close to the heart of the plot and much apparent detail tumbled out. It was a statement where names were named, class locations were revealed and a version of the plan outlined in great detail such that Holberry was in no position to question him or cast doubt.

Holberry attempted to draw Thompson out in his cross-examination as being heavily involved, and, by implication, unreliable, but without legal training he was unable to land any blows.

James Allen, the Rotherham leader turncoat and agent-provocateur, was spirited away, protected by the authorities as if he was never present. He was effectively air-brushed from the record, possibly to protect the role of the state in encouraging the rebellion, possibly for fear of backlash against Howard and fear on the part of his wife. *The Times* journalist covering the story did not seem to have received the censorship notice. In an editorial piece it said: "had it not been for the compunctious visitations of conscience in one of the delegates from the Rotherham Lord Howard, the town would, most probably, have been smoked and burned by this time."

During the week, search parties were looking for named participants (class leaders and others of Holberry's lieutenants) and some were rounded up and examined on Friday. John Clayton, William Booker, Samuel Bentley, Thomas Penthorpe, Joseph Bennison, John Marshall, James Duffy and William Wells were brought before the bench on lesser charges. Mary Holberry was released with no charge after 48 hours. Meanwhile more allegations spilled out into the public domain.[132]

There was a report in the London *Times* that there was a secret meeting in woodland outside the town (a quarry on Brincliffe Edge, three miles from the town centre) on the Sunday 19th.[133] Moderate WMA members like

Richard Otley and William Gill organised polite lectures in the Fig Tree Lane rooms and waited for the political storm to blow over.[134] The following week saw a failed Chartist rising in Bradford associated with the itinerant Scottish revolutionist, Robert Peddie.[135]

Charges were formalised at sessions in the Town Hall court chambers and Sheffield prisoners sent off to holding prisons awaiting the March Assizes in York or bailed for other court appearances. Holberry later stated later he was imprisoned for forty days before his trial.[136]

6. YORK – THE ASSIZES, MARCH 1840

Inside York Castle prison (demolished 1935)

Mid-March saw the Sheffield men arraigned for "seditious conspiracy" – the more serious charge of treason against Holberry and Thomas Booker having been reduced, so that they had something they could make stick.[137]

Holberry was represented by a Mr Watson – the men's defence having been paid for by public subscription. He faced a prosecution team that included the Attorney General, Sir John Campbell. Judge Erskine presided in hearings that commenced on 16th March. The impartiality of the jury probably left something to be desired, being made up of only of men of property who had probably already been influenced by the accounts like that of *The Times* in the newspapers, and easily led by the judge. Whilst on bail awaiting their own trial George White and William Ashton were in a local hotel and White said to Ashton that he thought the jury in the trial of the Sheffield men had been "composed of a parcel ignorant farmers; that I doubted whether some of them could write their names, and that where Chartists were concerned, I thought they could only pronounce the word 'Guilty'." They were shouted at by a farmer who was sitting in the room: "Thou's a leer! for oi been it Jury to-day and we acquitted six in um thought they were guilty reight enuf." When asked why they acquitted them then, he replied "because T' Judge said there wasn't sufficient evidence."

York assizes court

Watson's defence of Holberry was based around the following: that Foxhall and Thompson could not be regarded as reliable witnesses, and that the whole case hinged on that unreliable evidence, that the Attorney General had prejudiced the case in the eyes of the jury by his own statements rather than relying on the evidence led, that bringing Dewsbury into it was designed to play on the jury and lead to ideas of a wider conspiracy which was only speculation not evidenced, and that Chartists had the right to meet by night or day in large or small numbers and to use strong language. What it amounted to in sum was that none of what Holberry did was sufficient to meet the test of conspiring for treasonable object. He could not be guilty on the grounds of entertaining strong opinions, or expressing them in strong language, or even of having arms for defence, which was not a crime, but only if he had plotted to set "fire to the town and destroy the whole of the military force that was stationed there."

The jury retired at about 10 o'clock at night and returned a guilty verdict soon after.; thought them wanting their beds would surely not have influenced them!

Pressure was put on the judge to sentence them to be held in places furthest away from their homes. Holberry and several others were sent to Northallerton's ominously named, House of Correction in North Yorkshire.

The grounds for claims of political sentencing is in a letter from the clerk of the Assizes, Bayley, to George Maule at the Treasury in Whitehall dated 21st March 1840.

Bayley revealingly stated: "He (Erskine) could give hard labour to those only who were found actually rioting, but he gave it to all he could. Those who have got imprisonment only will fare but little better than those who have hard labour, for they will all be made to work, and put upon the silent system. I got Erskine to send them all the different Houses of Correction in the County that were furthest away form their own homes and all the worst are to go to Northallerton where they are worst fed and hard worked."[138]

Holberry ended up at the start of his sentence doing hard labour on the notorious treadwheel, despite not having been sentenced to hard labour. The sentences were: Holberry (4 years), John Clayton (2 years), Old Booker (3 years), Young Booker (2 years), Duffy (3 years) and Wells (1 year), William Martin (1 year). The prison governor, 53-year-old William Shepherd, aided by his 25-year-old son (Martin in his prison letters called him a "monster") as under-governor and "Superintendent of Silence," was known to be a law unto himself and, from later Chartist prisoner complaints, was not the only prison governor to run a rogue regime.[139]

7. NORTHALLERTON – A VOICE FROM THE HELL HOLE

Holberry was set to work daily on the treadwheel straight away for four to five weeks, as if in an attempt to break him. Martin who was with him described the first few weeks they shared in Northallerton in detail. They were told from the start that four hours a day on the treadmill that powered the prison corn mill was a normal condition of prisoners' obligations as there were limited other opportunities for prison work. The prison regime was endorsed by the prison's visiting magistrates. Holberry was not just subjected to the prison's version of the "associative" silent system, which banned verbal and symbolic human contact, but also himself in some instances for short periods was placed in solitary confinement. In his "Voice from the Hellhole" letters of 1841, he detailed the severity of the discipline. He emphasised the severity of the silent system, which was not simply about not speaking while being in routine contact with prisoners. It was also about being monitored for non-verbal communication and very early on he realised this also meant looking towards light. Later he wrote that he did not see the sun for 12 months in Northallerton. He recollected being reprimanded for the angle of his gaze and for the crime of "staring at the heavens." He wrote with some understandable bitterness, "I was looking as high as the prison windows when they were straight before me… you may form some idea of the comprehensive nature of the silent system."

A prison treadwheel. Note the partitions to stop prisoners communicating and breaching the silent system.

In May 1840, relatively early on in his confinement, he and the others were moved from the 4 hours daily ordeal on the "everlasting stairway" to silently picking oakum (breaking open the fibres of old ropes – itself a difficult task) seated eighteen inches apart from the next oakum-picking prisoner for nine hours a day, with only limited yard exercise. We don't know if he was told of his son's death, aged 18 weeks in September 1840. He was claimed in the 1843 biographical account in the Chartist press to have only been allowed one outside visitor in three months. He himself said in prison letters in late 1841 that he did not see any visitor for 16 months at Northallerton.[140]

His wife only once ever visited him in prison but it was unlikely to be while he was at Northallerton. Mary was traumatised for many months as several references to her desperate state of mind crop up in the biographical sketch of 1843. The Holberry and Cooper families were both in dire financial straits. The dead child had to be buried unmarked in a public grave (B47) which eventually held sixty bodies in the new Sheffield Nonconformist General Cemetery.[141]

The 1843 account in the *English Chartist Circular* was informed by various sources and, in respect of Northallerton, castigated the prison stating, "the accursed silent system is there established in all its rigour, the diet is coarse and scanty. Prisoners had to work on mindless repetitive tasks like picking oakum if they had no money for food."[142]

Holberry's health was under great strain from the start. In his letters, Holberry pinpointed changes. William Martin, Holberry's former associate, also imprisoned throughout 1840 but later transferred to Lancaster, later had a letter published in the *Northern Star* in March 1841. It was the first of several exposés of the Northallerton regime under the heading "Revelations from the Northallerton Hell Hole." This had confirmed the treadmill abuse in 1840 as "contrary to law" and experienced by several Sheffielders including Old Booker, Duffy, Holberry and Wells as well as Bradford's Brook and also Martin himself.[143]

A second 1841 letter with a similar *Northern Star* headline smuggled out and printed in the Star was from Holberry himself. This was in mid-1841. Holberry's letter, headed "Voice from the Hell Hole," noted that in those early 1840 months, Old Booker "was with us" (on the treadmill) till he could hardly crawl when the Surgeon ordered him out to the yard outside."[144] Martin had testified to Duffy and Bradford's William Brook falling off the tread wheel.

All this appeared hidden behind the walls of the House of Correction during 1840 but was an issue the state would not want to surface in the public domain. The sheer numbers of Chartist prisoners scattered across the prison system in 1840 is perhaps one reason why the end of the year saw the visit of a state appointed prison inspector.

Captain Williams visited Northallerton to complete a full inspection in mid-December 1840.[145] He filled a notebook with details regarding the Chartist prisoners which is held in the National Archives at Kew in series HO 20/10. The full summary of the prison report is found in the House of Lords sessions papers for 1840. The notebook report could well be muted on details of conditions. Williams interviewed and reported on the Sheffield internees. They and other Chartist prisoners were very guarded in their responses. He noted in his summary[146] of Holberry's conditions, his supposed diet:

Prisoners' Daily Allowance of Victuals.

	BREAKFAST.	DINNER.	SUPPER.
Sunday	A Quart of Oatmeal Porridge and One Half-pound of Wheaten Bread.	Six Ounces of Boiled Beef, a Quart of Potatoes, with Salt, and One Half-pound of Wheaten Bread.	A Quart of Oatmeal Porridge, and One Half-pound of Wheaten Bread.
Monday	Ditto.	A Quart of Stew made of Beef, Potatoes, Oatmeal, and Onions, with Pepper and Salt, and One Half-pound of Wheaten Bread.	Ditto.
Tuesday	Ditto.	A Quart of Stew made of Beef, Potatoes, Oatmeal, and Onions, with Pepper and Salt, and One Half-pound of Wheaten Bread.	Ditto.
Wednesday	Ditto.	A Quart of Broth, thickened with Oatmeal and Onions, with Pepper and Salt, and One Half-pound of Wheaten Bread.	Ditto.
Thursday	Ditto.	Six Ounces of Boiled Beef and a Quart of Potatoes, with Salt, and One Half-pound of Wheaten Bread.	Ditto.
Friday	Ditto.	A Quart of Stew made of Beef, Potatoes, Oatmeal, and Onions, with Pepper and Salt, and One Half-pound of Wheaten Bread.	Ditto.
Saturday	Ditto.	A Quart of Broth, thickened with Oatmeal and Onions, with Pepper and Salt, and One Half-pound of Wheaten Bread.	Ditto.

Williams described the regime in a matter of fact manner, stating:

"The discipline of silence is most strictly enforced (to those) in the house of correction confined within its walls. The only relaxation allowed to the prisoners confined for political offences is that they are not restricted either in the writing or receiving of letters or visits. The prisoners not sentenced to hard labour sit during the day in a room with a fire and are employed in picking oakum – they take exercise by walking round the yard in files. They are not permitted to introduce food. The magistrates have put this construction on the statute – that if they elect to avoid labour by maintaining themselves, they must pay for the gaol allowance. The prisoners at hard labour are at the tread wheel" (Holberry was not given a hard labour term but still put on the wheel at the start of his term.)

Holberry was not on the wheel by the time of Williams' report. His typical day centred on a workroom. By December 1840, on six days, from early light, after lining in single file at 6 a.m. to go outdoors to wash with a half ounce weekly soap ration, Holberry in his standard issue plum-coloured prison jacket and trousers proceeded to the mess to eat and listen to prayer. After this he would be attending the workroom picking oakum for hours with short meal and rest breaks and for most of the remaining eight hours. He would be sitting on a wooden form, as all were, tightly spaced from fellow prisoners in an atmosphere of stultifying silence and under constant scrutiny for "deviations" like "looking about," "constantly looking about" or "making signs and looking about." Punishments had been summary and acted on for every offence, but in late 1840 their numbers were falling with less "confinements" and "stoppage of diet" as the regime, it was claimed in the prison inspection report summary, had recently adopted a new more lenient three strikes and out approach with the first two offences seen only as warnings.

The prisoners were locked up at 5 p.m, again in social isolation. Sundays saw some difference. Chapel was the 9 a.m. substitute for the work room, with the rest of the middle of the day dedicated to solitary exercise, reading and reflection in the yard until the 2.30 religious service and then supper and returning to cells at 5 p.m.

Regarding Holberry, Captain Williams said there were no complaints about his behaviour. He added that, "he makes no complaint of his treatment. He wishes to be allowed half a pound of bread daily." Was this Holberry sending coded message that he wasn't in receipt of the diet reported?

Regarding his health, he reported of Holberry, "…he has been repeatedly afflicted with rheumatism, with a tendency to dropsy, but is now in improved health. The surgeon is on the opinion that he had better be removed to a more airy and elevated situation." The House of Lords summary had commented on Northallerton being a "low and damp place."

The inspector had been able to interview Holberry regarding his political role. Holberry was candid and talked about the rising but only talked about himself, his role in arms manufacture and testing. He had tried out one of their shells at Edge Bottom. He said he knew nothing of the rising till 15/16th November. He stated if he had been tried for his life he said he would have revealed where the money and combustibles came from. He again mentioned "the Frenchman." Holberry was recorded as saying, "he was a foreigner" who had arrived after Frost was taken in early November. "He had been to Wales and knew all our friends in the country, particularly Birmingham." This outsider was not at the Lambert Street pub meeting on the Saturday and this: "decided us not to go on; but it was too late to prevent some from going out." This may have sounded like a red herring to the inspector who might have seen this as an attempt to deflect attention as to the true authors of the plot, including Holberry himself. Another claim was that Turner, the then WMA secretary, had run off with the funds collected for Frost, the imprisoned Welsh leader. Thus, claimed Holberry, the Frost money wasn't spent on arms. One other potentially reliable insight was the statement that Chartist women, aided by the Fig Tree Lane woman keyholder, destroyed membership records to protect their husbands.

The Inspector's report contains information partly at variance with other recollections of Holberry's imprisonment. The hard labour, social isolation and the damp did their work, and the result could be evidenced shortly after Captain Williams departed. John Clayton, another Sheffield Chartist, died at Northallerton in early 1841.[147] Conditions were little improved during the next few months. The Chartist *Northern Star* paper ran several further articles in July, August and September 1841 under the heading "Voices from the Hell Hole." These feature Holberry's letters (some key points are cited above as they relate to his situation in 1840 and earlier 1841) and were his contribution to the public campaign to end the barbaric treatment of political prisoners.[148]

8. YORK CASTLE – SEPTEMBER 1841 TO JUNE 1842

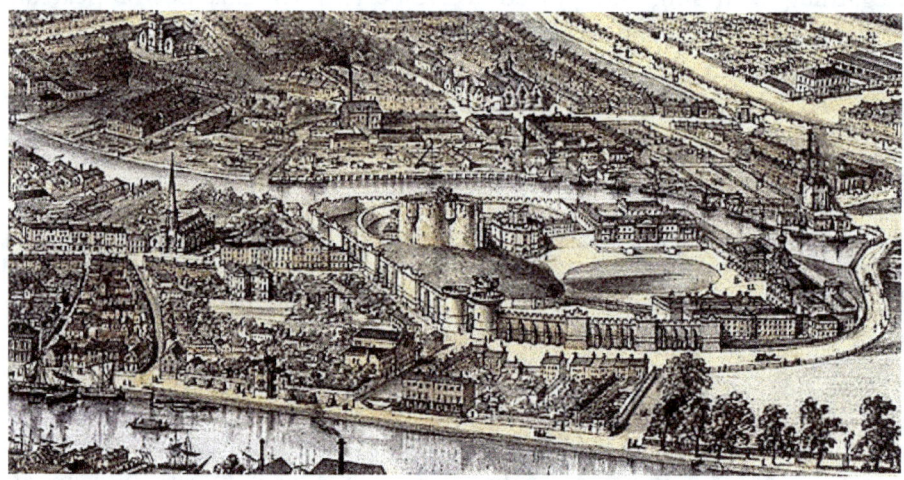

Holberry's health was seriously deteriorating in the summer of 1841 and Holberry ended up in Northallerton's prison hospital for four weeks in late August and early September. His letter to William Martin of 8th September, *Northern Star 18th September 1841*, details contradictory signs of his health. He had "no pain" but he, "had bad digestion and a bad appetite," which he saw as the result of "eighteen months close confinement." He was getting better food, and the hospital allowed exercise that he had been denied before, the lack of which he linked to his legs previously being so swollen. He talked about "twenty four still in prison" and that how could he complain when it was "scandalous" that such as Ashton and Crabtree (Barnsley Chartists) were still imprisoned. He concluded, "from the tender mercies of such miserable wretches as Normanby and Co, may the good Lord deliver us."

Inside York Castle Prison

In September 1841 the new Tory regime at the Home Office intervened and he was moved from Northallerton to premises in York Castle and offered a place in the hospital ward, which he initially declined. The correspondence from the Home Office indicating the new Home Secretary, Sir James Graham's concern about Holberry's health, and moving him, was dated 16th September.[149] The Surgeon at York Castle wrote that he met Holberry on the 22nd September, the day after his transfer, and stated that he, "was suffering from a bilious attack… his skin and eyes are still suffused with bile, his pulse is quick and his appetite bad. His diet is altered to suit his appetite and I have every reason to hope his health will gradually improve."[150]

A draft petition that was amongst Samuel Holberry's possessions returned to his wife upon his death and passed down through the Pearson family until given to the Holberry Society in the 1970s. A rare document containing Holberry's signature

Back in Sheffield, George Julian Harney had now, since July 1841, become the National Charter Association organiser in Sheffield. Amazingly, some of the militant Chartists connected to the rising re-appeared and were involved in Chartist activity in 1841. Holberry's wife and other prisoners' wives had appeared on Chartist platforms, especially when O'Connor was visiting. Harney combined his role as correspondent for O'Connor's paper from an office in Hartshead with leadership of the main NCA branch based in Fig Tree Lane.[151]

Membership was recovering from the collapse at the start of 1840. There was division and disagreement with moderates and some former associates of Holberry choosing to have a separate NCA group, the Political Institute branch. Holberry's reputation was somewhat diminished, early in his imprisonment. Old Booker had been released early and had said some damaging things, blaming Holberry for the failure.[152] This negative view was challenged in the local branch later in 1841 and knowledge of Holberry's condition resulting from the punitive actions of the State and his defiance gained him more sympathy and support.[153]

Holberry was being allowed some correspondence (subject to censorship usually involving a line struck through words or expressions not approved by the prison authorities) and occasional visitors and access to some books (subject to censorship).[154] It is to be presumed that only a fraction of the correspondence to Holberry survives.

In the late 1970s some of the prison correspondence held by Mary Holberry's descendents through her second marriage (the Pearson family) briefly came available for sale but half of it went into the private hands, now in York Archives. John Salt, then Head of History at Sheffield Polytechnic had bought most of the other half and was persuaded to donate them to Sheffield City Archives. A few other letters sold for their Victorian stamps also came into private hands but the contents, including two letters of his wife, were shared with the author and added to the publicly accessible Sheffield City Council archive collection. These latter fifteen accessible letters cover September 1841– April 1842.[155] They include three family letters (two from his wife and one from a married sister) and several from Edward Burley who, with other York Chartists, worked tirelessly during the spring of 1842 to better Holberry's York prison conditions. The York Chartists petitioned their two local MPs, one of whom was the eccentric radical Whig, Henry Yorke, son of the young firebrand Jacobin Henry Redhead Yorke (whose speech set the April 1794 Castle Hill Sheffield rally alight, but led to his imprisonment) to intervene on Holberry's behalf with Home Secretary Sir James Graham. Thomas

Duncombe MP, a friend of the working class, had submitted a petition in the House of Commons in March about Holberry.[156]

There are also several letters sent from a William Martin, a Derbyshire Chartist leader, but apparently not the ex-Bradford Chartist, active briefly alongside Holberry in Sheffield and arrested after the militant churchgoings, tried and sent to Northallerton with the Sheffield men. The latter Martin got a transfer to Lancaster where he finished his sentence. He had begun the public exposure of Northallerton's regime by writing in the *Northern Star* about its severe conditions.[157]

Most communication in later 1841 to the spring of 1842 suggested Holberry made some recovery and this lasted for a few months.[158] The authorities claimed later to have improved his weekly diet with three and a half pounds of mutton "when he could eat it" and regular provision of tea. In reality, the food provided was adding to his health problems but he appeared to recover in the early months of 1842.

A pocket made by Samuel Holberry (see letters HS6 and HS7) - also returned to Mary upon his death.

He received some low-key information from the outside world about the enthusiasm for the second national petition in the early months of 1842. There was clearly more communication than we can examine today. We are able to some of the letters returned by the prison authorities in a small fabric bag after his death that the Pearson family obtained through Mary's estate.[159] It is believed that this is actually a "pocket" made by Holberry in prison – two of the letters refer to such pockets made by him and given as gifts to friends. Holberry was hoping for progress with a petition in the Commons promoted by Duncombe, the radical MP who York Chartists had contacted. This followed the failure of a Christmas memorial. A letter to Burley on 1st April suggested he had not been given Burley's reply to his last letter. He asked about progress. He was suffering from severe coughing bouts and asked Burley to send a "stick of Spanish juice" (i.e. liquorice root) for his well-being. He also revealed, "my very dear wife is poorly."[160]

Holberry's health was going into reverse. The authorities claimed he was sent to the hospital ward on the 16th April. Holberry wrote of being, "very ill" on the 17th April. On the 21st he wrote of: "severe pains in his limbs and his stomach shockingly distended."[161] The Surgeon at York Castle wrote to Whitehall on 22 April 1842 that: "The health of Samuel Holberry… has not been so good as usual during the last two months. His appetite is at present bad and the functions of the stomach and liver are disordered, and I have thought it right to place him, for a time in the hospital"[162]

In a letter dated 24th April Holberry foresaw the completion of his murder by the State: "If they thought I deserved it, they would have put an end to all my suffering at once, instead of which they have destroyed my constitution until I am in such a state of bodily debility that I can hardly crawl, and, dear friend, you may be rest assured that I shall never serve two more years in prison. No! Before half that time has expired, I shall be in my grave."[163]

Some histories refer to Holberry suffering from tuberculosis (consumption). This is certainly possible since it was a prevalent disease and associated with poor, cramped living conditions and bad ventilation. There are a number of places where this infection could have been picked up, since the disease can progress slowly and even become latent, re-emerging later: the army, Sheffield, Northallerton. When he first arrived in York prior to the trial he "appeared a strong healthy man," according to the prison governor, if "rather pale in the face."

Poor nutrition would exacerbate the onset of disease and it can be seen just how bad the prison diet was, if he even received was he was supposed to. Vitamin D and C deficiencies are likely, affecting his bones and causing tiredness and aches. He was already suffering from dropsy (swelling of the legs) by late 1840. By the time he was transferred to York from Northallerton he had pains in his side, and back, shortness of breath and loss of appetite. The surgeon described him as weak and "his skin and eyes suffused with bile," i.e. jaundiced. TB can take different forms: not necessarily the coughing up blood seen in many period dramas: forms of the disease can affect other organs including the liver, leading to swelling of the liver. Following his death in June 1842, the deputy surgeon, Anderson, said it was caused by "chronic inflammation of the liver, which implicated some of the other abdominal viscera." Infection of the kidneys can also occur with TB. Kidney or liver disease could the account for the dropsy (swelling of the legs) from which he suffered from 1841 to his death. Another possibility is that he had a co-morbidity, possibly cancer which could explain his difficulties digesting food, if there was some obstruction.

The various "treatments" he was subjected to would have been useless. "Medicines" could have included things given for dropsy: emetics, such as ipecacuanha, to induce vomiting, followed by restriction of fluids. Diuretic medicines included nitre (potassium nitrate) or powdered squill (a toxic powder from bluebell roots). Seneca root was used to promote perspiration, as a diuretic and as an expectorant. Other drastic treatments would include draining of fluid from limbs by "tapping."

It is reported that his health returned for a brief few months in the winter of 1841–42.

He was later prescribed blistering. This involves applying a toxin such as cantharides powder (derived from crushed beetles) onto a plaster on the skin and leaving it for several hours to cause a chemical burn and blistering of the skin, which might then be punctured, in the misguided belief that this draws the fever away form the internal organs, when all it does, in fact, is to add horrific skin lesions to the victim's suffering.

In his last few weeks he was given a different diet: puddings made from egg, flour and milk, tea and milk to drink instead of gruel, and cuts of mutton leg, rather than the usual fatty bits of mutton he complained about. He was also given a frying pan and other implements so that he could cook things to his taste. It seems that the prison surgeons were trying their best. He also had the oranges bought for him from money sent by friends and purchased by Edward Burley.

Mary Holberry had just been to see Harney in his 11 Hartshead office to stress the urgent need for his intervention. He wrote to Holberry on the 22nd April in slightly apologetic but respectful terms.[164]

> "I have not hitherto written to you, because I was not personally acquainted with you, but you must not suppose that I have been indifferent to your situation; on the contrary (as Mrs Holberry can testify) I have been instrumental in getting adopted at public meetings, several petitions and testimonials on your behalf since I became a resident in Sheffield… I extremely regret that my efforts have been productive of little good."

He was persuading Mary Holberry to seek supportive statements from some Sheffield magistrates. He gave out to Holberry some encouraging news of Sheffield's 25,000 signatures on the national petition but said he would hold back other local information as it might prevent his letter getting past the censors.

Holberry was clearly considering a martyr's death stating in reply that: "I have no fear of death, I never felt more calm in my life."[165] This was a man who was reconciling with the apparently failing petitions for his release, rejections of support from Sheffield's two Whig MPs, Parker and Ward, and a faltering last minute deal brokering an early release which intensified in the next few weeks.

A letter written to York Chartist, Edward Burley, on the 30th April repeated the complaint that he was, "reduced to a skeleton" and that his mobility was reduced to crawling and that any food could not be digested unless he took medicine. "You will perhaps be surprised to hear that the Castle is a worse place, for a man in sickness, than Northallerton House of Correction. When I was ill there I had the food allowed as I could eat, but here the case is different; and if a man's stomach cannot take the food allowed, he must go without", he declaimed. He was only eating potatoes and these were not served every day. He said his eyes were sunken in his head and he had jaundice.[166]

Holberry's mail in May included a mid-May bulletin from Burley.[167] Holberry's reply, dated the 19th reveals severe health problems with an abscess on his side needing draining of "corruption." His lungs were affected and he was suffering "dropsy." Drinking quantities of water gave him no respite. He wanted a feather pillow sending in, as he was struggling to sleep and "sixpenny worth of oranges… which I will repay you as soon as I get some money." Even at this stage he was concerned about others asking Burley what the Chartist Convention was doing to support all the

Chartist prisoners wives and families and, "not leaving them destitute as they have been for months past."[168]

There was more communication with Harney in late May.[169] Holberry's health bulletin was negative saying, "I get worse in health every day; I cannot digest sufficient food to support my body; and all the medicine I have taken has not in the least benefited me; my side is very bad, and the blisters etc seem to do it no good. I am reduced to such a state that I can scarcely crawl. York Castle is a very bad place for a sick man." Holberry acknowledged the petitioning that Harney was organising saying, "I hope your endeavours will be crowned with success."

Burley received a similar letter from Holberry dated 28 May.[170] He had received the comforts asked for but was still favourably contrasting Northallerton with York Castle ("queer place for a sick man"). He complained the Castle had rules that prevented its staff buying anything that prisoners gave them money for and that the shilling sent with the pillow and oranges would not be able to be spent. One final bit of news was that Sir James Graham had written to him refusing release. Holberry noted: "he sends the same answer to a poor unfortunate convict that lays beside me (in the hospital) and is in the last stage of consumption." This was possibly a reply linked to Duncombe's March Commons petition or more likely to an April memorial got up to publicise his deteriorating health. Sir James Graham, Home Secretary, refused to respond to this.

He had now been committed to a bed in the hospital ward. It clearly wasn't easing his condition where he felt he was cooped up with the dying. He wrote another letter in late May echoing remarks made previously to Harney, "York Hospital is a queer place for a sick man… I wish I was back in Northallerton. Hospital mind," he added cryptically.[171]

Holberry again forbade his wife to visit him in an early June letter because of his deteriorating physical condition.[172] His final correspondence revealed little more about his chronic liver complaint which finally panicked the authorities wanting to avoid another imprisoned Chartist dying in prison to come up with a plan for pardon and release.

An intensely personal poignant mid-June letter sent to his wife a week before he died offered a brave face:

"My dear, you say you should like to come to York to see me; to that I cannot give my consent. In the first place we should have to look through the odious bars, and it would only make you more unhappy, to say nothing of myself, besides I have no complaint on me at present that is likely to terminate my existence; that my illness should bring me into consumption is all I am afraid of, but I believe they will not let me die here, except it will be by sudden visitation."[173]

Looking through "odious bars" (taken from The Illustrated Police News*)*

The petitions in May and early June did have an impact even though it was too late. An 11th June letter from the visiting magistrates responsible for the conditions of prisoners at York had been communicated to the Home Office. It contained the Castle surgeon's report of the 7th June stressing the seriousness of this turn in Holberry's health. Holberry, said the surgeon, was "in great danger." The problems with his liver, stomach and colon were said to be "an organic disease" and that his health had been impaired, of late by the length of confinement, and the great anxiety in his mind he appears to have suffered since his imprisonment."[174] Phillipps, at the Home Office, replied on the 17th June that Sir James Graham was advising the Queen to release Holberry with £100 bail agreed to be vouched for by Sheffield's magistrates.[175]

The possibility of release was forestalled by Holberry's severe turn for the worst on Monday 20th June. Mr Baxter Barker, under-gaoler at York, noted at the coroner's inquest on the 21st: "I saw the deceased yesterday (20th), I think he was delirious, and could not speak rationally." The deputy surgeon had been seeing Holberry daily and he had two hospital attendants watching over him in the last few weeks claimed Barker. He was woken up at 3.30 am on Tuesday 21st June. A watchman was calling out and the under gaoler went to the hospital ward. The other prisoners said Holberry was worse. Mr Anderson, the deputy surgeon, was sent for.[176] Anderson's bulletin from York related that Holberry had died. He wrote identifying the means and the moment, his report noting: "this morning at half past four of chronic inflammation of the liver, which implicated some other abdominal viscera."[177]

That evening an inquest was held before a coroner, Mr Wood, with a jury of respectable citizens from Fulford and with Mr Leeman, a York solicitor, in attendance as a "friend" or representative of Holberry's well-wishers. Mr Baxter Barker was questioned in relation to the contents of several letters from Holberry to Edward Burley (April 30th, May 19th and May 28th) which illustrated the straits Holberry was in. The letters detailed Holberry's concerns about his treatment. Next up was Anderson, as principal surgeon, Champney, was absent from the prison, as it turned out, sojourning in Paris during the last few weeks for his own health! There was a lengthy statement by Anderson stressing how accommodating the prison regime had been with Holberry's dietary requests, especially in the final weeks. It transpired in Anderson's testimony that the prison inspector and author of the 1840 report about Northallerton, Captain Williams, was inspecting at the York prison from 9–11th June, a fortnight before Holberry's death. He had twice met Holberry who he had first seen and interviewed at Northallerton. Possibly this contact may have been to do with the paperwork relating to Holberry's proposed release and the granting of a certificate of discharge which was then sent.

Leeman went over the history of the various appeals via petition that had been made, starting with one in September 1841, followed by Christmas 1841 and then March and April 1842. The authorities at the inquest responded with denials about Holberry's treatment and an alternative narrative of their sensitive and caring response to Holberry's illnesses. John Noble, the governor, who said some certificates were sent but was unsure if in the April–May period they were remitted, also stated, "my wife sent him pudding." (Everything is relative but it should be noted that the York Chartist Edward Burley said in a letter: "as what I have seen of the

Governor and officers of the prison they are Men possed {*sic*} of Humane + Kind hearts + tho the rules may be strict yet it is pleasant when you have such men to Enforce them." Also, chartist prisoner, George White, says to Holberry: "Please to give my requests {*ed. presumably 'respects'*} to Mr Noble the Governor of the Castle He is a worthy man.")

The prison authorities were defensive and evasive about the number of certificates of health sent to the Home Office as requested by Sir James Graham in respect of Holberry's health. The jury, presumably steered by the coroner, gave a verdict that Holberry: "died by the visitation of God… we are of the opinion that the deceased has had every attention paid to him."[178] It would have been extraordinary for any other verdict, in the context. It could be seen as the final act of denial by the State and its accomplices of what can be strongly argued to be effectively a political murder committed by the State.

Holberry's body was to be returned to Sheffield a few days later to lie in state at his wife's family's family home in Oakes Green, Attercliffe, two miles north of the town centre. Sheffield's Samuel Ludlam, a veteran in the cause and a personal friend of the Holberrys, arrived on Wednesday morning to demand the release of the body from the Castle. He was accompanied by several members of the York National Chartist Association including Holberry's friend and correspondent, Edward Burley, Robert Demaine a cabinet maker who was to make the coffin and Peter McLaughlen. Demaine made a death mask from the body and commissioned a lasting representation of Holberry, a plaster bust, which was placed in the Fig Tree Lane Chartist room.[179]

PART 2 – THE SPECTRE – HOLBERRY REMEMBERED

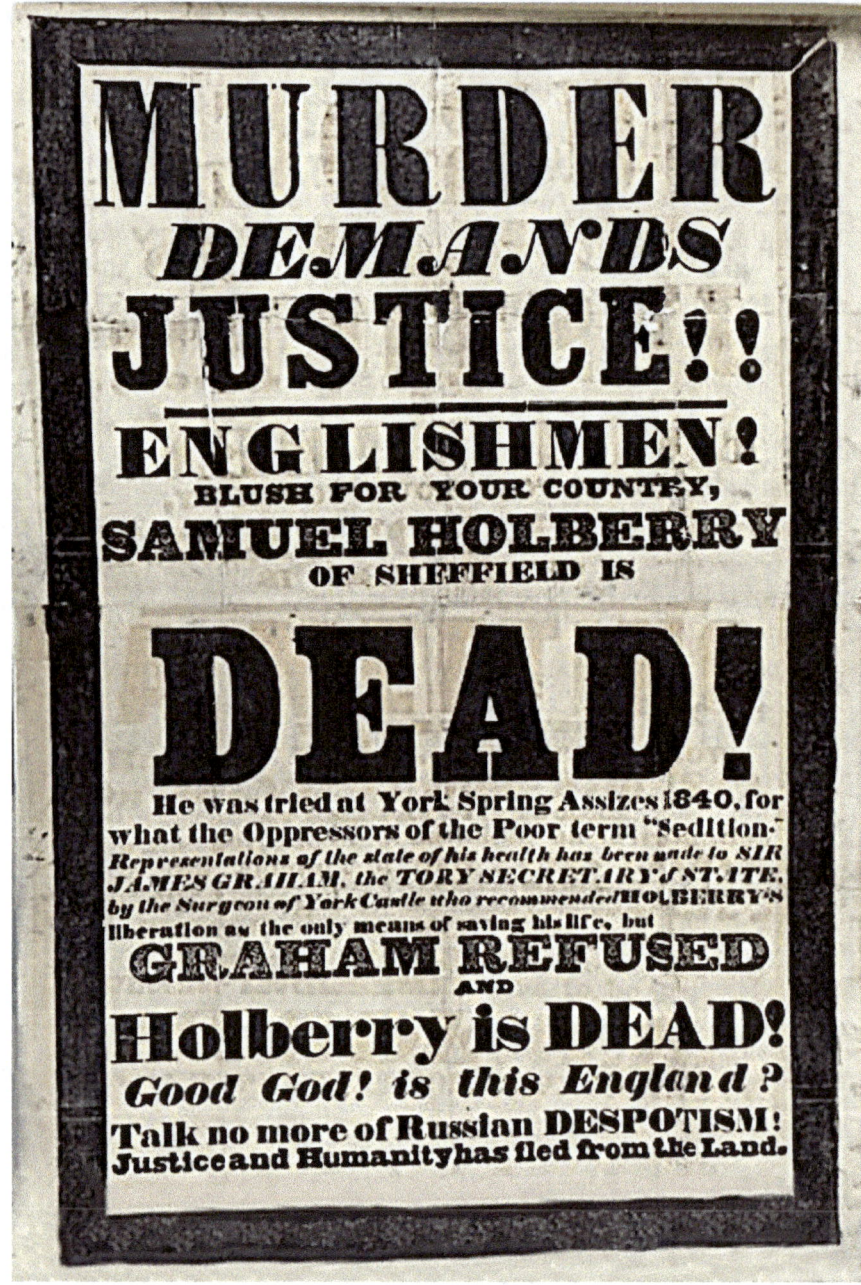

9. SHEFFIELD –THE FUNERAL – JUNE 1842

Sheffield's two NCA branches were riding on the crest of a wave of mobilisation in the summer of 1842. The economic context was even worse than the last months of 1839. Across the country 1842 was to see the highest levels unemployment and social distress in the 19th century. The *Northern Star*'s hugely partisan reports present Harney as a dynamic inspirational leader. He had strong backing from national leader, Feargus O'Connor. Harney had blazed a trail in London with the LDA but was arrested in 1839 and cooled his heels distancing himself from the winter insurgents like Holberry.[180] O'Connor had notoriously "called out" the "folly" of the post-Newport plans for risings with a *Northern Star* headline as the Sheffield rising was about to take place.[181] Holberry, the failed "insurgent," (one of a "knot of fools" as the *Star* had it) was no value to them, but now, Holberry, the dignified, suffering prisoner, displaying stoicism was, as a tortured and murdered Chartist prisoner, seen to have a risen stock value.

Reports from Sheffield in May and June[182] show significant recruiting meetings in the scattered villages and hamlets ringing the town. Meetings were held on familiar open spaces in the town including the once heavily contested Paradise Square. It was like the autumn of 1839 never happened. A programme of open-air Sunday meetings featured local Chartist artisan poet Edwin Gill alongside Harney. A mixture of moderate and centrist local leaders worked hard to build the movement, now petitioning for a second time, eventually signed by three million. Some ex-prisoners of the state like Duffy and Marshall were back in the town, busy proselytising. There was a Female Charter Association (originally set up by Wolstenholme in 1839), and a Chartist youth group had commenced in the town.

The movement was braced to capitalise on the tragedy of Holberry's death and placarded the town on Friday 25th June with green placards edged with black. These contained the words:

> "Funeral procession of Samuel Holberry, the martyr to Liberty – "Peace to his Soul." The friends of Freedom will assemble on Monday 27th June, 1842 in Paradise Square, at one o'clock, for the purpose of forming into procession, with band, banners, etc; and from thence will march to Attercliffe to meet the body of the departed Samuel Holberry, previous to its internment in the General Cemetery. Marshals are appointed to form the procession

and direct the route. It is particularly requested that all parties attending the funeral will abstain from intoxicating drinks, observing our Motto of "Peace, Law and Order," and all will observe the strict decorum which the solemnity of the occasion demands. Mr G.J. Harney and Mr S. Parkes will deliver appropriate addresses after the burial service."[183]

The day arrived which the *Northern Star* edition of 2nd July prophetically stated would be long remembered in Sheffield. The following section below largely mainly uses the *Northern Star*'s report almost verbatim in places.[184] The *Star* said 50,000 people were participants as funeral goers or sympathetic spectators. Reports claim many shops closed in parts of the town on the route of the procession. The town's smallest circulation paper, the largely Whig *Iris*, claimed 20,000 there and contained some sympathetic detail, confirming large scale community support.[185] The *Star* commented in its report, "when a Whig paper says 20,000, some idea may be formed of the real number." The *Independent*, the local paper with the largest circulation, did not mention numbers and carried only a small and exceptionally downbeat report which will be evaluated below.[186]

Holberry's funeral turned out to be probably one of the largest funeral events in British 19th century working class history, although American modern cultural historian, Thomas Lacqueur, who picked out aspects of Holberry's funeral in his recent book on the social celebration of death, notes that large scale funerals aping "bourgeois style" were a feature of Chartism up to 1848. Laqueur claims they were deliberately hyped up events to make political points.[187]

The funeral saw Harney play the showman. The *Star* reported an extravagantly proportioned poster in his office window to publicise the event. Harney was, in all likelihood, the writer of the coverage in the *Star* so his account would be highly partisan but it does contain intimate detail.[188] The police tried to request Harney to remove what they claimed was a provocatively worded poster but they were defied. Hundreds rapidly became thousands parading in Paradise Square from noon. At 1 p.m. the march to Attercliffe began. The marchers arrived at Oakes Green and the oak coffin (6 foot and 9 inches long, only two inches longer than the body later claimed Thomas Cooper, the Leicester Chartist leader) was brought out of the Coopers' cottage. The *Star* noted it was "handsomely decorated." It had been made in York under the commission of the York NCA. The inscription on its breast-plate read:

"SAMUEL HOLBERRY

Died a martyr to the cause of Democracy,
June 21st, 1842,
Aged 27"

All the mournful preparations having been completed, the procession started in the following order:

The band, playing the solemn air of Pleyel's
German Hymn.
Two undertakers.
Two mutes.
The hearse, beautifully decorated, containing
the body of the decreased Patriot.
Large magnificent, black banner of the National
Charter Association (Fig Tree Lane) with the
following inscription:
"Vengeance is mine, and I will repay it saith the
Lord"
"Clayton and Holberry,
The martyrs to the People's Charter"
On the reverse side –
" Thou shalt do no murder"
Two mourning coaches containing the female
relatives of the deceased.
An open carriage containing several female
mourners.
The male relatives of the deceased, on foot.
Members of the Council of the National Charter
Association, (Figtree Lane).
Members of the Association.
Females, two deep – Men, four deep.
Members of the Political Institute, two deep,
bearing a white banner, with the
following inscriptions:
"Political Institute,
Birks–Clayton–and Holberry, Martyrs to the Charter."
On the reverse
"The Lord hateth the hands that shed innocent blood"

The *Northern Star* continued its report:

"The procession commenced its solemn march about half-past two o'clock; of course it was not confined to the members of the Association, as some thousands accompanied it on either side. On reaching the town, the road along the Wicker, from the Railway Station to the Bridge {*Lady's Bridge*}, was densely crowded, and immense numbers continued to swell the mass, as it moved on. The pavement on each side of the road, the doorways, windows, and in some instances the roofs of houses were crowded with anxious gazers, even some of the chambers appeared to be literally crammed with human beings; and in every nook and corner where a view could be obtained there were men and women watching with seemingly intense interest the melancholy sight. We observed many, very many, females, unable to control themselves, giving vent to their feelings in tears."

The route took in Waingate , the Haymarket, High Street, Fargate, Barkers Pool, Coal Pit Lane and then onto a southerly route down Sheffield Moor before sharply turning left onto New Road leading to the Cemetery at Sharrow. By the time it was at the bottom of the Moor, the *Star* correspondent said, "the mighty multitude showed to the best advantage." It continued, "by the time the procession had reached this quarter, many thousands of persons were in advance of the band." The march stretched from the bottom of the Moor to the last marchers entering Coalpit Lane. This means over half a mile long and it was much wider than any local 21st century equivalents.

On arrival at the cemetery gates it was seen that hundreds were already inside. The band stayed at the gates, the hearse, coaches and mourners went to the chapel. The coffin was taken inside where only family and close mourners attended. Lee Croft Independent chapel minister, Mr Landells, conducted the service. The burial plot was close by, also at the top or higher end of a large, but as yet largely unused, new burial area which dropped steeply down almost a hundred yards to the northern boundary which was marked by a small stream, the Porter Brook, travelling eastwards towards the centre of the town and its eventual joining with the Sheaf and Don rivers.

The coffin was lowered, and a prayer given and a hymn sheet with Leicester Chartist, John Henry Bramwich's verses given out by Samuel Parkes and then sung to the air of the Old Hundredth.[189]

The *Star* printed the words and printed copies were widely circulated:

FUNERAL HYMN,

SUNG AT THE INTERMENT OF THE MURDERED AND LAMENTED PATRIOT,

SAMUEL HOLBERRY,

Who at the Age of 27, Died in York Castle on the 21st, of June 1842, after Two Years and Three Months Imprisonment. He was Buried in the Sheffield Cemetry on the 27th, of June, 1842.

COMPOSED BY JOHN HENRY BRAMARCH.—LEICESTER.

LONG METRE.

Great God! is this the Patriot's doom?
   Shall they who dare defend the Slave,
Be hurl'd within a prison's gloom,
   To fit them for an early grave?

Shall victim after victim fall,
   A prey to cruel class made laws?
Forbid it, Lord! on thee we call,
   Protect us and defend our cause.

In vain we pray'd the powers that be,
   To burst the drooping captives chain,
But mercy, Lord, belongs to Thee,
   For Thou hast freed him from all pain,

Is this the price of Liberty?
   Must Martyrs fall to gain the prize?
Then be it so, we will be free,
   Or all become a sacrifice.

Tho' Freedom mourns her murder'd son,
   And weeping friends surround his bier;
Tho' tears like mountain torrents run,
   Our cause is water'd by each tear.

O! may his fate cement the bond
   That binds us to our glorious cause;
Raise, raise the cry, let all respond,
   Justice, and pure, and equal laws.

[HARDCASTLE, PRINTER.]

Sheffield Local Studies Library collection

Many among the crowds remained on the road outside. Many occupied the space around the grave on plots owned but as yet unoccupied in this newly opened cemetery. A spiteful report in the *Sheffield Independent* said trees were damaged and some of the attendees were pickpockets. The following week there was a small page bottom retraction of these claims.[190]

Harney then followed with a powerful speech.[191] Many could not hear him, so vast was the assemblage but most knew why they were there and spoken words were not necessary to feeling connected to a collective outpouring of sympathetic political feeling.

Harney commenced addressing the crowds as, "Sisters and Brothers" and commenced stressing the qualities of the "departed brother" who was an "honest man" – "the noblest work of God." He stressed Holberry's "sterling honesty, his unbounded integrity, his thorough incorruptibility and dauntless courage."

He rhetorically asked, "What was his crime for which he has been sent to the cold grave? He saw his country enslaved, her sons in bondage and her daughters in misery. It was a time when oppression hovered over England."

Harney, in an interesting allusion to the attempted 1840 rising and Holberry's betrayal, attributed to him: "a heart without guile, he believed in the truth of all men; and confided in miscreants who betrayed him into the hands of the enemies of his country." Harney talked of the informers who were, "but the despicable tools of their base employers – the oppressors that pursued him to his grave."

The latter section of Harney's speech focussed on Holberry as inspiration for the future:

> "... the spirit of Holberry hovers over us, and smiles approval of the vow – swear, to unite in one countless moral phalanx, to put forward the giant strength which union will call into being, and aid, assist, and fraternise with each other to burst the bonds that bind ye. Swear as I now swear, that neither persecution, nor scorn, nor calumny – neither bolts, nor bars, nor chains, nor racks nor gibbets – neither the tortures of a prison death-bed, nor the terrors of the scaffold, shall sever us from our principles, affright us from our duty, or cause us to leave the onward path of freedom; but that, come weal, come woe, we swear, with hearts uplifted to the throne of eternal justice, to have retribution for the death of Holberry! Swear to have our Charter law! and to annihilate forever the blood-stained despotism that has slain its thousands of martyrs, and tens

of thousands of patriots, and immolated at its shrine the lovers of liberty and truth! If ye do this and act upon your vow, while we mourn the death of Holberry, our children will rejoice that he died not in vain! But from his ashes rose, phoenix-like, his dauntless spirit, inspiring you with the love of freedom! and the stern resolve to set your country free"

The crowd listened spellbound in total silence, absorbing the essential message.

Samuel Parkes, another local Chartist, made a short speech echoing Harney and linking Holberry to others who had died like Shell, killed at Newport. He connected him to a survivor, Frost the Newport leader, who had been transported and Sheffield's John Clayton, who died in Northallerton early in 1841. A visitor from Scotland, Thomason, a travelling NCA lecturer, gave a shorter final speech and the crowds began dispersing. The struggle was to go on for the living. That night at 7 p.m. many thousands attended a meeting in the Square to memorialise the Queen about the Chartist prisoners still suffering the degrading conditions in Northallerton and Beverley Houses of Correction. The next phase of Holberry's existence, his transcendent significance from the grave was commencing.

10. BRITAIN – THE BREAKING WAVE OF SOLIDARITY – IMMEDIATE RECOGNITION: JUNE – OCTOBER 1842

Even before the Sheffield funeral, Chartists in some localities enacted open displays of recognition of Holberry's passing. York Chartists (and probably Birmingham Chartists) were among the first with an indoor rally in York where many leading NCA members had organised petitions to their MPs and constantly liaised with leading national radical MP, Thomas Duncombe, member for Finsbury, the most supportive member of the House of Commons.[192] Birmingham, if we accept the story in the *Star* of 2nd July which claimed that the news of Holberry's death reached Birmingham two days after his death and George White was able to act immediately to arrange a procession and open air rally attended by thousands on 23rd June. If the *Star* misreported, this was held on 30th June.[193] In Hull on the Sunday night (26th) before the Sheffield funeral, a sermon was preached by Reverend William Hill, close confident of Feargus O'Connor and sometime editor of the *Northern Star*.[194] This type of religious meeting, some using the half penny sheets of Bramwich's funeral hymn, was to spread.

Many responses are documented in the columns of the weekly *Northern Star* for the next fifteen weeks. For a lot of this time, which followed the 3 million name national petition, rejected in May, the movement shifted gear in late summer towards a replay of "ulterior measures" based strategies. These months saw a huge revival of Chartist branch membership at a time of deep and deepening recession. From late July there was spontaneous industrial unrest that coalesced into a general strike for the Charter. The NCA was caught out by a largely autonomous independent rank and file surge led by some Chartist "ultras." On top of arrests in Staffordshire and then in August throughout many industrial areas, the official movement, in adjusting to the political-industrial surge, found itself too closely scrutinised by the State, and was rocked by arrests of its key leaders.[195]

Early 20th century mass meeting in Paradise Square, Sheffield Local Studies Library, Picture Sheffield y 00766

Holberry commemoration events played some part in assisting membership revival and the general political credibility of Chartism. Sheffield NCA, with the dynamic Harney organising almost daily recruiting activities, grew from 200 members in May to 1400 in August. Harney on 8th July had sent off the Paradise Square memorial of the 27th June, concerning the investigation of Holberry's "murder," to Thomas Duncombe MP, for presentation to the Commons. Harney stated, "the death (murder it is considered here) of poor Holberry, at the age of only twenty-seven, has excited the greatest indignation of the people of Sheffield against the Government… upon the occasion of the funeral, a mass of people had assembled such as within the living memory of the oldest inhabitant as never been seen in Sheffield".

In Sheffield it was as if 1839's repression by the local elite never happened. Chartists gathered confidently in all the once contested sites of Paradise Square and Doctor's Fields. Roscoe Fields was frequently used and included the presence of Mary Holberry when Thomas Cooper from Leicester preached there on the evening of 17th July (see below). They freely entered over a dozen out-villages to recruit. They ascended the heights of Sky Edge unchallenged for camp meetings.[196]

Recruitment at the Sunday orations and at camp meetings and the collections for the Widow Holberry were part of connecting ordinary people with the human misery the State enforced through political repression. Activities combined the actual commemoration of Holberry and the underlying moral and practical issue of support for his widow. Studying the *Northern Star*'s pages over fifteen weeks from Holberry's death reveals varying commemorative activity that range from open public rallies relating to Chartist prisoners, promoting petitions and memorials to the Government as well as specific religious-type political funeral sermons delivered using his funeral oration and the hymn written by Bramwich leading to room, chapel, street and other outdoor collections for his widow's benefit.[197] Sunday evening indoor religious style events in meeting rooms and chapel premises were by far the most common but also several outdoor camp meetings on moorland or in fields grabbed the attention of numbers in the low thousands. Street meetings at regular locations (like the open space next to the railway station on Duddeston Row and open land by the Vulcan foundry in Summer Lane) in Birmingham to promote local activity were also used to collect money for Holberry's widow.[198] Across England and parts of Scotland meeting room and public house collections made in the course of meetings of working class groups with social welfare and industrial roles like unions and benefit clubs were another format of respectful acknowledgement of Holberry and his family.

Over a hundred locations featured in making commitment to Holberry's memory.[199] Peak numbers of events were centred on Sundays. There were ten reported on the 3rd July, fourteen on the 10th, seven on the 17th, six on the 24th and eight on the 31st July. Thereafter numbers of Sunday events dwindled to insignificance. Several places were acting similarly for consecutive weeks as with Sheffield, Birmingham and York. Many others featured activity in at least two weeks. In total the *Star* identified over 150 Holberry connected activities over fifteen weeks. Locations ranged from east to west, from Sheerness to Plymouth and north to south from Aberdeen to Brighton.

In alphabetic order from late June to late September these included: Aberdeen, Adwalton Moor (nr Bradford), Armley, Arnold, Barnsley, Bath, Batley, Bingley, Birmingham, Bishop Auckland, Bradford, Brighton, Brinscombe, Bristol, Brockmoor (Bilston), Brompton, Calverton, Carlisle, Carrington, Chelmsford, Cheltenham, Chowbent, Clitheroe, Colchester, Congleton, Coventry, Dartford, Derby, Dewsbury, Durham, Earlsheaton, Elland Edge, Fenton, Halifax, Handsworth, Woodhouse, Hawick, Hayward (Staffs), Holbeck, Holme Lane, Hucknal Torquet, Huddersfield, Hull, Hyson Green, Idle, Intake, Keighley, Kettering, Leeds, Lees, Leicester, Leith, Liverpool, London (Camberwell, Hammersmith, Kentish Town, Mile End, Somerstown and trade union branches in pubs associated with masons, stuff hatters and shoemakers), Longton, Malton, Manchester, Mansfield, Marple, Miles Platting, Millbridge, Morley, Nantwich, Newark, Newbattle Abbey, Newcastle, New Lenton, Newport (IOW), Newton Heath, Northallerton, Northampton, Nottingham, Oldham, Plymouth, Rotherham, Rothwell, Selby, Sheerness, Sheffield (two NCA branches and Shoemakers branch), Somerstowe, South Shields, Stockton, Stroud, Sunderland, Sutton-in-Ashfield, Swinton (S Yorks), Thornely, Todmorden, Tonbridge Wells, Upper Elland, Vale of Leven, Walsall, Warrington, West Bromwich and York.

The general messaging about Holberry was that he was a "patriot" of unimpeachable character and that he had shown great dignity, bravery and resilience in prison in the face of the horrors and abuses of the state's prison regime. He was seen as being murdered by the state. In the few instances where speakers alluded to the winter rising of 1840, they emphasised his betrayal by unnamed others and there were a few allusions to the rising as a mistake. At least two large meeting speakers, Bartlett, in Bath, who used a provocative yet sympathetic rhetorical analysis of

Holberry as an "assassin,"[200] and Williams at South Shields (see below) made detailed analyses of Holberry's motivation.

Speakers connected his case to the other martyr deaths, the still suffering remaining prisoners taken in 1839 – 40 and the new sufferings of recent Chartist prisoners on what turned out to be the eve of a wave of further prosecutions of key leading national figures from the late July to early September phase of political-industrial insurgency and consequent repression.

Some of the speakers had first hand experience of the prison regime. James Duffy had been released earlier and probably burnt himself out in his lecturing activity in the East Midlands.[201] George White who moved from the West Riding to be a key figure in Birmingham was somebody who knew the inner secrets of the planning of late 1839 and knew he had escaped detection by a hair's breadth.[202] Both gave a great deal of commitment as propagandists for Holberry's treatment. E.P. Mead, "the Commodore," was also a widely-travelled Midlands speaker on Holberry's behalf. Thomason from the Vale of Leven in Scotland was a frequent officiate at the funeral oration deliveries. Many well established hard line militants and advocates of armed resistance from 1839 like Ashton-Under-Lyne's William Aitken remained in place as determined community leaders and gave sterling service organising support for Holberry's widow.[203]

Many gatherings were modest, but well-attended branch meetings. Outdoors, in market places, on uncontested urban wasteland sites, urban public squares, in fields, on hilly outcrops and moors, there were larger crowds.

The following selected reports represent a mixture of types of commemorative activity from a wide geographic area. They contain a few hints at a backlash against the perceived ambivalence of movement leader Feargus O'Connor towards "Poor Holberry."

Birmingham 23rd (or 30th) June – the procession (*Northern Star* 2nd July)

Birmingham's first Holberry focussed meeting started at a familiar meeting place on Duddeston-row. It led to a march after a larger gathering of several thousand listening to key local speakers introduce a memorial to the government about Holberry's prison treatment and the actions of Sir James Graham. York and Sheffield were with other centres continuing this approach. Speakers included White and John Mason, an itinerant shoemaker from the North-East. Mason was now active in his new West

Midlands home and was to be a central figure in the Staffordshire strikes in late July. One stand-out feature of this display was John Barrett's huge black flag on which were painted the words: "Samuel Holberry, died in York Castle on Tuesday, 21st June. Shall we have Justice?" The meeting was described as a "bumper" and a source of frustration to the police who tried to remove some of the giant six foot wide black bordered posters to publicise the rally and procession. The *Star* picked up the story of the procession which came out of the meeting:

> "As soon as the black flag was placed in the centre of the road, opposite the Liverpool Station (railway station), the working men commenced forming in a quiet and orderly manner, six-a-breast, and proceeded through the principal streets of the town in solemn silence, and halted at the National Charter Association room, Aston Street, where they were addressed by Mr White, who declared his determination of organising every working man who desired liberty, and told them he would meet them again at Duddleston-row the following Monday.
>
> The multitude then separated in a peaceful and orderly manner; and this ended the most important and numerous meeting, which was well-conducted throughout, and evinced the love which the men of Birmingham have for sound democracy, and their determination to have justice for the death of Samuel Holberry."

Adwalton Moor, near Bradford Sunday 3rd July (*Northern Star* 9th July)

> "On Sunday afternoon last, a Chartist camp meeting was held at this place. At two o'clock Mr Jennings gave out a hymn sung at poor Holberry's funeral, and afterwards read the oration delivered by Mr Harney at the graveside of our departed brother. Mr Jennings also spoke on the subject. Mr Henry Hodgson followed and spoke for upwards of half an hour on the benefits that would result from the extension of the suffrage to every male adult of twenty-one years of age"

Sugar Loaf public house, Church Street, Mile End, London 3rd July– harassment by Metropolitan Police (*Northern Star* 9th July 1842)

Chartist branch meeting describes collections in the more hostile environment of heavily policed London in this report:

"An audience assembled on Sunday evening in the large room of the above place to hear a lecture from Mr Anderson, Mr Shaw having previously requested the attendance of Mr Ruffey Ridley to make an appeal on behalf of his brother victims; the result was that although 10 shillings and four pence was raised for the widow of the martyr Holberry on that week previously, the meeting responded to the noble call with a subscription of 8 shillings and 6 pence. This was only the second meeting at the Sugar Loaf. The police who are always at our local meetings, either in their private or public dress, worked upon the landlord's timidity to cause him to give our friends notice that they should not meet on his premises again. We are hunted like beasts of prey by this unconstitutional force."

Newark, 5th July – grim humour in lecture by James Duffy, political lecturer and ex-inmate of Holberry at Northallerton(*Northern Star* 9th July 1842)

"Mr James Duffy arrived here unexpectedly on Tuesday night, and lectured on the following night in a very humorous manner; he told a tale of grief of the cruelties of the infernal silent system, and the horrors of a Whig boarding school; he also alluded in a feeling manner to the case of the never-to-be-forgotten Holberry"

South Shields , Sunday 10th July gathering on the " Bents" (*Northern Star* 16th July)

"On Sunday afternoon, Mr Williams, in compliance with an invitation, visited this place, for the purpose of delivering an address on the death of Holberry. The place selected was on the Bents, or Sea Banks, opposite Tynemouth. It was admirably adapted for the purpose, and a noble assembly there was. It was estimated there were upwards of two thousand people present

Mr Williams, after briefly stating the facts relative to Holberry's conduct, arrest, trial and conviction, then proceed to show why Holberry had embraced Chartist principles, and, why in an erring moment, he had been led to use the weapons of his oppressors in endeavouring to arrest by night what had been denied to the calm demands of justice. The general scope of the address was as follows: Holberry was a working man, a producer of wealth. That which he and his brother millions, produced, he was not permitted to enjoy; instead of that, poverty and toil, and suffering was his portion – while he saw privileged idlers, wallowing in the superabundant wealth which he and his class had produced. Common sense and a sentiment of justice, taught him this was a grievous wrong. Oppression, therefore, made him feel, feeling prompted him to inquire, and to think about the causes, of such an unnatural and unjust state of things – inquiry and reflection led to a discovery of the grand, of the all-comprehensive cause of his sufferings. That cause he found to be that he was subjected to the operation of the laws affecting his labour liberty and happiness, which laws were made by others, by the idlers, the drones; and therefore for them, and not for him. He laboured for the benefit of his brethren, to make known the cause, and with the friends of human right, he combined to remove it. His petition and the petitions of millions, was treated with contempt, and insultingly rejected.

He was told by one of those privileged lawmakers, that he, "might as well petition the rock of Gibraltar" as that body. Their acts proved its truth and Holberry believed it. He not only saw the petition of plundered millions treated with cruel neglect, but he also saw that those who had dared to advocate the cause of the oppressed, seized upon, dragged before the tribunals of the oppressors, there condemned and consigned to a dungeon residence and a felon's treatment. This acting upon his sensitive sympathetic nature, maddened him. Having seen that this fraud and oppression was committed by force, he concluded that as the oppressors were deaf to reason and honour, they might be alive to fear the fear of being compelled to disgorge by force what they had got or maintained by force.

The vile oppressors knew what was working in the mind of Holberry and his brethren, and they therefore sent among them the insidious and perfidious spy to fan the flames of patriot indignation and the progress of their hellish work. Plots were formed, but their secrets were made known, the enemy was prepared and when the hour for action arrived, the oppressors pounced on their unsuspecting victims: Holberry was such a victim. For this he was, convicted, condemned, imprisoned, tortured, destroyed… the evidence given before the jury, which clearly proved that the parties holding Holberry in bond, knew that the disease was making rapid inroads on a once powerful constitution. They knew that the disease was the result of mental agony, by long confinement, unsuitable diet and other privations to which Holberry was subjected, knowing the fact of the disease, the cause of its progress, and his approaching death, according to all the ordinary and just processes, of reasoning, it must be inferred that they either intended that Holberry should be destroyed, or they were altogether indifferent to the result."

On the Forest at Nottingham Sunday 17th July – George Harrison preaching about Holberry to 10–12,000 people (*Northern Star* 23rd July.)

"We are hunted like beasts of prey by this uncontrollable fire kept up by the oligarchy whose main object is to oppress the people and tyrannise over their liberties."

Thomas Cooper of Leicester preaches the Holberry sermon outdoors in Roscoe Fields to 6–7000 on the evening of 17th July in the presence of the Widow Holberry (*Northern Star* 23rd July)

"I preached twice to the Sheffielders, in the open air Sunday last. In the evening the death of Holberry was part of the theme. His faithful widow sat in a chair close by the table on which I stood and with a perseverance and an ardour which prove her to be a woman of no ordinary value. She sat through the whole of the discourse, surrounded by six or seven thousand people, and would not move from the ground till I had enrolled one hundred and fifteen Chartists.

I thought as I gave her my arm to conduct her off the ground, amid the thronging of hundreds, who crowded round to gaze, that if every Chartist in England could have seen that brave, bereaved and noble woman, they would have sworn, as I did in my innermost soul, either to compass the downfall of the horrid tyranny by which her husband was martyred or to spend life in the attempt."

At the "Byron Oak", propaganda by self-promoting Feargus O'Connor on his two day "procession" from Nottingham towards Calverton on 25th July and on this second day heading towards Mansfield 26th July.

The *Northern Star* of the 30th July describes the theatrical use of young "juvenile Mercuries" to head up the route into Sutton on the second day (Tuesday 26th August) of O'Connor's regal tour and the arrival of great numbers of branch banners and contingents from outside Nottingham prior to entry into Sutton with a claim of 30–40,000 supporters:

"Within three miles of Mansfield stands Byron's Oak, at the gate leading to Newstead Abbey; here the avant-couriers of the day's grand spectacle met us, like so many running epistles of Chartism, each containing a pithy paragraph printed upon various slips of coloured paper, fluttering in the breeze, from the napless hats, tattered caps, and bare poles of these juvenile Mercuries of Chartism.

Amongst the pithy sentences were of the following:

"More fat pigs, and fewer parsons," "Holberry and Clayton were martyred by the Whigs," "The judgement of Kings is toil and starvation," "Welcome, welcome, O brave O'Connor," "Frost, Williams and Jones – never forget them," "We will, we will, we will be free," "Down with the Corn Law Humbug, and up with the Charter," "A tear of sympathy for the martyrs – Clayton and Holberry."

The number of these living epistles, read and understood by all men, was surprising; from six or eight to eighteen or twenty years of age, we suppose more than 400 met us a mile or two in advance of the procession, and ran along with the carriage. At length we came up with the vanguard headed by a fine band, and the black banner used at poor Holberry's funeral, and numerous flags of all sizes, colours, devices, and tints, from the toy paper one of the young Fearguses of which sort there were a pretty considerable number, to banners taking up the breadth of the road. The entrée into the town of Mansfield was splendid."

Bairstow preaching in Cheltenham 7th August 1842 – *Northern Star* 13th August.

"Mr Bairstow preached a sermon in the open air in a field adjoining the town of Cheltenham, kindly lent by a friend, to upwards of 1000 persons who were apparently highly delighted. The service began at three o'clock. One pound was collected at the close of the service for Mason and his fellow prisoners. In the evening, at seven o'clock, the Mechanics Institute was excessively crowded, as well as every avenue leading to it, and even the street opposite to the room to hear Mr Bairstow's funeral sermon on behalf of the brave, departed Holberry – from the words "He being dead yet speaketh" {*Hebrews 11:4 – focus on virtuous Abel murdered by his brother Cain, both the offspring of Adam and Eve.*} He spoke for nearly two hours, in such a strain of overpowering and brilliant eloquence, that he not only carried all hearts, but riveted every eye upon him. All admitted that the concluding part of his discourses to be without parallel for its grasping force, its eloquent energy, and its touching, impassioned, pathetic appeals. The absorption of the speaker of his subject evidently was not lost on the audience; they were alternately electrified melted into sympathy, or burning with vehement indignation, as Mr Bairstow successfully showed how the departed Holberry, being dead, yet spoke of our principles – of his own unswerving consistency – of his indomitable perseverance – of his fortitude under persecution – of the majestic embodiment of and the triumph of the truth – his life, imprisonment and glorious death. Mr Bairstow's address will never be forgot by them who enjoyed the high intellectual treat. At the conclusion of the discourse, one guinea was collected at the door for Mrs Holberry."

11. COLLECTIONS FOR MARY HOLBERRY COME TO AN END

The collections for Holberry's widow continued to almost the end of the year. The donations were reduced to a trickle as the movement found many other prisoners and their dependents needing help. Holberry was rarely invoked but Mary Holberry was not forgotten. The *Star* noted 2 shillings and sixpence from "Friends at Colchester on 3rd September." The 10th September listed 12 shillings from "Rationalists in Newcastle via Mr Holyoake." In the 24th September edition a few Chartists at Warrington sent one shilling and ten pence. Subsequently small sums like this trickled in from Coventry, Nantwich, Vale of Leven, Leeds, Long Buckby, Brighton, Chesterfield, Coventry, Leeds, Rotherham, Sheffield Cordwainer NCA branch and Todmorden. The final published record of a donation was of "a few masons from London" who sent 8 shillings and a penny as reported in the *Star* of 1st October.

12. COMMEMORATIONS: THE GRAVESTONE, THE BUST AND VERSE 1842–44

The Holberrys' grave

Late in 1842 the Sheffield NCA, already heavily involved in supporting the national Victim Fund which was a conduit for funds for Mary Holberry, started supporting the widow of John Clayton, who was seeking help in getting her husband's body removed from its 1841 burial place at

Northallerton House of Correction. Funds were handed over after the national fund gave permission to the Sheffield NCA in February 1843.[204] Mary Holberry was now seen as having the shadow of the workhouse pass her by. The NCA branch had purchased Holberry's burial plot and they funded the gravestone monument that was erected, months after the funeral. Mary Holberry was involved in piecing together Holberry's story possibly with local activists for the *English Chartist Circular* which ran a series of articles between May and June 1843 on Holberry's life. They drew on earlier comments in the press including this view expressed by Thomas Cooper when he visited her on the Sunday 17th July 1842 before his Roscoe Fields oration:

> "She is a remarkably fine looking woman, and in spite of all her heart-rending sufferings, wears a latent fire in her eye and a dignity in her carriage, that tells you she is worthy to have been the wife of the unconquerable patriot, Samuel Holberry"

The *English Chartist Circular* echoed and added to this twelve months later stating:

> "After three years of heart corroding activity and mental anguish, she is still a truly fine woman, tall in stature, of graceful deportment, handsome expression and possesses an excellent temper, and considering the defects of education, a mind of no mean order"[205]

The records of the General Cemetery contain evidence that Mary authored the words in the gravestone, which was executed by a local stonemason in 1842. A long-time volunteer still working on the site once told John Baxter that she was confident Mary had composed the dedication. The words read to this day:

SACRED
TO THE MEMORY OF
SAMUEL HOLBERRY
WHO AT THE EARLY AGE OF 27 DIED
IN YORK CASTLE. AFTER SUFFERING
AN IMPRISONMENT OF 2 YEARS AND 3
MONTHS. JUNE 21ST 1842.
FOR ADVOCATING WHAT TO HIM APPEARED
TO BE THE TRUE INTEREST OF THE PEOPLE OF
ENGLAND
VANISH'D IS THE FEVERISH DREAM OF LIFE
THE RICH AND THE POOR FIND NO DISTINCTION HERE
THE GREAT AND LOWLY AND THEIR CARE AND STRIFE

> THE WELL BELOVED MAY HAVE AFFECTIONS TEAR
> BUT, AT THE LAST THE OPPRESSOR AND THE SLAVE
> SHALL EQUAL STAND BEFORE THE BAR OF GOD
> OF HIM, WHO LIFE, AND HOPE, AND FREEDOM GAVE
> TO ALL THAT THROUGH THE VALE OF TEARS HAVE TROD
> LET NONE THEN MURMUR AGAINST THE WISE DECREE
> THAT OPEN'D THE DOOR AND SET THE CAPTIVE FREE
> ALSO OF SAMUEL JOHN, HIS SON WHO
> DIED IN HIS INFANCY
> THIS TABLET WAS ERECTED BY HIS BEREFT WIDOW

Holberry was also invoked positively as a heroic exemplar to motivate commitment and for joining the burgeoning movement of 1842. Verse earlier appeared July in the *Northern Star* which idealised Holberry. L.T. Clancy had produced a four verse " Elegiac Lines on the death of Samuel Holberry, who died a Martyr to Democracy, 21st June, 1842, aged 27.[206] It commenced:

> "Peace to thy shade! immortal youth,
> Our Charter's martyr, rest!
> Thy spirit's gone, but like the sun's
> Diurnal in the West,
> Thy name shall long illume the land;
> And when the sky – the sea,
> Are vengeful on this world of ours,
> Then will I think on thee."

Holberry continued to be invoked in Chartist poetry in middle years of the 1840s even though the movement appeared to be fragmenting into a pluralist multi-directional movement with the extension of "new moves" into Christian Chartism, Temperance Chartism, accommodation with middle class reform Chartism, Land Plan Chartism and Municipal Chartism.[207] In terms of the Sheffield Chartists, they remained active but still operating as two separate NCA branches, the Fig Tree Lane O'Connorite loyalists (led by Harney and the more moderate and "respectable" Political Institute branch based on an Exchange Street reading room.[208] Social difference had been very much emphasised in the June 1842 *Sheffield Independent*'s funeral report which favourably commented on their smarter funeral garb including universally worn black scarves.[209] The real difference was those who followed O'Connor through thick and thin and those that had doubts about his honesty and some who remembered the *Northern Star*'s betrayal of the rising.

Holberry, in one sense "came home" to the O'Connorite loyalists in early 1843. The York-made Holberry bust had been completed and was newly installed on a podium in Fig Tree Lane. In the *Northern Star* of the 15th April 1843 the Sheffield Fig Tree Lane NCA branch recommended following their example of brightening up their meeting rooms. They described the makeover of their headquarters. They revealed the installation of the bust in pride of place on a rostrum with a scroll bearing the words "The Charter and No Surrender."[210] At the head of the room was a large paper banner with "Universal Suffrage" and then on the left side of the room were the other key Chartist demands: "Annual Parliaments," "Vote by Ballot," "No Property Qualifications," "Equal Electoral Districts" and "Payment of Members."

Under these were graphic inscriptions of the names; Paine, Wallace, Muir, Sydney, and Emmett. At the head of the room to the left was the name "Tyler" with a hammer surmounted by a cap of liberty (Phrygian cap – red cap given to freed slaves in ancient Rome that became a symbol of liberty in the French Revolution). Lower down was the name "Tell" displayed with two crossed arrows above also capped by the cap of liberty.

On the other side of the room were inscriptions of the names "Frost, Williams and Jones" (transported for their role in the November 1839 Welsh rising at Newport).

A few poetic lines were displayed below:

> "Tis Liberty alone that gives the flower
> Of fleeting life, its lustre and perfume,
> And we are the weeds without it"

More names followed further along the wall. These were those of Hampden, Fitzgerald, Washington, Jefferson, Franklin, Byron and Shelley. At the low end of the room were huge letters proclaiming, "Clayton and Holberry, Martyrs to the cause of Freedom."

Poetic inscriptions were inscribed at the side

> "Far dearer the grave or the prison
> Illuminated by one patriot's name
> Than the trophies of all that have risen,
> On Liberty's ruins to fame."

Below was the name "O'Connor" and underneath more lines:

"O where's the slave so lowly
Condemned to chains unholy
Who could be burst
His bonds at first
Would pine beneath them slowly"

For the next two years while the Fig Tree Lane branch stayed in these headquarters the bust remained, but its later whereabouts is unclear. The bust had been attributed to Demaine of York "a young Chartist of great natural genius" by Thomas Cooper at the time of his stop-over in Sheffield on 16–17th July 1842. The bust placed Holberry, for them, in the Chartist pantheon where the militant radical and democratic radicals of struggles in 17th and 18th century England, Ireland and America were honoured alongside Chartist contemporaries, but also seen to have distant ancestry in 14th century Scottish, English and Swiss freedom struggles. The room was an unashamed internationalist celebration of some of the ideologues and practitioners of armed resistance. A tradition that Byron and Shelley, as early 19th century radical poets and political adventurers, helped promote.[211]

Now in the dimmed political landscape of the post-busted flush of national petitioning and ulterior measure strike sanctions, the decorated meeting room might enhance the ambience of the tea-drinking soirees and thoughtful discussion meetings as the struggle continued, but was it now consigned to be a museum?

The local NCA struggled through the early to mid-1840s and years of falling sales of the *Northern Star*, and locally the NCA faced the national challenges from Joseph Sturge's middle class Complete Suffrage Union seeking working class collaboration with the middle class for lesser goals than the Charter. Irish Repealers also made claims on the local Irish communities. Anti-Corn Law campaigning was not a new feature but the middle class-led Anti-Corn Law League also posed a threat to working class Chartist loyalties.[212]

Harney, while still operating in Sheffield as NCA organiser, shifted the tactics to working to build better links with the unions that had either backed away from the general strike calls of 1839 and 1842 or were, in a few cases in 1842, ahead of the Chartists and their calls for strikes to win the Charter in August 1842. He led popular campaigning, drawing in unions, the Political Institute anti-O'Connorites and even some of the more radical CSU Free Trade campaigners in May 1843.[213] The Irish question also figured and was taken up but soon forgotten. Harney was ordered to Leeds to be *the Northern Star*'s deputy editor and was replaced by a new organiser, the capable John West.[214] The movement on the whole was in the doldrums as was illustrated at the start of 1844 by a half empty Paradise Square annual showdown between the local NCA and local MP, H.G. Ward on his annual visit to the town.[215]

What brought the Sheffield Chartists back to life in 1844 was their early work rebuilding links with local trade unions. The national miners' strike of 1844 saw Chartists mobilise and work with other local unions to give real help to the miners. This is the context in which the most celebrated Holberry Chartist poem was written by a Sheffield Chartist called J. Mc Owen, though this may have been a pen name. The poem is called "Father, who are the Chartists?" and appeared in the *Northern Star* on the 10th February 1844. It reads as a reply to the question:

> Millions who labour with skill, my child,
> On the land – at the loom – in the mill, my child.
>   Whom bigots and knaves
>   Would keep as their slaves;
> Whom tyrants would punish and kill, my child
>
> Millions whom suffering draws, my child
> To unite in a glorious cause, my child:
>   Their object, their end
>   Is mankind to befriend
> By gaining for all equal laws, my child
>
> Millions who ever hath sought, my child
> For freedom of speech and of thought, my child
>   Tho stripp'd of each right
>   By the strong hand of might
> They ne'er can be vanquish'd or bought, my child
>
> Millions who *earnestly* call, my child
> For freedom to each and to all, my child
>   They have truth for their shield
>   And never will yield
> Till they triumph in tyranny's fall, my child
>
> And they've sworn at a Holberry's grave , my child

(That martyr so noble and brave, my child)
  That come weal or come woe,
  Still onward they'll go
Till Freedom be won for the slave, my child!"[216]

The summer of 1844 brought Chartist organisations back into public view at a critical moment in the national miners' strike which had begun with short-time working in February and soon escalated to full blown strikes at many pits in the locality. The town's trade unions gave the newly fledged Miners Association support and this climaxed on 29th July 1844 with the arrival of T.S. Duncombe MP, Feargus O'Connor and George Julian Harney. A huge procession assembled on the Moor amid a sea of banners. John Baxter's 1986 pamphlet on the South Yorkshire Strike of 1844 used Sheffield and Chartist press sources to capture this moment and the Chartists arrival to show solidarity in public view.

> "It was the largest class demonstration ever seen (and up to 40,000 had witnessed Holberry's funeral in June 1842). The procession was headed by the friendly societies and sick clubs with their banners. These included the Labourers' Accidental Burial Society (motto – "Unite with Liberty and with Love") and the Duncombe Provident Sick Society which had that morning changed its name from the Brougham Sick Society. These were followed by what the middle class Whig Sheffield paper admitted were the banners and flags of "nearly every trade" (the town had over 50 separate unions). The trade union banners included those of The United Scissor Trade ("United to support, and not combined to injure"–"Aristocracy sucking the vitals of the People"), Pen Blade Grinders (" T.S. Duncombe, the fairest and most disinterested advocate of the Rights of Labour"), United Body of saw Grinders ("Firm as a Rock" – "T.S. Duncombe – the Servant's Friend and the people's future happiness"), United Razor Trade ("Labour is the source of all wealth") and the new Sheffield Miners Association ("Let us live by our labour"). Following this contingent came a miscellaneous group of banners quoting all varieties of wisdom – "Thus shall it be done unto a man whom the working classes delight to honour." "Wolves (bishops) in sheep's clothing – for they devour widows houses," "Britons strike home," "Thou shalt not vex the stranger nor oppress him," "God and our rights," "God made us free, tyrants would enslave us but Duncombe interposed" and a tricolour proclaimed republican

sympathies. Then a banner emblazoned with a woodman chopping a rotten oak proclaimed, "As are the rotten hollows of an oak, so are the rotten hollows of the State."[217]

This account then focused on the Chartist presence noting that at the rear: "came the Chartist contingent with their own banners and some borrowed from Manchester and Leeds". They carried standard messages featuring the key demands of the Chartist programme. The picture given contrasts the Chartists with the vitality of the trades and wider welfare organisations in the town. That is not to say the Chartist leadership presence with Duncombe, O'Connor and Harney was not of significance but the borrowing of banners was a feature of the weak state of Chartism in Sheffield in 1838 at the Roscoe Fields rally. The local movement was reverting back to being of lesser significance in the organisational mix of working class struggle. They lost their Fig Tree Lane meeting room a couple of months later and were meeting in Watson's Walk (possibly Harney's old campaign office). A merger was affected with the Political Institute and the combined branches eventually found a new home at 33 Queen's Street designated the Sheffield Democratic Temperance Reading Room.[218]

13. SHEFFIELD – CHARTISM'S PASSING 1845–54

The Sheffield Chartists stayed connected to the national body. Some leading figures involved themselves in municipal issues and built up ward-based electoral caucus activity with the result than in the three years 1846–49 the number of councillors elected on the Chartist "Democratic" ticket on to the newly created Town Council rose from 2 to 23. Most, partly because of the qualification required, were small tradesmen and employers and among them were the three key players in late Chartism in the town. Thomas Briggs, a joiner who had been active in Chartism in Derby earlier in the 1840s, Isaac Ironside, an accountant, with an Owenite background and Richard Otley (once a tobacconist and former bankrupt newsagent later a whitesmith), the moderate who was opposed to the 1840 rising and was instrumental in warning some leaders off.[219]

These three and few other "survivors" were found speaking out still in Paradise Square rallies that were few and far in between. A rally for the Holytown Miners in September 1847 found attendance in the low hundreds while it was claimed thousands were off watching cricket at a the huge Hyde Park cricket ground (itself a stone's throw from the once Chartist-populated Park Hill/Sky Edge rocky outcrops).[220] As a third national petition was mounted in the spring of 1848 against the background of a popular revolution in France, Paradise Square saw a largely petit bourgeois Chartist leaders revert to the older language of the earlier 19th century "platform" calling on "the People" and locating the problems of the masses in politically regressive terms as "taxation," rather than in capitalist exploitation which the unions of the town still recognised and were developing new strategies to mitigate through involvement in the mid-late 1840s "Labour Parliament organised by the National Association for the Protection of Labour."[221]

The national Chartist petition was presented on the 10th April 1848 in London but was soon rejected. A new Convention and then a Chartist National Assembly saw 10,000 in Paradise Square on the 13th June to hear O'Connor one more time. Chartism was in full retreat but it took another five years for its NCA branch to disappear. Two years later, Harney, now in London again, raised the cruel imprisonment treatment and the deaths of Holberry and Clayton in 1841–2 in the context of Chartist prisoners subject to the same 'silent system' and sensory deprivation prison methods in the case of Ernest Jones and other prisoners of the state arrested in 1848.[222]

Another important legacy of Chartism in the city is its possible carry-forward into women's suffrage. Women were prominent in Sheffield Chartism, being present at mass meetings, and processions and in one account being in the vanguard. On 26th February 1851 Sheffield working women formed the first women's suffrage society, the Sheffield Women's Rights Association, foreshadowing the later organisations by many years. It was launched with a soiree – no doubt similar to the ones organised by the FRA. They petitioned Parliament on women's suffrage. We don't know if there is any link in personnel between the earlier FRA and the WRA, but it is hard to believe there wasn't at least a transference of ideas and organisational know-how. It would be a fascinating area for further research.

What happened to the bust? Did it stay in the Chartist rooms till the end? Was it an embarrassing talisman for the "Democratic Party" striving to control the town council? The answer is possibly wrapped up in Mary Holberry' new life. Mary found peace and a new a few years later. She had met a widower, Charles Pearson, who was five years older, with a son. He ran a beerhouse on High Street, Park, then the Plumpers Inn at 51 Duke Street, Park, at least up until 1849, before becoming proprietor of the Seven Stars pub in Trippet Lane by the time of the 1851 census. Pearson had Chartist sympathies. They married in November 1843 and had a son they christened Holberry Pearson. John Cooper, previously a labourer but now a retired maltster, Mary's father, lived at the pub after his wife died. The pub, with a revered and respected landlady, became a focal point for trade union gatherings. In the early 1850s, when the 'father' of the trades council, Joseph Kirk, who led the trades to the Peterloo protest in October 1819, died his colleagues chose the Seven Stars for the wake.

Holberry Pearson's family, decades later, became the long-term owners of the bust and held it until the 1970s but it may have been in Mary's possession first when the Chartists disbanded. The bust was wrapped in a cloth and kept in a workshop for several post-Chartist decades but ended up in a suburban loft.[223]

The bust of Samuel Holberry in a suburban Sheffield garden in the 1970s

Mary and Charles Pearson had more children, Frances (1847), Ann(1851), Cooper (1853) and finally Rodgers(1855). The public house thrived. Charles lived till 1877 and Mary died in 1883 aged sixty-seven. The trustees of the Chartist Association had transferred the title deed of the plot Holberry was buried in to the Pearson family in 1872. The grave of Holberry contains Charles, Mary and three other Cooper family members. The headstone only indicates Holberry's presence but is also dedicated in words on the final line to the "lost son" Samuel John who died while Holberry was in Northallerton, though his remains are in a public grave with over sixty other bodies.[224]

14. HOLBERRY IN POPULAR MEMORY: 1855–1900

In 1864 a historical paper was read by Mr John Taylor to members of the Townhead Street Young Men's Book Society at its quarterly meeting on February 16th. Its main purpose was to see public acclaim for Mr Bland, Rotherham's police chief in the way he had "played" James Allen, Rotherham Chartist leader in the events leading up to the 11/12th January 1840 Chartist rising. It was now deemed safe to expose the key role of Lord Howard as he no longer lived in the area. The lecture mentioned Holberry by name once and was generally sycophantic towards the authorities and hostile to Chartism, starting with the claim the plan was to "give the town over to pillage, anarchy and fire."

It drew a response in the next edition of the *Sheffield Telegraph* newspaper which had publicised the lecture in its previous edition. This was in the form of a letter from Richard Otley. He was angry that the *agent provocateur* aspect of Allen's behaviour had been minimised in Taylor's paper. Otley cited Allen's behaviour towards William Gill who was in 1840 a moderate WMA member who had been the first delegate sent to the Convention in the spring of 1839. (Interestingly Gill had re-entered public life in 1860 and been a town councillor for three years.) Otley claimed Allen had tried to get Gill, "to take part in this desperate and disgraceful enterprise" in early 1840 and asked him to do so in front of "five or six in the room." He also recalled himself being propositioned by a person when leaving Peter Foden's Bank Street bakery. He stated, "a person came out of Foden's shop and tapped me on the shoulder saying, 'I wish to speak to you… we are going to rise, and you are to take a part with us and become our leader.' I replied, 'Indeed.' He stated, 'We know you have much influence; we can trust you and put our confidence in you; will you become one of us?' 'Where are your arms?, I replied. 'Oh, we have plenty ready.' 'Do you think

I am such a fool as to put my head in a noose for the Government to pull it tight and hang me?' This man, I have always been led to believe was this infamous Allen. I did not know him personally, but had a knowledge of most, if not all, the other leaders. The above also should be matter of history."[225]

It is worth offering recall of the earlier account in this biography of Holberry's arrest: that the police knocking at the door Mary Holberry opened named "Ottley" or a close version of his name as their target.

Ten years later the Sheffield and Rotherham Independent ran for several weeks on a bi-weekly basis, in July–August 1874 a serialised sixteen chapter melodrama entitled "Samuel Holberry, the Chartist or Sheffield up in arms."[226] This was a crime caper story whose central figures were a villainous uncle figure, an innocent nephew and a young Dragoon officer. Some of the rising's plans and plotting were written into the script and Holberry and Old Booker ("Bowker senior") were presented as central figures in the rising. Holberry and Booker (with his white greatcoat on which three medals were pinned) were sympathetically presented as honest, principled men (they turn down the proceeds of crime offered to help them buy weapons) but the rising was included as a sensational event adding drama to the plot. The final chapter, set in India, predictably reconciles the innocent nephew and the Dragoon officer when the former saves the life of the latter in fierce imperialist encounter with a Moslem prince's cavalry. In the penultimate chapter Holberry is summed up thus:

> "Poor Sam Holberry – we say poor, because he was a merely misguided enthusiast and not a criminal, a man who had high aspirations and a true regard for the happiness and welfare of his fellow beings, whom he strove to deliver from bondage, though in a mistaken and unlawful manner."[227]

The world of the mid-1870s with urban voting rights extended to all male householders, more positive trade union legislation and the emergence of trade unionists in Parliament as Lib-Lab MPs found Robert Leader's paper more sympathetic than it was in the 1840s where it had minimally reported Holberry's funeral and disrespected the behaviour of some attendees. In the same supplement of August as the final chapters of the Victorian melodrama played out, the paper respectfully reported Joseph Arch, the Norfolk based national farmworkers' leader, marching into Sheffield with some of his members and being politely received in Paradise Square.[228]

Two years later, the Independent's owner, Robert Leader, was involved in another publication where Holberry and the rising featured. This was in what even today is valued as an informed, detailed work of local Sheffield history, *Reminiscences of Old Sheffield*. Leader created a work that systematically wandered through micro districts of 18th and early 19th century Sheffield using the recollections of several elders to weave a rich, colourful and detailed text. The section on the rising lacks the authenticity in other parts of the book and involves "Leonard" reading out a section from Taylor's pamphlet including the derogatory phrase, "the wild extremes of their hot-headed leaders." It has some value in tracing Peter Foden's time on the run and eventual success in a new life across the Atlantic in St Louis but it reinforces the hostile stereotype.[229]

There is no sign of Chartist ancestry being explicitly honoured in Sheffield's Labour movement as socialist parties emerged from the early 1880s in the form of the Socialist Democratic Federation, Socialist League, Independent Labour Party, or among the reformist and revolutionary socialist groups of the earlier 20th century. Many stones remain unturned but it looks as if the nascent "modern" labour movement held to a "Pilgrims Progress" model of struggle where unions, co-operatives and other welfare vehicles of struggle dominated a sanitised narrative of forward movement.

15. HOLBERRY IN THE 20TH CENTURY TO TODAY: COLLECTIVE MEMORY AND HISTORY FROM BELOW

There are fragmentary recollections of collective memory carrying from the 19th into the 20th century. Sam Holmes, born 1909 and later in life a building trades union representative, Communist Party member and later, post-1956, Trotskyite activist into the late 1970s, helped the rediscovery of the Holberry grave. In an example of his sharp observational writing (published in 1978), he recalled his childhood:

> "The "Moor" area at the turn of the century had not changed at all in the previous sixty or eighty years. The picture I have in my mind is very much the scene as it was in Chartist times – mean little streets, rows of "back-to-back" houses, the "shops" of the "little mesters" in the cutlery trades, horse-drawn traffic and in consequence of them stables, the blacksmiths' shops that shod them and the hay and corn merchants that fed them, all lying check to cheek.
>
> I was born there in 1909 in Thomas Street in the "Big Yard" in

one of fourteen back-to-backs. Opposite the houses were stables, open middens, outdoor "closets" and a blacksmith's shop. It was in fact a "big yard," about an acre. The drays and carts that parked there overnight were useful as seats where men could get together and on occasion were a suitable rostrum for a speaker. The big yard was then a traditional assembly point for the district, it was here that many times I heard the story of Samuel Holberry."[230]

The Chartists and Holberry lacked recognition among the labourist organised mainstream in the inter-war years. The Communist Party which appeared from 1920 was more interested in the 19th century radical working class past. Bill Moore, in the late 1930s, secretary of the Peace Campaign, and a Communist Party member, said that in one instance he was involved in a party-organised march into the City centre through Netherthorpe carrying specially designed banners recording activists from the Jacobin past to the Chartists. Leading from the front was an 80-year-old Tom Mann, lifelong militant trade unionist and revolutionary with a Marxist pedigree in SDF, BSP and Communist Party incarnations.[231]

Individuals in the local labour movement knew the Holberry story. Sam Holmes, recalled a retired member who acted as "doorkeeper" of the branch who he described as "the spirit" of Samuel Holberry. This was Charlie Jackson who was born in the later 19th century, one generation on from those with Chartist memory. Sam recalled that, "Charlie would buttonhole members to give them a lecture on Holberry and the Chartists and that in one instance, on the publication of a new centenary edition of Marx's Communist Manifesto in 1948 by the Labour Party, Charlie spoke to the whole branch on the links between Chartism and the Manifesto."[232]

Two decades passed but in the mid-1970s several individuals from contrasting generations and from different socialist viewpoints met to commence a rediscovery of Holberry and to utilise his story to throw light into the dustbin of history to which the radical past had been consigned . John Baxter a London-born, young PhD student researching working class struggle in early 19th century Sheffield, was a member of the Sheffield Free Press Collective. He had met Steve Bond in the Collective. Tom Owen, Nigel Clark and Sue Owen were friends and political associates of Sam Holmes. The final piece of an unlikely political jigsaw was Bill Moore, a veteran Sheffield Communist, a former teacher and then full-time organiser for the Communist Party in the West Riding who had just retired back home to Sheffield. Bill knew where the grave was in the Cemetery. Bill had a good relationship with George Caborn, the local leader of the engineers union AEU, and this meant support from the Trades Council.[233]

John had written some articles in the earlier 1970s in the local press including one on Holberry. The Pearson family, after some time, got in touch and indicated they wished the bust could be recognised as part of the City's heritage. Baxter and a photographer friend visited the Pearsons and saw the bust that had been in an attic after years being wrapped in a sheet in a workshop. It had experienced some damage including a broken nose. Its discovery was caught on Yorkshire Television's Calendar programme and written about in the local press. The arrangements took a couple of years to finalise and involved the newly formed Holberry Society as brokers, offering a permanent loan to the city museums, as long as the item was put on permanent display. John Baxter was a political associate of Councillor Enid Hattersley, then Chair of Libraries and Arts; she took the acquisition seriously and oversaw the museum service's restoration.

The Holberry Society was officially founded as a trade union based socialist history group on 11 January 1978. It organised an annual lecture and graveside orations from 1978 to the mid-1980s. It published a journal, pamphlets and set up local history classes, organised exhibitions, promoted curriculum discussions with teachers and with its banner participated in political and industrial struggles. The Society organised "history workshop" conferences and helped host the national History Workshop Conference when it was held in the City in November 1982.[234] This was also the year of its organisation of the Sheffield Worker exhibition which ran alongside a touring national exhibition "The British Worker."[235]

Alternative street walks were designed not just by the Society but by an independent Women's History group with Cathy Burke, a research postgraduate, studying women in late 19th/early 20th politics and trade unionism. The Holberry Society's strongest support came from AEU branches and the Sheffield Trades Council as well as from political party branches and individuals. It promoted the naming of new streets commemorating local working class leaders from the past. Havelock Square was renamed Holberry Gardens. Holberry Close was newly adjacent. The fountains under the supporting pillars of then town hall extension (the "egg box") saw the erection of an octagonal steel plate to commemorate Holberry in 1979.

The Society campaigned for the commemoration of the town's volunteers for Spain in the late 1930s and a plaque was erected in the mid-1980s. By now support from some Old Labour stalwarts like the late Reg Munn of the Co-op Party, County Councillors John Cornwall and Bill Michie (later MP for Heeley) helped with some public funding of publications. It was the larger than life Chair of Libraries and Arts, the late Councillor Enid Hattersley, that commissioned the restoration of the bust which had spent some years in Weston Park museum's stores. By the mid-1980s the public now could share this unique object. It is now held in storage and is not currently on display.[236]

The bust restored

Bill Moore continued to use his influence with the "City fathers" and was supported by sympathetic local journalists like Stephen McClarence. At the start of the 21st century the re-vamped "Heart of the City" re-development in the Peace Gardens saw some new public space architecture. The Peace Gardens gained a new water feature with a series of raised bronze urns spilling water down through water channels: "the

Holberry Cascades" which replicate Sheffield's rivers, running towards the central multi-jet fountain area so beloved of young people on hot August afternoons. Bill's only disappointment was that the fountain was called the Goodwin Fountains ("a mere bloody businessman") as Bill described him in 1998, so-called as the original one was removed from the other side of the Town Hall.[237] A new slate plaque for Holberry, attached to one of the bases of the urns replaced the steel plaque.

Maybe it was not all bad news. The Heart of the City might unintentionally demonstrate the paradigm of capitalist exploitation: the urns and flowing channels representing the endeavour of the workpeople and the surplus value they create flowing to the capitalists who celebrate their accumulation with spectacular cooling water jets for their 21st century wage slaves and their children. I think Bill and Sam might break into a smile at that thought.

16. HISTORIANS AND HOLBERRY

Chartism was being written about before it had ended. R. G. Gammage, a moderate activist, produced his book in 1854. It was re-issued and extended in 1894.[238] From the First World war to the present, some professional historians have attempted overarching national studies from Mark Hovell (1918) to Malcolm Chase (2007).[239] There have been single town and regional studies, Chartist biographies, books exploring themes like economic influences, religious influences, Chartist alternative-society building, Chartist songs, poetry and other cultural manifestations, ideology and class consciousness, state responses to Chartism, explorations of Chartist space and more. Chartist newspapers and periodicals and literature are more available with digitisation. There are thousands of books, pamphlets and other new media projections. The Society for the Study of Labour History organises an annual Chartism Day Conference.

How has Holberry's reputation fared with historians? A leader with a clear working class perspective and whose rising plan might have impressed 20th century Marxist revolutionaries who had to physically fight for socialism as with Trotsky, Mao, Che and Fidel Castro among others. Has he been written out for being part of a deviant strain?

The answer is mainly no, but he is largely recognised in the same ways his movement contemporaries regarded him. Many historians are squeamish about Chartist revolutionary violence, however much some might recognise the constitutionalist reasoning behind general risings in the 19th

century.[240] Holberry planned to literally decapitate the local state, one that was dominated by an elite in which the emergent local bourgeoisie played a considerable role. Historians, like Feargus O'Connor before them, are more comfortable with Holberry the imprisoned martyr. The Holberry Society's various publications relating to Holberry didn't remain in this compromised default position. Some of the five thousand copies of the Holberry Society pamphlet (1978, 1980, 1986 editions) found their way out of the city. It has been cited in academic work as has an essay on South Yorkshire Chartism 1837–40 (1976) featuring a detailed analysis of the rising, also a study of Chartist armed resistance in the West Riding.[241]

Holberry has been included in the *Dictionary of Labour Biography*. He is included in the more recent *Oxford Dictionary of National Biography*. The late Professor Malcolm Chase in the excellent general history of Chartism gave Holberry a dedicated biographical summary as an addendum to a key chapter. Writer and radical educationalist, Chris Searle wrote a multicultural play about him performed at his school in Sheffield[242]. There is a screenplay with a film option gathering dust.

I was at a Chartist Day conference a few years ago in Sheffield; an out-of-town, internationally respected Chartist expert was musing on commemoration at the Friday evening warm-up and was using two Sheffield Chartist connected figures, Ebenezer Elliot and Samuel Holberry to expressed surprise about the lack of personal biographical information. I got the microphone passed to me and had something to say that night because I thought 4–5,000 words in the original pamphlet contained a lot of detail for somebody with a short, if spectacular trajectory. Some of this older work was context and some of the 30,000 words here are context too. I was irritated then, but I have thought more constructively on the criticism. Here, I have tried to creatively expand on the subject of Holberry's life and actions. It would be good to have succeeded in writing the definitive work.

John Baxter 2025

PRIMARY SOURCES FOR THE STUDY OF SAMUEL HOLBERRY

Notes

The following was originally going to be published as a separate book: this was originally just research for a novel (which is still in progress). Having found that John Baxter had a work in progress, it was decided that it made sense to collaborate on a single definitive history of Samuel Holberry. The documents are placed in chronological order.

The main sources of information are:
- Statements taken at the time of the committal hearing/ trial contained in T.S. 11/816/2688 held at the National Archives. There must be some circumspection when studying these statements. They would clearly not pass modern standards of reliability of evidence.
- Contemporaneous newspaper accounts of the hearings. These are probably fairly accurate accounts of what was said in court, but as with the written statements, they would not survive modern standards of evidence. Witness collusion was a common practice – it is something that alarmed Holberry in court (it is also as evidenced by the almost identical wording in statements in earlier Sheffield Chartist hearings, that have echoes of later 1980s SY Police malpractice!)
- Records made by Captain W. J. Williams, Prison Inspector, who carried out a series of interviews with chartist prisoners in response to Parliamentary (i.e. public) concern of their treatment. These are also held at the National Archives at: HO/20/10.
- Surviving letters sent to Holberry in York Castle and given to Mary Holberry on his death, then passed down through the family. These re-emerged in the 1970s, along with the bust. It would appear the descendents of Holberry Pearson sold at least some of the letters for the value of their stamps! The letters were not offered to the Holberry Society, who were for several years unaware of their existence. The pocket, and draft petition signed by Holberry, were also in their possession and given to the Holberry Society. The letters at Sheffield Archives. (HS 1-15), were purchased by John Salt, then Head of Sheffield Polytechnic's History Department and given to the city. These have been

- made available online by Sheffield Archives (https://www.calmview.eu/SheffieldArchives/CalmView). In addition Sheffield City Archives have photocopies of three letters: PhC 494/1, 494/2 and 494/3. It is not clear where the originals of these letters are – probably still in private hands: they were mentioned in the *Sheffield Star* on January 19 1980 when someone "wishing to remain anonymous" spoke to the *Star*. If the current owner were to come forward we would be very grateful. The letters at York Archives are numbered HBY 1-30. These letters were purchased by Alfred Peacock, Head of York Educational Settlement and eventually donated to York Archives. They also have some that are from the same original source that are numbered CPR 1-5.
- The biography contained in *English Chartist Circular* May–June 1843 vol 2 nos.118–122. This is not open to be easily publicly viewed online. Leeds University hold a digitised version behind a hugely expensive paywall and there is a facsimile version, which the Wellcome Collection hold a copy of. It is believed that this a reliable source of information, and the author seems to have obtained details direct from Mary herself.
- Other letters to and from Holberry were printed in the press.

Only a fraction of the correspondence can have survived. There is not a single original letter sent by Holberry to anyone that remains, so far as we know. The surviving letters were all presumably kept by Holberry and returned to Mary upon his death in the "pocket." There were presumably also a number of other letters etc. that were destroyed by the prison authorities and too subversive to have been allowed through: everything was subject to censorship.

<u>Footnotes in this section.</u> The footnotes in the statements are contained in the original handwritten statements, except the ones in italics which are editorial.

<u>Transcription</u> Transcribing these nearly 200 year old handwritten letters and documents, often written by people without the benefit of much education is an art, and required a deal of patience. It is not always possible to be certain of what is said. I have retained original spellings and punctuation, rather than trying to correct it. Where I think I understand what the author meant, but it may be less obvious to a non-native Yorkshire speaker, I have added some notes. Some parts are missing: these

are marked with an em dash (—), other words have defeated me (after much gnashing of teeth), and are marked {...} or in some cases I have less confidence in my translation, these are marked {?}. Should anyone succeed in solving these puzzles, or spot errors I have probably made, it would be great to hear from you.

S. Kay 2025

Snig Hill: the route the dragoons would take from the barracks up into town, Sheffield Local Studies Library, Picture Sheffield w00335

A sample of the letters:

> Rockingham Norto Sep 7th/41
>
> My Dear Hollis,
>
> It was with much surprise and regret that I heard from Mr Needham you had not received my last Letter which I sent according to promise, soon after I heard from you; with surprise because as I put the Letter in the post myself I cannot conceive how it is that have never recieved it. and with regret because I am ware that in your present circumstances it would be a source of great grief to you if you thought I had not answered your Letter. I speak according to my own feelings when placed in the same position as yourself."

From T.S. 11/816/2688

<u>Samuel Foxhall</u> I[1] am a Native of Staffordshire 24 years of age and married – It is 6 years since I first came to Sheffield – I came to my brother I am a file cutter by Trade and I first worked at Mr Thomas Wyng's till he died – Afterwards I worked for Messrs Pease & Ibbotson for about 2 years – since that time I went to work with Messrs Vickers & Co. as a file cutter and have continued with them ever since – Myself and Wife have lived in Button Lane in Sheffield Moor with my Wifes Father Francis Hough for the last 12 months – I joined the Chartists about 6 weeks before the disturbance in Sheffield – I had been at their public Meetings and the time I first joined them I went to one of the public Meetings in Fig Tree Lane and when the Meeting was over they said All were to go out but the Committee – I went down and stop't some time with several others about the Door, most of them went away – Then a person came to me and said he thought there had been a spy and he followed him and he told me to go after him. I went according to his directions and then met the man again who brought me back to the Room and laid hold of me by the collar and said there was a new association formed and asked me if I would be a Member. He said there was a person inside the door to receive a Password. Then he gave the Password "Truth" to the person inside, he said this is a new one and took me into the Room having still hold of me by the collar – I dont know who this person was never having seen him since – When I got into the Room I saw Bradwell there whom I had known before – I and several others stood round Bradwell and he went through a Ceremony the substance of it was to promise that we were to assassinate any one who should divulge the secret – I believe McKetterick (whom I afterwards became acquainted with) was there. I and the new Members were told (I think by McKetterick) where the Classes were and which was the gainest[2] to each person – A person of the name of Rose told me my class was at Clayton's in Porter Street, he told me the number of the Door and said he would take me there he said the number was 87 as I believe – While I was there Peter Foden came into the room with two new Members as he said – I heard Foden given them the Ceremony – I believe that night was a Wednesday night – The next night I went to Claytons, there were 8 or 9 there – Clayton was one of them – Rose was there Danl Hands was also there – Then there was a Conversation amongst them how they should attack the Military – Clayton said he had

---

1 The first part of this examination was taken with a view of shewing the previous course of life of this witness

2 i.e. nearest

been a Soldier – Hands said he had been a Soldier – The Class Meeting Nights at Claytons were Tuesdays & Thursdays I think I went regularly for about 3 weeks on the Tuesdays & Thursdays at Clayton's – I have seen both old and young Booker at some of these Meetings – The talk at Clayton's used to be about what Arms we had – and the Members Names were written down in a Book and where each lived – Danl Hands was our Class leader and he wrote most of the Names and Bradwell the remainder. I remember hearing Old Booker say that he had been a Soldier – Besides the Meetings at Claytons I attended Meetings in Fig Tree Lane – They were private Meetings – I think I attended 10 or a dozen times – I had seen Holberry at the public meetings before I joined so as to become acquainted with his Person. I remember his coming to our Class Meetings at Claytons about a Fortnight before the disturbance – Clayton was there and Bradwell and Francis Rose, those were all I remember – Holberry said he had been as a Delegate to different parts, he named Chesterfield, Mansfield, Dewsbury and other places which I dont recollect. He said he had got a pound for the defence of Frost and he was to see it was laid out in something that would defend him – That they were all Chartists at Dewsbury that when they were about searching for Arms there – they had pawned them to a Chartist Pawnbroker for small sums – that he had told them at Dewsbury and other places that the time for a General Rise was fixed and that they said they should sleep better that night than they had done for the last six months – I think that Holberry said the Rise was fixed for the 31st December – He said there would be 3 to lead we on – One was to be a sort of Field Marshall the other two were to be lower and the three would be distinguished so that we should know them from any one else – That each man was to put two shirts on to keep him warm and to save every halfpenny he could to provide a Sixpenny dram as probably it would be very cold That the Field Marshall would take possession of Sheffield in an hour and a half and that he would lead them on the next day. Soon after that time we used to meet every night at the Class at Claytons – I took my gun twice to Claytons in consequence of directions to bring what arms I had – I shewed it to the class people. I took it in my hand it was dark I saw others in at the class shew both guns and pistols. I remember Francis Rose brought a pike head to the class and William England a pistol and afterwards a gun and he also brought an axe and a dagger. I think I saw 6 or 7 guns shewn at the class and about the same number of pistols and some pikes and daggers We were called on to pay 2^d a week which was said to be for the defence of Frost. I paid it twice and it was put down in a book It was said to be for the defence of Frost that no one might have hold of it. Hands received the subscriptions and entered them in the book. And afterwards he produced powder and caps which he said he had bought with the money. The powder was divided and I received 2 oz & a half and it was distributed to the others in the same parcels. I received also from Hands some percussion caps. One of the Members gave me some lead and Saml Bentley lent me a bullet mould to make it into bullets. I have seen Bradwell at Claytons making ball cartridge. About 30 while I was there I think that was about a week before the disturbance. I heard young Booker at Claytons say that he had a gun at their House but it wanted a screw or two put in the lock and said he must get it done and the others said the time was short. I believe that Clayton was present at all the class meetings I have spoken to. The place where I live is about 2 or 3 minutes walk to Claytons I have merely to cross one street. I attended the private meetings in Fig Tree Lane on the Wednesday Thursday & Friday before the disturbance. On the Wednesday, James Boardman was Chairman, Bradwell, England, Saml Bentley and Duffey were there. The chairman gave out that we were to shew up our small arms at the classes on Friday night those arms that could be concealed Duffey made a speech and told them that the reason he left them before was because they mixed religion with Politics – he said he was as dear to his religion as any man – he alluded to their mixing up religion with politics in Ireland. He said he had an Irish class but he should not tell them the number that night as there was not sufficient order kept at the door. that he should continue to meet as long as they met. I observed that Duffey had under his top coat about ½ a dozen daggers in rough handles and I saw some of the Irishmen there with similar daggers. The pass word was changed that night. there were two men to keep the door, one about half way down the steps and the other inside the door. The new pass word was for him on the steps outside "Union" and for him inside the door "Strength" I remember that Powell Thompson was there that night I went to the meeting again on Thursday night Saml Bentley, Bradwell, England, Duffey and some others of our class were there. I heard Duffey tell the number of his class that he had 64. Holberry was also there that night. He said he had a motion to propose that there should be 50 bills printed for a scotch Delegate to come and lecture on the Monday night, and that a sermon would be preached on the Sunday he said it would do them good if they heard them. I cannot say whether Foden was there that night or not but I remember one of the nights he came in and got into the pulpit and said the news had arrived about Mr Frost that he was brought in guilty – that it was in Mr Wyley's Window but they were to take no notice of it, it would be a fine handle to work upon and then he left the pulpit. I attended again a private meeting on the Friday[3] Bradwell, McKetterick, old and young Booker, Duffey and England were there Holberry was not there while I was there Duffey was the Chairman. About 100 were there. Duffey was speaking and while he was doing so some one came in and said he believed there was a Policeman underneath a spy and Bradwell got up and said he would put a cloak on it and he made a sort of Moral speech very loud. Duffey then got up and took a pistol from his bosom and held it in his hand and said lead me to the spy and Ill stop him from spying. I left about ½ past 10 O Clock before the meeting broke up. On Saturday night about 10 O Clock I went to the class at Claytons. I took nothing with me the first time. I went there in consequence of hearing the Night before at the Class that I was to be in attendance at that time – When I got to Clayton's I found there Clayton, Bradwell, and about a dozen others – Bradwell had a Dagger in His Hand and I saw others with Arms, some had Pikes on handles – I was asked whether I had brought my Gun – I said No but I hadn't far to fetch it – Duffey came in and Bradwell and he exchanged some words and Duffey said the Soldiers were out and after exchanging a few words with Bradwell Duffey went away – I then went and fetched my Gun, I remember hearing Bradwell say he would go out as a Spy – he went out – he came back about 12 o'clock, and he said an Irishman had stabbed a Watchman or a Policeman and almost throttled him & kicked him on the head. Old and Young Booker had come in before them – They both had daggers. Between 12 & 1 o'clock Bradwell and Hands went out together – While they were gone our Class moved to Old Booker's House within 3 or 4 minutes Walk of Clayton's – The Party began to be afraid that if they remained at Clayton's they should be found out, that it would be better to remain and so they went to Bookers – They took their arms with them – I remained with 4 or 5 others to the last. In a Back Room a Slop Kitchen there were about ½ doz Hand Grenades and 2 large Shells and we took them all to Bookers – I took one of the Shells – Two or three went at one time & 2 or 3 came afterwards – That must have been about 1 o'clock or after – We waited at Old Bookers till between 2 & 3 o'clock when Bradwell came in, and said the Orders were to Moscow the Town that each one was to set Fire to his own House – A dispute arose on this – some of them objected to it – After this dispute was over Clayton said he would go back to his own house and fetch Hands as he did not know where Booker lived – Bradwell said the Orders were that if they saw a Watchman they were to assassinate him, and if the Watchman produced a Pistol they were to shoot him – That Hands was hard of hearing and

---

3   10th January

Bradwell moved that Swallow should take his place as Leader – Swallow was appointed instead of Hands and then Bradwell said we were to go to the Top of Watery Lane to meet the other Bodies – Before Bradwell proposed that Hands should be displaced, Hands and Clayton had come into Bookers – Swallow was one of our Class men. He brought to Clayton's some Cats that Night in an Apron – One of our Class men was a Stout Man and lame and he said as he could not run he should not go with us. Bradwell and he talked together about it and it was agreed to leave him behind. He had a Gun and a Pistol – he lent Bradwell his Pistol, and to Hands his Gun, and Hands lent his pistol to one of the other Men. We then set off, leaving Old Booker and another or two in the House – Young Booker took two Hand Grenades and a Box of Lucifers and he had a dagger – The Party were all armed – They then went to Watery Lane. We arrived there about 3 o'clock. We only saw one there who said he belonged to McKetterick's Class. We waited there an hour I should think.. Then we moved further on toward Crook's Moor Workhouse having heard a Gun or two fired in that direction. We went past the Workhouse and there met a part of Boardman's class – Peter Foden was with them I both heard him speak & saw him. They were most of them armed – Old Booker and those that were left behind joined us near the Dams – Booker had a dagger – the others had Pistols – some of Boardman's Class said that Holberry was taken at 12 o'clock and that Boardman had gone off to Barnsley – Boardman's class and ours then parted – As we were going on we heard the sound of Horses' Feet. Bradwell said they were the Soldiers. Then Young Booker, Bradwell, myself and 2 others parted from the rest and went together, and kept the Field roads as much as we could, and then got into the Road by the botanical Gardens. I hid 40 rounds of Ball Cartridges in a Field which adjoins the wall of the botanical Gardens. I covered them with some Grass and a Stone over it and a little lower down I flung the dagger over the wall into the same Field – Young Booker hid near that spot two Hand Grenades and another hid a Pike not a great way from the same place. Bradwell and the other person left us and I and young Booker returned to his Father's house – It was near five o'clock when we got there.

Young Booker knock'd at the door and his Mother got up and let us both in – He mended the Fire and we sat by it till the Police came in and took us – I remember at a Class meeting at Clayton's on Friday Night before this disturbance that an account of the Arms was taken. Bradwell said those who have Guns hold up your hands – Several held them up I was one – Then he asked as to Pistols in the same manner and others held up their hands. Then he asked as to Pikes and hands were held up. Bradwell took the numbers down on paper – and also the number of Ball Cartridges – Clayton having told him that he thought he had about 100 – and Clayton turned to Hands and said I think there will be about 100 for thee – Bentley said he had 50 or more – the Stout lame man said he had 40 – others said they had 40 – Bradwell took it all down on paper and said it was for the Council.

I have heard it said many times both in the Class Meetings and at the other Meetings that the object of the General Rise was to gain the Charter. I never heard the Charter explained.

The Night I gave my promise Wells acted as Door Keeper inside and received the Pass word – I saw him afterwards at the private meetings several times – I have heard him reading the Newspaper aloud – I have seen Marshall both at the Secret and public Meetings in Fig Tree Lane. I have heard him say he was a Class Leader and have seen him speak to others about the Class – I have heard him mention his Class.

<u>Samuel Powell Thompson</u> I[4] was apprenticed for seven years to Messrs Kidd & Law at Stockport as an Iron Turner – I once went before a magistrate when serving them and lodged a complaint against Kidd for beating me got a Warrant from Mr Coppock the Town Clerk –My master didn't appear and the Case was never heard – I then left my apprenticeship and came over to Sheffield – This was 3 years ago last September – About a week or a fortnight before the Christmas following Kidd and a Policeman named Earlham came to my father's in search of me – While I was in Sheffield I went to work with Booth & Co. as an Iron Turner and left them about a fortnight before – Kidd and the Policeman came – I was married at Stockport during my apprenticeship and when I quitted Stockport – I left my wife with her child to support herself as she could – I went to Stockport to fetch my goods a few days before Kidd and the policeman came over to Sheffield as above stated and returned to Sheffield the Sunday before they came – I left my wife still at Stockport – She was in a good place of work as a reeler.

When Kidd and the policeman came to my father's house they took me away to Ashley's the Waterloo Tavern and kept me there till the next morning and then took me by the coach to Stockport – There I went to work again with my Master Kidd and continued till he failed which was in the following March. My time would have been up the following July – That would have completed my seven years – On my Master's failure I

---

4 The first part of this examination was taken with a view of shewing the previous course of life of this witness

came over to Sheffield leaving my wife at Stockport and went to work with the Milton Iron Company about 8 miles from Sheffield – I continued there better than 3 months and while there I fetched my wife from Stockport – I parted from the Company by reason of my putting a screw into the fire for which I was turned off by the Engineer – I then came to Sheffield and worked for Mr Revill in his Sugar House as Engine Tenter – I continued there better than four months – I left the service on account of a quarrel between myself and the Sugar Boiler – Mr Revill gave me a written character when I left – Then I continued out of work some time – Afterwards I worked at Woods a Boiler Makers – Afterwards at Sandfords of Rotherham in the Iron way – I left him by reason of a quarrel with Fox the foreman – Then I came to Mr Parker of the Pond Forge and worked with him till the day before I was taken up – On that day I left my service having given a month's previous notice in order to go back to Sandford – Fox having then left his service and I being applied to by Michael Hessle the Foreman – I was to have started for my work on the Monday following – I worked for Parker About 9 months – I went to work there in March and left in January – During that time I became a Chartist. The first time I attended was the day they went to the Parish Church – It was soon after Peter Foden was taken[5] – I attended a meeting in Paradise Square where thousands were assembled previously to going to church on the Sunday Morning – they were singing a hymn – I accompanied them to church – they took possession of the pews and filled the church – I went the next night to a meeting in Fig Tree Lane – It was notorious that the Chartists held their meetings there – At first I went through curiosity – It was a full meeting – the room was full – it was about 8 o'clock at night – I heard speeches made – After this I attended the evening meetings as regularly as I could – I first became acquainted with Holberry at Church – it was on the third Sunday after the first that I attended the Chartists to the Church – I saw Holberry frequently at the Meetings – he was a leading Speaker – I remember being at a Meeting in the Fig Tree Lane on Saturday Night the 4th January this was the Saturday week previous to the Sunday when I was taken up – There was first a public meeting and a Private one was held afterwards – at the public meetings the Newspapers were read and Speeches made – Then the room was cleared and those who were made members were admitted to the private meeting. Members were admitted to the private meeting by a Sign and a Pass Word at the Private Meeting that night it was said (but by whom I do not know) that Holberry was expected home that night – I have attended the Private Meetings during the whole

---

5   13th August 1839

of that week and had learned there that Holberry was gone to Dewsbury and was expected home first on the Tuesday and afterwards daily – At the meeting on the Saturday Night Holberry not having arrived I and Peter Foden were at first delegated by the Committee to go in a gig to Dewsbury after him – Afterwards James Boardman was substituted for Foden – James Boardman Peter Foden, Birks, James McKetterick and James Marshall were at that meeting – Peter Foden went out to get a gig and returned saying he could not get one till 6 the next morning – Soon after the meeting broke up.[6] I went home and at 5 in the morning – Boardman and Birks came to my house – I was up waiting – they told me at first to get ready – but afterwards said that Holberry was come back – I went out with them – Birks left us and then we went to Bentley's House – and there saw a man whose name I understand to be Law and to be a Delegate who had come up with Holberry from Dewsbury – we breakfasted with him at Bentley's and walked to the Coach Office with him – and I saw him take his place for London and get on the coach – about 1 o'clock on that day I went to Holberry's House in Eyre Lane, and found there two men, and afterwards 2 or 3 more came in – I knew them all by sight having seen them at the Meetings – but did not know their names – Holberry told us that he had been a Delegate to Dewsbury – and they had settled when the general rise should take place – that only two men in every town should know the time besides the Delegate that brought the News – that there was a courier gone up to London from Dewsbury – I told him I had seen him off on the coach – Holberry named also that he had pledged his word at Dewsbury that no place of Worship or Provision Store should be injured – We all came away together from Holberry's to the room This was between 2 and 3 o'clock in the afternoon – There were a few people at the room and the Meeting was a secret one – Holberry called on the Meeting for a collection to carry him round by Nottingham and that way – he said he only set off with 6/ – When he went to Dewsbury and had but 5/s. of it to keep him there – That they had made a collection there to send a Delegate off elsewhere and he had given 1/ towards it – a collection was then made and I believe 10/ and some odd pence were collected – I gave sixpence – we met again on that Sunday night – that was a Public Meeting – Holberry was there, and another collection was made for the same purpose – Bradwell made known its object. I think about 4/ were collected. After the collection was made we gave Holberry the money in the Committee Room. he said he should go to Nottingham and round that District and should be back on Tuesday night if he could but he should be

---

6   5th January - Sunday

at home on Thursday without fail. I attended Meetings on the Monday Tuesday and the Wednesday. I don't recollect what passed on the Monday. On the Tuesday Duffy was at the Meetings both public and secret. He made a Speech about Daniel O'Connell becoming an universal suffrage advocate – On the Wednesday Duffy attended again and told the people at the secret meeting that he had got a Class of Irishmen together but he said he should not give the meeting any information as to their numbers or names until such a time as there was better order kept at the door as he did not consider it safe. He said they could hardly know who was admitted seeing the manner which the Door was tyled. In order to satisfy Duffy I proposed a new pass word 'Union is strength' and that two Tylers should be placed one on the outside and the other within the outside man to receive the word 'Union' and the inside 'strength'.

On Thursday night[7] I was at the Meeting. It was a secret meeting and a good many attended Holberry, Boardman, Duffy, Bradwell and Young Benison were there Duffy spoke first. He told the number of his Class he said they were 64, Holberry spoke, he said he had been round by Nottingham to warn them of the time when the general rise was to take place and to give information of the decision of the Convention. That the rise was to gain the Charter, that as to Mr Frost he was but an individual and the news of Frost would arrive correctly on Friday night but they must take no notice of that the Charter was their motto. That they must all be punctual at their Class on Friday night. He then brought forward a proposition that 50 Bills should be printed to announce a Sermon on Sunday night and a Lecture on Monday night by a Scotch Delegate. He said he hoped no person would ask him any questions about these Bills for time would show. Boardman spoke but I don't recollect what he said. When the Meeting broke up I and Boardman went to a Public House in Dixon Lane kept by Kirk.[8] We found Holberry there and Law and a man whom I learnt had been a Delegate from Barnsley whose name was Ashton – We were in a Back room There was a talk about the rise and Law said he was glad they should have Wales with them at the same moment, they talked about Arms and Holberry produced a dagger from his pocket it was on a red Morocco Sheath it had an Ivory handle tipt with silver, Law asked me if I had got that dagger ready for him (that was in allusion to something that had passed between him and me when I accompanied him to the coach) I answered No but told him to come down to my House the next morning I would try and get him one I was again at the secret

---

7   9th January

8   *Thos Kirk ran the Rock Tavern. A "T. Kirk" was also a witness at the Holberry's wedding.*

Meeting on Friday night[9] Duffy was in the Chair Holberry, Bradwell, Birks, Marshall, Boardman, McKetterick were there and Foden came in afterwards late. Duffy spoke something about his Class I don't remember what he said. While he was speaking a person who was a Stranger to me came in and said a policeman was underneath as a Spy – Duffy pulled out a Pistol from his Breast and said lead me to the Spy and I'll stop him from spying as soon as he said that Bradwell got up and said he would put a Cloak on the Meeting and then spoke in a loud voice a kind of moral lecture he spoke for three or four Minutes in that way after that they went to business again Holberry then spoke he stood on a Form in the middle of the Room he had a Pistol in his hand he said that every Man must be punctual at his Class at 10 o'clock on Saturday Night and if he found any man out in the Streets that was a Chartist after that time he would certainly blow his Brains out he said that every man must put two Shirts on and whatever Clothing they could to keep them warm he said they must get a 6d Dram to keep out the cold and that the class meeting was for an inspection of Arms and there was a man who was a Frenchman and was in the French Revolution who would go and inspect the Arms that they must all take their Arms whatever they could secretly but not pikes. The Frenchman was in the Room Before the Meeting broke up it was made known there was to be a Meeting at 7 o'clock as usual on Saturday and that there was to be an inspection of arms also there. After the Secret Meeting a few stopped and discussed about the arms Holberry was one – The Frenchman spoke English during that discussion. We learnt from Holberry that the rise was to be on Sunday morning at 2 o'clock – There was also a talk about what ammunition there was – Boardman said he had a thousand rounds of Ball Cartridges – James Marshall said he had about 400 rounds – I said I had about 400 rounds, Birks said he had but a few Holberry said he had a deal Hand Grenades and if I am not mistaken he said 12 dozen and a quantity of Fire Balls – Then we talked about arms – Boardman said that he could bring about 6 or 8 guns – I said we had three Marshall stated he had either 3 or 4 – Birks said they had only 3 or 4 guns – Boardman Marshall Birks and myself were respectively Leaders of Classes and McKetterick was another leader – Then they talked about attacking the soldiers, at first it was suggested that they should fire on them as they were coming by the Infirmary, then another place was mentioned by Johnson's Waggon Warehouse in Gibralter Street, but it was left at last to the Council to determine. Then it was talked about money to buy powder and they asked Birks to get them 5/ and he said that he had not it and they asked

---

[9] 10th January

him to pawn his Sunday Clothes, Birks said he would get them 5/ either by pawning his clothes or in some other way. They asked me for some money and I said I would see what I could do for them. It was after 12 before the Meeting broke up and then I went home – and on Saturday forenoon Boardman came to our house and asked if I had money, I said I had not got any for him and he desired me to come to the room at 3 o'clock – I went and found a man of the name of Cooper there and others – Holberry came in afterwards and asked me and Cooper to go with him – Holberry left the room and we followed him and he took us to a Public House in Lambert Street the Reuben's Head – he took us into a large room up stairs. We found there McKetterick, Boardman, Duffy and a few more Irishmen and a man whom I afterwards found to be a Rotherham man – Birks came in afterwards, Holberry got up up and addressed the Meeting – he stated the Plan – First he spoke about taking the Town Hall and the Tontine.

He said every man must be at his Post exactly as the clock struck 2 – He spoke about the best plan of coming to take them that they must calculate the time they would be in coming from the Meeting House so they all might be there as the Clock struck two. The plan was that one man of every Class should come first and then two of every Class but still all to keep in sight. that that was to prevent alarm since they would not be alarmed at one or two as they would at a whole Body, that the one and the two's were to assassinate every Watchman they came across – He said that my Class, James Boardman's, McKetterick's and Birks classes and the Eckington Friends were to attack the Town Hall – Duffy's Marshall's and the Forty Row the Bridgehouse and the Rotherham People and the Attercliffe people were to take the Tontine – That the Rotherham and Attercliffe were to meet at a Beer house below the twelve o'clock public house and by the Weir head about this time Boardman interposed and said he could bring about fifty and I could bring about fifty, Birks said he could bring about twenty and McKetterick said about forty. Duffy said sixty four – It was put to the vote by Boardman which classes should go to the different places and it was voted according to the arrangement laid down by Holberry as before stated – Holberry said now we have said nothing about what should be done if we are put off and he said he should say to begin to Moscow the Town and all the party seemed to approve of it – Then we discussed about getting arms for those who had none – One of the Irishmen said we have picked upon Ward's shop the corner of Church Street – I said I should like to go after Naylors and Boardman mentioned Mr Yeardley's at West Bar – Holberry seemed to object to this and said there were arms enough and he should object to break into any Shops there was a long haggling about it but it was put to the vote by Boardman whether they should go to the Shops or not, and it was carried we should go – Boardman having suggested that instead of the whole class going eight out of each Class should go and then Holberry consented. It was agreed that the Irish party should take Ward's, Boardman's Yeardley's, and mine Naylors and they were to break into the Shops exactly as the clock struck two and then return to the main body with what they had got each party knowing where they had to come to as arranged. Holberry then went on to say that as soon as the party got in to the Tontine they were to shut the Gates and barricade them with the Coaches that were in the yard and those who got into the Town Hall one party was to occupy the Ground floor and the other party were to go on the top outside. If the Soldiers brought their big Guns to fire at the Town Hall or Tontine would be able to knock them off before they would be able to plant them and to load and the Hand Grenades were to be divided amongst those of the Classes who had no Guns to throw amongst the Soldiers. That the Government and all the authorities were a property Government and as soon as their property was destroyed they would become as poor as us, and when they heard it was destroyed they would leave Town and go and protect their own property and they would also give in towards giving the people the Charter. It was then discussed about throwing the Cats some proposed that they should be thrown on Sing Hill on account of its being so narrow it would be sure to lame every horse that came up, Sing Hill {*i.e. Snig Hill*} is on the Road between the Barracks and the Tontine. Sing Hill was not approved of and an amendment was made that the Cats should be laid from Woolhouses' Corner to the Corner of the Town Hall and from thence across the Albion, that was put to the vote and carried. Holberry then stated the plan he had adopted for firing the Barracks. He said that he and 8 more he had picked on one of whom could climb the spouting would go and throw a Fire Ball into the Straw Chamber at the Barracks as soon as the Soldiers were called out and that he would set fire to the Riding School which was built of timber and they then would throw a hand Grenade or two into the Barracks he said the hand Grenades were to be distributed amongst the Classes that from the Barracks they would go to Albert Smiths House and fire that and so on with the remainder of the Magistrates A person then asked him if he could manage to get to Mr Parkers as that was a wide distance. Holberry said leave that to me. I will look after that business if you will look after the Town during the time that all this was going on in the Room. I saw the Landlord there. He was there the greatest part of the time and only went in and out for Beer & Liquors. I knew him to be the Landlord because there was a dispute at one part of the time about paying for the Beer which he supplied & he said they had a mind they should have it for nothing he was a stranger to me at the time but I have seen him a time or two since I don't know his name. In the course of the Meetings that took place I learnt that there were various Classes I was the Leader of one Class which met at Valentine Benison's in the Park. James Boardman was the Leader of another Class which met at his own house in St Phillips Road, Birks was another Leader that Class met at his house in Mill Lane. I have been there myself Joseph McKetterick was Leader of another Class that was held at Penthorpes in Spring Street John Marshall was Leader of a Class which met at his house the top of Coal Pit Lane. There was a Class held in Forty Row I don't know who was its Leader There was another in Bridges houses & I don't know that Leader and Duffeys class. I don't know where that met. We left Lambert Street about 6 o'clock when the Meeting broke up. I went to my Masters Mr Parker to settle with him and received my wages and then went home to my Fathers I remained there until I went out to meet my class. I left home about 9 o'clock and took with me a Sword which I had borrowed from my Brother concealed in my Trousers I went to the room and found no meeting there from thence I went to my former house in Forge Lane expecting to meet some of my Class there but found none I then went to Valentine Benisons in the Park where I met about a dozen of my class (young Benison was one of them) & led them to the house in Forge Lane. When we got to Forge Lane I inspected the Men and found them all armed except young Benison most with daggers & some with Pike Heads which they carried concealed while we remained at Forge Lane William Wells came in he was one of our Class he brought three Dirks with him they were in red Morroco Sheaths and had Ivory handles tipt with Silver he asked me if I had got a dirk. I said no and he then gave me the 3. he asked if We had a file in the house to file out the Mark on the Dirk George Morton another of my Class came in and said the Soldiers were out and hearing the file asked for looked on the dirks and said he would go & fetch a file he fetched one and gave it to one of my Men & I gave that Man the Dirks & he filed out the marks. Hearing the Soldiers were out I ordered the Men to stop where they were till I returned and then I went out to Birks in Mill Lane who sent me to the Public House in Lambert street, I found there James Boardman, Duffey and the Landlord. I first went into the Bar and saw the Landlord. he took me up Stairs into the room and then went down and fetched up Boardman and Duffey the Landlord remained in the room. I told them the Soldiers were out and asked them what was to be done now. They said they knew that and the Landlord said they could not see any choice now but Moscowing the Town it was at this time about Eleven o'clock Boardman gave me orders to come or send every half hour, and I returned to Birks and agreed with him that my Class should join his – Two of his Men had a Gun apiece and another had a Sword. Birks was engaged in dipping Torches in Turpentine. I saw him dip about half a dozen I then returned to my own Class in Forge Lane, and brought my Class to Birks and we made when united about 20 or 24 while we remained at Birks young Benison went home and brought back his father's pistol & some ball cartridges A person went backwards and forwards to Lambert Street for orders and at last brought an order that we were to go to the top of Water Lane to meet the other Classes. Birks had a torch and a dagger. We went there and found nobody – We returned to Birks and then it was determined that Watery Lane must have been meant for Water Lane and then we went there up Spring Street, Allen Street and Tobacco Box Walk. We found nobody there. We were about 20 or 24 then it was turned 3 o'clock. Then we returned into Tobacco Box Walk & met with a few Irishmen seeking after Duffey. I and two of my party went with the Irishmen to Duffey's house. We found Duffey there and stayed till between 4 and 5 o'clock. There was some wrangling between him and the Irishmen A great many Irishmen were in the house – they charged him with not coming forward as he ought and he excused himself by saying he had been to the Council and appealed to me for the truth of it. All of them were armed with daggers. I left Duffeys with young Benison another Man and went to Birks and found he was not at Home. I was then making my way home to my Fathers when I was collared by a Policeman on the Bridge from whom I got away and ran down towards the Wicker when I was stopt by a Body of Police and brought to the Town Hall I had then on my person two Swords, two Daggers and a box of Lucifer matches and a box of percussion Caps. I remember to have seen Old Booker at secret meetings during the week before I was taken, but I cannot tell how often or at which

Before a member was admitted to a secret meeting he was obliged to make a promise. I made that promise and I have heard others make it. More than forty made it to me – I made my promise the Second Sunday after the disturbance in Wales it was at Penthorpes house in Spring Street Peter Foden was Chairman Holbery and Bradwell were present. Foden put the question to me whether I had any objection to join a Secret Society I said No then he said will you do all that lies in your power towards gaining the people's Charter even to the loss of your own life and shedding of the Blood of the Tyrants. I said I will. Holbery mentioned that when he was a Soldier the Soldiers had been putting down secret Meetings where they had taken oaths, but he mentioned one place the name of which I don't remember where they could not put own because they had taken a promise instead of an Oath and therefore he recommended a promise. Then Holberry and Bradwell settled a form of promise but which Bradwell wrote down and read over several times and when it was approved he gave it to Foden. Then I and several others stood round him Holbery Bradwell and Penthorpe being three of them. Foden read the form and we repeated it after him – As well as I can recollect the form was this. Each man beginning with his own name "do most solemnly and sincerely promise that in the sight of Almighty God that I never will on any occasion make known any matters that are to be kept secret and I therefore pledge thee my troth that I will assassinate any one that shall betray the secrets of these Meetings and bear assassination if I shall betray them"

I got the promise off by heart and I saw the paper from which I read the form put into the fire and destroyed that night.

James Molyneux of 19 Newcastle Street Sheffield Labourer and Watchman Says

It is my duty to be out at night – on Friday 10th of January I was sent by order of Mr Raynor to a room in Fig Tree Lane to attend a Meeting there – I went to the room about a quarter past 9 I found an assembly of People that – I had never been there before – the People appeared to be of the lower Class – I should think there were about 130 – they consisted of men and boys from about 14 and 15 upwards – The Room is a large one – the People kept coming and going – when I went there was a man stationed there – he was stationed after I came in – I didn't observe he prevented any one from going – he appeared to be keeping the door – I stopped about an hour and a half – I saw a man there whom I have afterwards seen in custody and learned his name was Holberry – I saw him stand up above the rest and I heard him tell the people there that night was not a night of very great importance He told them to be steady – they knew their duty and not to be afraid of watchmen – He told them not to be daunted – he said they knew their duty before hand and he need not tell them then – I didn't stay in the room an hour and a half but was in and out – I went down stairs and made an attempt to go in at the door of the room underneath but there were three or four men standing near it in the passage and they told me they thought I should not get in without a Ticket – I said I wished to getting to join the Society as a Member – then one of them tapped on the door and said a person wanted to get him – a man opened the door and asked me what I wanted – I said I wanted to get in as a Member – he said that was not a night for that purpose – I left the place about a ¼ to 11 – I observed there was a little man[10] standing by the outside door below inviting people to come – I saw him again in custody and then knew him and I shall know him when I see him again – I went by the same directions the next night (Saturday) it was after 10 o'clock – I went to the Great Room up stairs – I found there about 20 lads and I heard one of them say they were waiting for a Prayer Meeting – they were at one end of the room – Afterwards I saw 4 or 5 men come into the room and stand together at the far corner of the room as if they were in full conversation – one of them drew from underneath his coat something that looked like a bayonet – then I saw one of the other 5 go to a corner of the room and take a wooden shaft and bring it to the man with the bayonet who tried it on and said it would do very well I observed four or five other shafts of the same description in the corner of the room – In about 10 minutes afterwards a man came in and said there would be no Class Meeting that night and they then dispersed this was about 10:30 – I then went away.

On the Friday Evening I saw a man walking up and down in front of the Meeting House – That man[11] I afterwards saw in custody and knew him and I shall know him again when I see him – I saw him pacing up and down for half an hour and once I saw him open the door and look into the room upstairs as if looking round

<u>Mr Edward Smith</u> of 72 Far Gate Printer says that on Friday, January 10 Holberry brought to Witness the MS No.13 now produced and desired 100 to be printed Holberry fetched some of them and desired Witness to get the remainder Posted on Saturday a good height He called upon witness on Saturday noon to ascertain whether they were printed. They were not finished and he then and directed witness to get a person to post them and Holberry said that if the man posted them a good height & well & would call out of the Room in Fig Tree Lane on Monday evening they would pay him 6/ for posting them Witness got them printed on Saturday and they were posted Witness asked Holberry his name

13
Universal Suffrage v Anti Corn Laws

---

10 This man is Wells

11 This was Pensthorpe

The public of Sheffield is respectfully informed that a Lecture on the above important questions will be delivered in the room of the Chartist Association Fig Tree Lane on Monday, January 13th 1840 at 7 o'clock in the evening by Mr Lowery of Forfar Scotland who will be proud to meet any Gentleman connected with the Anti Corn Law Association to discuss the merits of the Corn Law question in juxta-position with that of the Franchise

On Sunday, January 12 the Revd William Hill (Editor of the Northern Star) will deliver a Sermon in the above Room during Divine Service to commence at 10 o'clock in the Fore noon

A collection will be made after the sermon and lecture towards defraying the expenses of Messrs Foden and Fox's trial

100 Dbl Crown
ES

<u>Ann Salt</u> of Lambert Street a Servant to Mr Saunders sign of Reuben's Head and also Birmingham Arms has lived with Mr Saunders about 9 months – there was on the ground floor a room called the Box – the Bar and Front room also a kitchen which was not a Company Room and up stairs there was a Lodge Room for the Odd Fellows who met once a fortnight on a Tuesday night – on the Saturday afternoon the day before the disturbances being the Saturday before Mr Saunders was apprehended Witness saw 2 persons coming down stairs from the Lodge Room about ½ past 3 o'clock one was drest in a blue coat[12] a stout person and Witness thinks he walked a little lame on the right foot – he was not a regular customer – another person was with him a youngish person should know both of them again – the stout person was dressed in a blue woollen coat – he had a stoutish face and dark complexion – the young person was dressed decently – they both went into the yard neither of the two persons were lodge people – Witness remembers seeing Mr Saunders going upstairs to the Lodge Room with a half gallon jug of ale – this would be about 6 o'clock as near as Witness recollects – Witness was coming out of the cellar at the time and had been all the afternoon in the back kitchen cleaning – Last Saturday (8th February) Mr Saunders came in about 5 o'clock and Mrs Saunders told him that Mr Bland the Constable had been saying he wanted to speak to him and that she had promised he should go at 6 o'clock and when she said so he went and dressed himself that Mrs Saunders said William where are you going and he said he must be off directly, and has never been back since – Witness has never seen either of

---

12 Cooper {*This may be one of Mary Holberry's brothers, or perhaps, father.*}

the 2 persons she saw on the Saturday either before or since. Before Mr Saunders was taken Witness has frequently heard Mrs Saunders speaking to him and telling him not to have anything to do with the Chartists and he has told her to hold her noise and not to interfere and to mind her own business and he would mind his

James Gunn lives in lodgings near Castlefolds in Sheffield is Bookkeeper at the Albion Hotel Coach office in Sheffield – that on the morning of Sunday, 5th January last a man of the name of Law took an outside place to London by the Rapid which started at 10 in the morning and paid 18/ for fare – that Witness put it down in his Book in his own handwriting and also in the Way Bill – witness will produce either his Book or Way Bill

Samuel Simpson of Forge Lane, Stock Taker proves that he knows the Witness Thompson – Has been a Moral force Chartist from soon after they held their out door meetings on a Sunday – Did not go much amongst them till after Peter Foden came back from York – got to know the Pass Word from Thompson and used to attend the Secret Meetings in Fig Tree Lane occasionally – Was a Member of Thompson's Class – saw Holberry at one of the meetings in Fig Tree Lane before the new password was made and afterwards also. The new pass word was made at night or two before the Saturday when the disturbance was, it was made in consequence of a complaint of Duffy's that the door was not properly titled. Has seen the Spear in Thompson's possession and heard it had been given to Duffy – Saw Duffy one night in the Chair. Heard him speak about the Door being better taken care of – Has always said he would not go out

Letters

HBY 1

(Letter sent from Pontefract to Sheffield – a stray envelope in the CPR numbered files, which has become separated from this, is postmarked "Pontefract May 28" and has this written in pencil on it: "Uncle William had his ancle crushed by a waggon")
May 27th 1840 Atcliff
Dear Farther and Mother Sisters and Brothers we send our best respects to you hoping to find you in good helth as this levs me at present but my Brother Whilam has got run hover last Friday 22 May a loaded whagen run hover his hankle and crushed it very bad but thank God he is Gating bater and i hop he whil sun be rady for work you have no {?} to mak your selns un esey a bout him but my Dear prans {*parents*} hat is not the worst i have to tal you poor Whilham Smith has got run hover with 12 whagens with the hingen {*engine*} On the 26th May and he is Dad he only lived a bout 8 hours after he got run hover i hop he did hapey and we think hare goig to barey him on the Thorsday the 28 May and we sent a later to his Farthes this moring so Dear Farther and Mother you musent mak your selns unes a bout us and with this and the road been nearly fineshed you must exquse us and we think we sharnt cum while the Fest give mie best rspets to Ann and hole in {?} prans {*parents*} aye sa no more from youre Deer suns at present

CPR4

Postmark:June 23 1840

Addressed to:

John Cooper
Hork Green
Attercliff Near
Sheffield

Dear Father and Mother we send these fue lins to you hoping to find you in Good helth as this levs us at present thank God for it we thout you would have sent a latter to us bee fore now lating us now ow you Whos geting on for when Smiths Brothes com tha cod not tal us a deal a bout you you must Excus me for not riting you by Parmes wife for i whos so

besey just then and we never Got to here til last wek whether my Sister Mary had a sun or a doter til Ann rote to mee we tould Smith brothes to cole at youre house and lat you nouw how my brother bill whos but i rit to you to tal you hat he his a deal beter then he whos but he has not got to work yet but hope he whil bee hable vee fore lougn we gather him 12 shillens a weak we send oure best respecks to hole oure brothes and sisthers hoping tha ar hole in good helth at present pleas to send a latter to us to leat us nouw wheather you have had a latter fro Holbrey or not and if you have send us word how his is getting on please to sen us word when Attercliff feast is for we think of comming this railway is going to bee hopinged on the weadnesday the 1 July 1840 and we do not now how we ar going on yet Marster and Mistress and James Horn sens there best respeks to you Giv my best respects to in qiring frands
So no mor from youre
Afectionate sons Thomas and Willaham Cooper

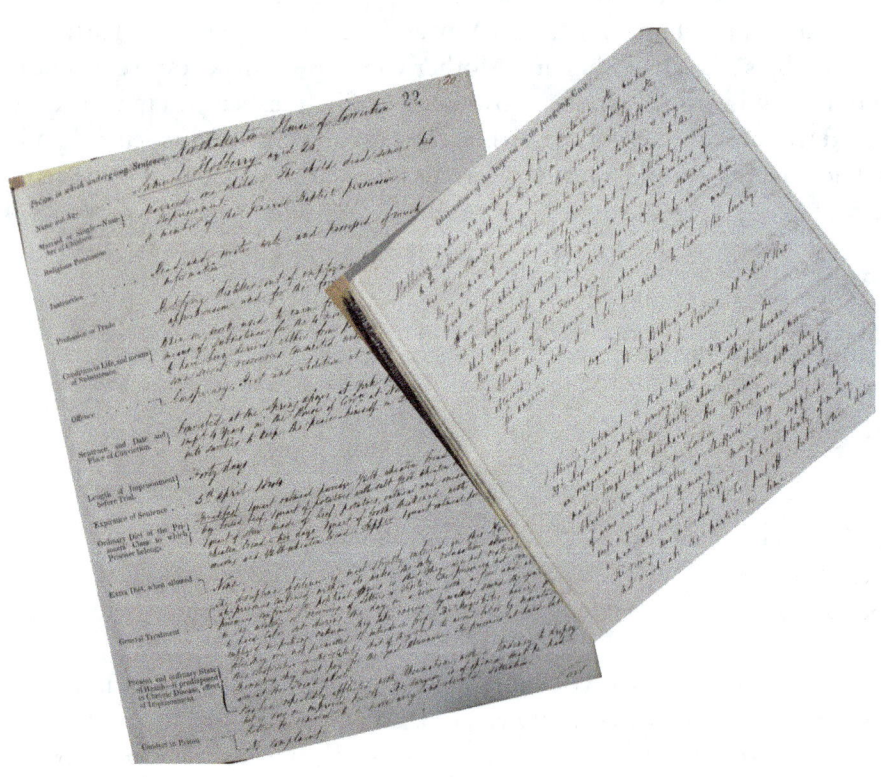

Report of Captain W J Williams, Prison Inspector, from HO/20/10

Prison in which undergoing sentence... Northallerton House of Correction

Name and Age..... Samuel Holberry Aged 26

Married or Single/ Number of Children – Married one child – The child dead since his imprisonment

Religious Persuasion..... A member of the General Baptist persuasion

Instruction... Read and write well – and possessed of much general information

Profession or trade.... Rectifying distiller – out of employment at the time of apprehension and for the four months previous

Condition in life, and means of subsistence When in work used to earn from 25/ to 30/ a week. His means of subsistence for the 4 months before apprehended appear to have been derived either from pawning his furniture or from some secret ressources {*sic*} connected with the agitation

Offence ... Conspiracy, Riot and Sedition at Sheffield

Sentence and Date and Place of Conviction/ Place of Conviction Convicted at the Spring Assizes at York 1840 and Sentenced to be imp^d 4 years in the House of Correction at Northallerton and to enter into sureties to keep the peace – himself in £50 and two in £310 each

Length of Imprisonment before Trial Forty days

Expiration of Sentence.... 5th April 1840

Ordinary Diet of the Prisoners' Class to which Prisoner belongs Breakfast. 1 quart oatmeal porridge ½ lb wheaten bread. Dinner – 2 days of 6oz boiled beef, 1 quart of potatoes with salt ½ lb wheaten bread – three days 1 quart of stew made of beef, potatoes, oatmeal and onions with ½ lb of wheaten bread – two days 1 quart of broth thickened with oatmeal and onions and ½ lb wheaten bread – Supper 1 quart oatmeal porridge ½ lb bread

Extra diet, when allowed.... None

General Treatment... The discipline of silence is most strictly enforced in this Ho: Corr: when all prisoners confined within its wall – the only relaxation allowed to the prisoners confined for political offences is that they are not restricted either in the writing or receiving of letters or visits. The prisoners not sentenced to hard labor sit during the day in a room with a fire and are employed in picking oakum – they take exercise by walking round the yard in files. They are not permitted to introduce food. The Magistrates having put the construction on the statute that if they elect to avoid labor by maintaining themselves they must pay for the Gaol allowance. The prisoners of hard labor are at the Tread-wheel.

Present and ordinary State of Health – if predisposed to Chronic Disease, effect of Imprisonment... Has been repeatedly afflicted with rheumatism, with a tendency to dropsy but is now in improved health. The surgeon is of the opinion that he had better be removed to a more airy and elevated situation

Conduct in prison... No complaint.

Observation of the Inspector on the foregoing case.

Holberry makes no complaint of his treatment. He wishes to be allowed ½ lb of bread in addition daily. He was the ostensible principal in the rising at Sheffield. He is a man of considerable resolution and talent – is every frank in communicating every particular relating to the offence for which he is suffering – but is extremely guarded as to compromising others. I annex a few particulars of what appears the most important part of his statement. His mention of the Frenchman I conceive to be an invention to blind the true source from whence the money was obtained. He states it to be his wish to leave the Country for America.

(signed) W. J. Williams
Inspector of Prisons 18th Dec 1840

Holberry's statement is that he was 2 years in the 33rd Regt and while serving, with many others became an orangeman – left the society when the disclosures were made – bought his discharge – his connexion with the Chartists commenced in London – there were a quantity of arms and combustibles at Sheffield – they must have cost a great deal of money money was supplied by a man who seemed a foreigner – he had plenty of money. The rising was intended to be put off but notice did not reach all the parties in time. December 1840 Notes taken by W J Williams Inspector of Prisons HO 40/10

<u>Notes of Samuel Holberrys statement.</u>
Samuel Holberry – am a native of Nottinghamshire being from near Retford where my father and mother still reside renting a Cottage belonging to the Duke of Newcastle. I have been a soldier in the 33rd Regt was in the army for three years when my friends purchased my discharge. I once belonged to the Orange Society, I was first made an Orangeman at Northampton when in the Army. There were many in the Regiment who belonged to the Society. I split away from them when the the Duke of Cumberland business and Colonel Fairman took place. The split took

place at the Albion Public House. All my relations are Conservatives. I was a Chartist when in London. I went twice away in connexion with Chartism from Sheffield in the month of December 1835. {*sic -probably was 1839*} I went to Nottingham, Sutton, Dewsbury and other places. I know that arms were sent, and money who found it I do not know. If I had been tried for my life I should have done pretty well to show where the money and combustibles came from. I did not know what to do at the time. There was a deal of arms and combustibles in Sheffield they must have cost a deal of money. It is a mystery where the money came from. The petards could not have cost less than 10/ each, There were two men at work in my garret. There are many arms now in Sheffield. We never thought of arms till after the Magistrates stopped the meetings. I never knew any thing of a rising to take place late November, about the 15th or 16th, the association did furnish the money, they could not get enough to pay their rent of 10/ a week for their room. There was a Council, but I do not know who they were, I only know the "one man". The "one man" was selected by the committee, and he chose the Council. The combustibles were tried, I tried one of the shells at Edge Bottom, it tore all the ground up. One reason why we did not succeed was that the news came from Wales that they were not able to rise at that time. They did not know it at Sheffield, the person did not arrive in time. They knew it at Dewsbury. It was a very extensive concern had it gone on the man knew all about where the money came from (Otley or Hartley) he had plenty of money, I knew him, he was not known to many. It was after Frost was taken when he came to Sheffield. He was a foreigner I think. I do not know where he stayed. He never was at the committee meeting but once. When he wanted any thing he always stood in the entry. He was between 30 and 40 a {...} {...} man with dark hair, a gentlemanly looking man and well dressed. He had been to Wales and knew our friends in all parts of the Country particularly at Birmingham. He was to have met me with others at --- to have gone to Lambert Street. His not being there made us all awry and decided us not to go on, but it was too late to prevent some from going out. If he had made his appearance in time we should have carried it in Sheffield

I know it has been stated that we made use of the subscription for Frost to buy arms, but this is wholly untrue, for Turner the man who collected it, ran away with the whole amount.

The keys of the Chartist Committee Room were kept by a woman and the women being apprehensive that the entries in the books might affect their husbands, got the keys through her and destroyed them at the time when enquiries were being made by the Police.

Notes of William Wells's Statement

William Wells. I became acquainted with Holberry from attending the meetings about the sacred month, he saw me better dressed, I sought his company and he mine. I have mentioned to several persons, and have always been surprised how he always had money at command. I have been at Holberry's house. I have been in the house when they were engaged upstairs, I went with Holberry to his house on the Saturday before the rise, while there a man came down with Bradwell, they brought some cartridge paper to dry at the fire, which they were using upstairs I have heard Holberry say there was a respectable man in Sheffield engaged in it but we would not tell his name. I heard him also speak of a Frenchman, he told me he had communication with a Polish Officer whom he had seen at the convention in London, but that he would not come down until a few days after the first {…} his name was Benzowski, he said they could not trust Dr Taylor from when he got a little drunk he let every thing out Holberry had the management of the Town Lamps for a few days, it was merely a blind to become acquainted with the police office, he said one person had engaged to take one of the balls and throw it into the police office he Holberry was to fire the barracks and then to take the {…} I believe Holberry had some correspondence with Birmingham about money. The men of Sheffield were given by Holberry to understand that the whole country was going to rise and that they were the smallest in number. A great deal that he brought from the Counties was either exaggerated or altogether untrue. There was a delegate came before the rise from Dewsbury to see our situation and he was quite surprised to see how few we had He told us a great deal about the quantity of arms and amunition they had at Dewsbury, and I have also heard from Holberry and others that they had considerable quantities there, I said to Holberry the day before the rise "I am afraid it will all end in smoke if Sheffield were the only town". He replied "It might end in smoke but there were plenty of other towns" It was expected that the rise would have taken place the Saturday before Holberry had indeed sent a letter to fix it for the Saturday before. I saw the letter which was "That the classes were preparing and that it was expected the wedding would take place the next Saturday, and he hoped to be home in time to be present at it. The letter was shown to me by a man of the name of Mr Carlty who disappeared, the reason why it was put off was understood to be in consequence of some arrangements with Dr Taylor. I first heard that this rise was to take place in a few days after the Sheffield Fair, a few weeks after the Welsh business. They made some of the shells from Macerone's book and the history of the Irish Rebellion. I believe a great many combustibles and arms are still about.

Marshall had vast many ball cartridges. He told me he had all sorts and all sizes, and if I knew any that had pieces they were to come to him. Marshall lived at the top of Coal Pit Lane, his house was a kind of armoury – it was a rendezvous for all the Physical Force men. Pikes were sent out to Barnsley from Sheffield. On the night of the rise the Saturday I went to my Class but did not stay I went home to bed, the reason I did not go, was that I thought what it would end in, but I did not dare to express my opinion. I believe some of the Powder was bought of Mr {...} a druggist in Barkers Pool, but I dont know whether it was a large quantity. the night when at Holberry's, he shewed me a large bag, which he could hardly lift full of powder. I went to Barnsley on the Monday after the break up. I then went among the Chartists, they said that Ashton had been at hand to lead them, they did not rise because the Sheffielders had failed they said there were 50 men out on the road to see if the mail did not arrive when Ashton was to be sent for he being within ten minutes call. The Toll keeper who was a Chartist had engaged to barricade the Toll bar and prevent the military getting through into the Town, which from its situation would have been a matter of great difficulty for them to do. When I was in York Castle Ashton Crabtree and Peter {...} were there in the same ward with me as well as this Ashton said he was one of 12 who had engaged to stop the three judges who were sent down to Wales. One of the number declared he would not go down in the coach to meet the judges for there was one of the 12 of whom he was not quite sure, Ashton said this to the others to show how little trust was to be placed in people giving this as an instance. I learnt from Marshall and Holberry while in York Castle that there was a sort of committee which acted by Tally, when my thing was to be done it was written on a Tally and drawn from. From their conversation I understand that Marshall was one of those engaged in throwing the fire balls into St Phillips church, he said he knew how the fire balls were constructed, that he had had some and that they were cleverly made.

Letter published in Northern Star 3/7/41

A VOICE FROM THE HELL HOLE
TO MR. WM. MARTIN
Northallerton, June 17th 1841

Dear Martin, - I am extremely sorry that I have not been able to receive your letters in consequence of the severe restrictions we are under. It is natural that I should choose such letters as contained a communication from my wife; but, my friends informed me of your persevering conduct in our behalf, I do not know of anything that has given me so much pleasure since I have been in prison, as your manly conduct in confronting the big Beggarman,[13] at the Crown and Anchor, and charging him with his gross inconsistency to his face. I am sure you are deserving of the thanks of all the Chartists in the kingdom, for that one act alone; but, I have been further informed that it was you who first brought forward the utility of Petitioning and a Prisoners' Convention; and as an individual deeply concerned in it, I feel it is my duty to return you my sincere and hearty thanks.

And if it has not accomplished all we could wish, it will have been the means of sending the Chartists' muster-roll within the walls of St Stephen's, and proved to demonstration that Chartism is on the increase, in spite of the unparalleled persecution by the Government, and threat and intimidation of masters, and such as think it their interest to keep the industrious millions in a state of political bondage.

Sir, I sincerely hope that the Chartists will split their vote with the Tories, and where there is no Chartist candidate, they will vote for them solely; not that I think there is a pin to choose between them; but to convince the Whig Government that the prayer of two millions of men, who are the sinews of the country, is not to be treated with contempt, on so slight a matter of the releasement of a few political prisoners, who have been so severely treated, I shall rejoice if you can get them out of office; all they think of is place, pension and patronage; the starving poor are only mentioned to serve party purpose. Sir, when the election squabble is over, I hope you will endeavour to get us removed from here. You can scarcely conceive the pain that my legs are to me with being so much confined, and the quantity of medicine I am obliged to take to keep the swelling down; but yourself has experienced something of close confinement and will, I have no doubt, feel for others. Remember, my friend, that I have two years and nine months yet to serve, being nine months longer than the worst felon in the jail. Poor old Booker kept with us till he could barely crawl, and the surgeon ordered him to be in the yard instead of at work, and gave him extra diet; but I am sorry to inform you that after all, he could stand no longer and has gone to take up Duffy's quarters. No wonder on the inactivity of the muscle that we are obliged to put up with, is sufficient to break the strongest constitution, if subjected to it for any length of time.

---

13 14th May 1841. Meeting called by Daniel O'Connell where entrance was controlled by a sixpence fee.

I shall be glad to hear of you bringing the matter before the public. My wife will be in Sheffield at the latter end of this month, and will be sending me a parcel, if you have got a few Temperance tracts I should be obliged to you if you would let her have them to send to me. If you favour me with an answer, you must send it to Brampton, to be there on or before the first Sunday in July, to be put in the letter – I cannot receive it any other way. I have not room for any more, so I conclude with my best wishes for your health, that you may be able to advocate the glorious cause of the unenfranchised millions; my prayer is, that the Chartists will be true to themselves, that unity will prevail amongst them, and denounce any man who brings forward any half measures – the Charter, the whole charter is the only thing that can bring any lasting benefit to the working classes.

Yours truly S Holberry

P.S. Let me know if you have heard any thing of Mr Peddie – he is an honest man, and when you write to him, give my respects.

CPR3

Letter addressed to:

John Cooper
Attercliff Ner
Sheffield
Yorkshire

Postmark: April 12 1841

Dear Farther and Mother
We send thes Few lins to you hoping to find you in good health as this levs us at prasent thank god for it we fon them at Castleford hole in good helth we let on Wilham Farmer at Rotham and we all whent to gather and we ad a very plasent gerney and we got ther all safe Deear Sisters and Brothes we send ore kind love to you and hoping you all ar in good helth Dear Mother we hop that you are beter My Brother Wilham started an working last Monday and the wether as been very fine sines we cold at Ann Tompson and we Got our deener ther before we started of. So No More at prasent from your loven sons Thomas and Willam Cooper

CPR1 Postmarked July 4, 1841

Dear Farther and Mother Sisters and Brothers we send oure best respects to you hoping to find you hole whel as this leves us at present thank God for it we receved your kind later you must exrues us for not coming it Christmas for we could not comfuble pleas Marey send us work a but Samuel how he is coming on we so it in the paper a bout the Chartes shifting from Northealant to Nancaster[14] so send us word wheather he is a not. Give oure best repsects to Johiney {?} and teal im i dont now how is landladey is for we have not spoaken since the night bee fore he com a way but hole is rit Give my best respeachs to Ann Toadd and tal her not to bee so hard harted tal her how i think she whil for Give if not for gat.
So no more at present from youre
loven sones

Thomas and Whialam Cooper

Letter published in Northern Star 14/8/41

July 29th 1841

To Mr William Martin[15], Brampton, Chesterfield

---

14 Northallerton to Lancaster

15 The original newspaper letter has the name Walsingham Martin on it. This was corrected in the errata of the following week. There would seem to be two William Martins which is confusing for historians. The preceding Martin letter would appear to be addressed to the Irishman William Martin who was imprisoned in Northallerton alongside Holberry. It refers to his intervention at the Crown and Anchor Meeting of the 14th May 1841 (Northern Star, 22nd May 1841). In the report of this meeting William Martin is declared as the "representative of the Birmingham Frost Committee" and in a document at: https://chartist-ancestors.blogspot.com/2018/06/a-list-of-chartist-leaders-but-where.html, there is a signature of William Martin using that same title. It is however, a different signature to that used on the letters in the York and Sheffield archives collection (HS/1/1, to which the letter in the Northern Star of 18/9/41 is clearly a reply, and HS1/3 and HBY 12). These appear to be to a different William Martin of Brampton, Chesterfield. HBY 12, written on the 16th January 1842, disparages the two Martin brothers ("the Great Walsingham has never been amongst us since October 4th there is a Chartist & Republican for you His brother Bill...") Letter HBY/6 corroborates this, written on the 5th December 1841 it says: " Mr William Martin last late prison at Northallerton goal {sic} is on the Road to America" In HBY 11 George Flynn says "Mr William Martin has Left Bradford and I think Removed to London" We know

Respected Friend, - I received your kind letter and was pleased to hear of your being at Attercliffe Feast. I should have liked to have been there too, or anywhere but in this miserable place.

Sir, I confess I felt rather surprised when I read your letter. I thought you had known me better than to have such an opinion of me, as to think for a moment that I am afraid to speak what I think or know upon the silent system. I am aware I have never entered into any detail to it, but it was not through fear or any restraint I am under, for I knew my inability to do justice to my thoughts on the subject; and I am aware that others, who knew as much of it as I do, are well qualified to treat the matter in all its odious forms.

I cannot but think our friends take a wrong view on the subject: it is our rascally Government that is to blame for sending a set of men to such places, and treating them as felons, for a political offence. The new rules were revised and altered, as they now stand, by the Marquis of Normanby this last week, backed, as you must know by the statute law; and you may depend it is useless trying to get them altered. Talk of convicts: I would rather ten times be one of them, than be under the severe discipline of this place. They are allowed social intercourse with each other, and it is not a breach of discipline, with them, to cast a look at the heavens.

I do assure you, Sir, I have not seen the sun for above twelve months. I was reported the other day for looking as high as the prison windows, when they were straight before me. So you may form some idea of the comprehensive nature of the silent system.

Sir, I cannot say that I have been treated in any manner contrary to the rules of the prison; but I do say that the severity of the rules has given my health such a shock as I shall perhaps feel whilst I live. I am sorry to inform you that my back is no better: it has been coming on me for months: it is the same complaint that I have had so long in my legs – at least, I think so, as I am taking the same medicine for it as for my legs. My friend, I have enclosed you a copy of a petition that I have sent to the Marquis of Normanby this last week. I perhaps need not inform you that his Lordship can ascertain how far it is true if he thinks it proper. I think that if Sheffield was to get up a public meeting, and send a petition, signed by the Chairman, to the Home office, perhaps most of us might be

---

that William Martin of Chesterfield was a hatter and the other Martin a shoemaker, and there is a hatter of that name in the 1841 census in Brampton. The Irish William Martin was living in Bradford after his release from Lancaster gaol in March 1841 and was put up as a candidate in the 1841 General Election.

forgiven, and the others removed: at least, it is worth trying for. Will you have the kindness to write a Sheffield on the subject?

Sir when you receive a copy of the Bradford petition send me one, but do not write anything else on, so as to make a letter of it: if you do, it will prevent me receiving it, as the prison rules will not allow us to receive or send a letter oftener than once in three weeks.

My dear Sir, I am heartily glad that the Whigs are in so great a minority. I received the half dozen stamps for which I return my friend thanks. You must excuse the rambling, unconnected manner that I have wrote this letter: you are not aware how painful stooping to write is to me.

I will endeavour to do the next better.

Give my respects to Mrs Martin and all friends; and before I conclude, let me beg of you, my friends to use your endeavours to get us removed. Health and strength is the only property I have; and if it is destroyed, how, in the name of God, and I to get any bread, if ever I live to get my liberty? Let me know in your next what exertions had been made.

I am, Sir,
Yours faithfully,

Samuel Holberry

To the Right honourable the Marquis of Normanby, secretary of state

The humble petition of Samuel Holberry, a prisoner in the House of Correction, in Northallerton, in the North Riding of the County of York

Sheweth, – that your Lordship's petitioner was convicted of conspiracy and sedition at the York Spring Assizes, of 1840, and sentenced to four years imprisonment in the above mentioned in jail.

That the severe confinement he is enduring is not only ruining his health, but daily diminishing his strength; and to give your lordship an idea of his afflictions, and that his person he is undergoing a considerable change for the worse, his legs are subject to continual swellings, and his appetite has lost all relish for the prison diet.

That your Lordship will feel convinced from these circumstances that your petitioner must be considerably debilitated, and hourly feeling his afflictions more and more.

That your Lordship's petitioner having been subject to the severe restrictions of the silent system, for so long a period, and having, by his sentence, yet to undergo two years and a half imprisonment in the very closest of confinement, he feels it a duty he owes to himself for the protection of his health, nay, his very life, to petition your Lordship for a mitigation of his punishment; not that he prays for that almost unhoped for favour at this stage of his sentence of a total remission of it, but for a relaxation of the prison discipline by being sent to some other gaol where the silent system is not enforced, wholly on the ground of protection to his health.

That your Lordship's petitioner, having now stated the ground of his petition, he will rest in full hope of confidence in your Lordship's humanity to take the above circumstances into consideration; that is – the length of time he has served under the most severe prison discipline – the time he has served under the decline of health – and the present state of his health: and may your Lordship, under the circumstances, see the absolute necessity of granting his humble petition, by removing him to some place where the restrictions are less severe, thereby holding how to the hope that his health may be protected, and his life spared; and your petitioners will ever pray.

Samuel Holberry, Prisoner

Letter published in Northern Star 4/9/41

Northallerton College, August 29th 1841

To Mr William Martin, Brampton, near Chesterfield.

DEAR FRIEND

I received your letter, and am happy to inform you that my back is a deal better. I have been troubled with a pain in my side and stomach and shortness of breath for several weeks, which has taken away my appetite and reduced me very much, and I have been in hospital since the 10th instant, but fresh air and plenty of good food have done me a deal of good, and I hope soon to regain my strength, but I am very weak at present. I have not found the prison hospital such a place as I had anticipated, but comfortable, with a beautiful prospect, and allowed social intercourse with its inmates.

Sir, I have received no answer from the Home Secretary to my petition. I wrote a respectful letter to him on the 14th instant, requesting one, and informing him of my being in the hospital.

You will be apprised of the liberation of my four companions leaving only myself, Marshall and Brook, in this hell-hole.

My friend, I believe that personal good conduct, since we have been confined here, has not been the criterion by which my Lord Normanby has been guided. I did not expect my liberty, but am surprised that Marshall did not get his: feeling convinced that there is no chance of my pardon being granted, I shall persevere in trying to get removed to some other place, as I cannot stand close confinement any longer, accompanied by the silent system.

Sir, you informed me in your letter, which I received from you in April last, that Sheffield* was only waiting to see the results of the national petition, and if nothing was done, they would set up a meeting and petition the Home Secretary for our removal.

Now, Sir, I think, considering what has transpired, the committee has shown a supineness as to what becomes of us; that I did not expect, and I feel as if I could not ask them any more to petition for me.

Sir, have the kindness to inform me in your next how many of my Chartist brothers have got their liberty, and how many are in prison yet.

Sir, you may wish to know what becomes of my letters. I am not stinted to as to the time I keep letters in my possession: and when I am done with them they are put away until I get my liberty: and if I want I can see them at any time I have occasion.

Sir, you sent a copy of my petition in the hope that Sheffield would endeavour to to get me its prayer granted, which I think might be done if you write to G.J. Harney the next time he visits that place, to take the subject up.

Sir, I am not daunted at trifles, but I do confess that I dread the close confinement of another winter – it does a man more harm than hard labour in winter time.

Sir, excuse me, (you wish me to speak my mind freely), I cannot but think that it was known to many of the Chartist delegates, whom I have had the pleasure, of meeting with, that there was a manifest disposition on the part of the Government not to pardon me, and considering the state of my health, and the length of time I have to serve, (and other things not necessary to name here), they ought to have endeavoured to have got me removed.

My friend, this is plain; but you are not aware of what I have suffered in this close confinement. Let me have a good long letter with all the news possible, and as soon as I get to know that Normanby is out of office, I shall petition again.

Give my Respects to Mrs H {*presumably "M" incorrectly transposed*} and all friends in the cause of liberty, and accept the same from,
Your sincere friend and well-wisher
S Holberry

* According to the letter that I received from Sheffield, from one of the Council, dated April 20, 1841, the first paragraph runs thus:
"Last night, being our general meeting night, I read your letter; there was a feeling of sympathy for the fate of poor Holberry and his suffering companions. We resolved to memorialise Normanby, having it signed by as many householders as possible, their names and places of residence. I hope our friends will take this subject up as soon as possible.
P.S. Since writing the foregoing, I have received an answer from my Lord Normanby. His lordship says he has fully considered my petition, and that he does not see sufficient reasons to advise her Majesty to grant its prayer. What a mockery! Why make use of Her Majesty's name! Is it not he, by virtue of his office, prison-master general? Could not he have ordered my removal if he thought proper? After such a division in the House of Commons, to turn a deaf ear to such a request as relaxation from the severity of the silent system and close confinement, wholly on the grounds of protection of my already injured health (bear in mind, Sir, that I was not sentenced to labour), I feel that any comment of mine would be far from doing justice to my feelings, I therefore refrain from saying more, and leave you, Sir, and others, to form your own opinions of the tender mercies of a Whig Government.
Let me have a bit of Chartism in your next; should be very glad to hear of the Chartists using their endeavours to get the remainder of us removed to the County gaol.
Yours S. H. August 21, 1841

HS/1/1

Brampton Moor September 5th 1841
Respectful Friend
I again take up my pen hoping to find you better than when you wrote last I was very sorry to hear that you was in hospital for I know you must be very bad or else you would not of become an inmate of that place you must keep up your spirits and cheer yourself up as well as you can in your Dreary Cell you said in you last you were not daunted at trifles I am very glad to see that you have some Courage Left I have some Good Tidings to tell you The Brave Champion of the Peoples Rights is at Liberty – F O Connor the Whigs liberated him on Thursday last being Prince Albert's Birth Day[16]

---

16 The meeting in York was addressed by William Martin "of Bradford" – it appears our William Martin wasn't there himself

Last Monday was the Day Announced for his liberation and he stopt in York until the Monday when delegates for all Parts of England & Scotland where there to meet him at one o clock upward of 200!! in number!!! They built a car expreſsly for the occasion drawn by six Horses and formed in procefsion. through all the principal Streets in the City to the Grand Stand on the Race Course where he addreſsed 30,000 persons!!!! Such an afsembly There never was in York before above 1200 {?} to a tea supper in the stand and they separated about Eleven o clock at night. Highly satisfied with the Days proceedings He will be in Sheffield on Wednesday the 29th inst when there will be a Grand Display there oh How i could like to meet you there once more. I hope the Day will not be long friend May God Grant that it may. I have a Bit more Good news for you that is the Base Bloody & Brutal Whigs are out of office and the Tories are In so you must set to work and petition again The Home Secretary is Sir James Graham upon the addrefs to the Queen's Speech an Amendment to it were Proposed both in the Lords & Commons The Tories carried their amendment in the Lords by 71 and the Commons there by 91 so you see what a Majority they have in Each House the houses have adjourned until the 24th inst Mr Sharman Crawford posed an addition to the amendment upon the addrefs the words i write {?} you which are That we further Respectfully Represent to Your Majesty that in our opinion the Distrefs which Your Majesty deplored is mainly attributable to the circumstances of your Whole people not being able to be fully represented in the House and we feel it will be our duty to consider the means of so Extending and regulating the suffrage and of adopting such improvements in the system of voting as will confer on the working clafses that just weight in the Representative body which is necefsary to secure a due consideration of their interest and which their present endurance of suffering gives them the strongest Title to Claim. Seconded by Thomas Duncombe Esq. amongst some that took part in the Debates and left the House and voted neither for or against is George Henry Ward of Sheffield and Mr Roebuck for Bath out upon Such Trafficing Politicians of Course it was lost but 39 Consistent members voted for the Peoples rights My Dear Fellow you wish to know how many of our Brother Chartists are in the Hell Holes yet i will inform you Lancaster 1 York 0 Devizes 0 Northallerton 3 Beverly 1 Wakefield 5 Millbank Penitentiary 8 Brecon 6 Total 24 Transported Seven But i hope soon to see the {?...} Bronterre {?} O'Brien agreement the 25th Inst. A Meeting will be Held in Figtree Lane Room Tomorrow Evng to memorialize her Majesty to Cause our Enquiry to be made into the silent system Enforced in Wakefield Beverley Northallerton & other Prisons in England Mr Harney will be there almost all Parts are Getting up meetings

for the same purpose which i have no doubt will be attended with succefs we are about petitioning individually upon this subject there is about 419 Petitions been presented this Sefsion By Mr Dunscombe from Nottingham. You no doubt heard of the Notorious Harrison the Bradford spy who was employed by the Whigs to entrap honest men in 39 he his Caught in is own Trap at Last this notorious vilain would not say that he had not received 80 Pound from the Government for Entrapping the Chartists this Roue has been stealing a Horse from a field in Ribolden located{?} near Preston and hired two boys to drive it to Blackburn When{?} he was given them a shilling each and their suppers and after giving them Sevenpence to pay the Toll beers he goes straight off to Blackburn and gets there before the lads and Gives information to the Police that his suspicions rested upon 2 lads of stealing a Horse and told the police where they might find them accordingly the police went to the Public House where this vilain told them drive it to and took them both into custody both in Seperate cells and when they were Examined the boys told the Magistrate what i have stated above and they immediately took Mr Harrison and committed him for Trial So you see by trying to Get these lads sent out of the County he has fell into the trap himself and probably he may be sent off i have just Read a letter from John Walker of Wakefield. Hell it is most horrible to read i am anxious that you should let Me have a Statement of Your Dietary table for Each day in the week with all particulars possible with your opinions feelings & wishes with respect to any treatment if of a harsh kind you may have received at any of their hands whilst you have been in that <u>Hell</u> i had thot of giving you a Extract or two out of Walkers letter and then i thought it be better not as it would harrow upon your feelings Send me word wether you sit to pick Oakum and what quantity you pick in a day and if you are Stinted and wether it is Soaked or warmed or how you have it i hope your Principle still remains firm to the Charter of our Liberties you may Depend upon it tha[17]—
nor Whigs will be able to carry on the Goverment—
Country without conceding to the Working Clafses—
& Long witheld Rights i will Give You Your Dear—
which is not so well put together owing i think—
person writing it for her Attercliffe Sept 3rd—
My Dear Husband I hope these lines will find—
health than when you wrote Last i was very sorry—
of you being in hospital—
They came home and a—

---

[17] A section of this letter is missing.

My Dear I hope you wri—
I think something will—
Esqr will in Sheffield—
will be such a meeting—
place i have had a a le—
& Wm Rhodes send the—
from Gamston and you—
all well and send th—
At Bedford has got a Da—
to you Mr and Mrs Be—
send word in your n—
Like the— all no—
mother —& sis—
accept the— from—
Holberry My Dear Frie—
at the Baths he has been—
Legs and Body swells so —
again the Infernal Syste—
that his Constitution is—
communication from Wm—
him he is at Bradford—
at Woolwich to see a La—
orders for the Liberation—
this needs no comment fr—
doors and let all Politic—
act for which her Peop—
I was to let you have a —
an agitation made S—
A Seventy Towns Em—
are opening branches—
Cards of Membership the Same My Dear Fellow loze no time in
forwarding a memorial to Sir Jas Graham Home Secretary for Her Majesty
My wife sends her Best Respects to say the time is not far distant when we
shall have you among us again and says now the Tories have got in we shall
be able to get something out of the mess though i think it is High time we
had this Last fortnight there is four of our men gone to america they
cannot get a living here and they are gone in hopes of Getting a Better our
Friends desire to be remembered to you I shall conclude with a line or to
from Goldsmith which are appropriate to the times
I have seen a calculation made today that if the people were addmitted to
their share in the soil this Country could maintain a population of

100,000,000!!! and at present it cannot maintain 20,000,000 Oh shame where is they Blush. My Friend I must conclude with my Best Respects and remain your sincere Friend Wm Martin
PS Direct all your letter for the at. B Goodlads Cowleys Yard, Holiwell St, Chestefield

Ill fares the Land to Hastening ill a prey
Where wealth accumulates and men decay
A Time there was, Ere Englands' griefs began
When every Rood of Ground Maintained its man
Princes & Lords May Flourish or May fade
A Breath can Make them, as a breath has made

Criminal Petitions: Series II 1840-1846 HO18/048

To the Right Honourable Sir James Graham
Secretary of State for the Home Department
We the undersigned being members of the Convention of the industrious classes assembled in London beg most respectfully to submit to your serious consideration the cases of the following persons who have been imprisoned for political offences.
That in the Assizes for the County of York held in March 1840, Samuel Holberry was convicted of conspiracy and riot, and sentenced to four years imprisonment in Northallerton House of Correction and that in consequence of the severe discipline of the said prison his health was so much impaired as to induce her Majesty through your kind interference to cause his removal to York Castle. That your memorialists have heard with the pain and regret that the said Samuel Holberry is now confined to a bed of sickness. And your memorialists are of the opinion that if his imprisonment be persevered in, it will totally incapacitate him from any kind of labour hereafter and make him a burthen to his friends or to society.
We would therefore earnestly press upon your attention the necessity of your recommending to Hr Majesty to discharge the said prisoner for the above reasons and we believe that whatever might have been the nature of his crime, he has suffered a punishment more than commensurate to it. From the effect which the said imprisonment has had upon him, and which we understand has been communicated to you by the surgeon of the prison wherein he has been confined, we have every reason to suppose that unless her Majesty be graciously induced to extend her mercy to be

said prisoner by ordering his discharge that death will speedily terminate his sufferings.

Your memorialists also consider the case of Robert Peddie who was tried at the same Assizes convicted of riot and sentenced to three years imprisonment in Beverley house of correction to be one of great hardship. We understand the prisoner has been subjected to hard labour and the other degrading and inhuman regulations practised under the silent system which have caused him to endure extreme suffering. We would beg to remind you that the chief witness upon whose evidence he was convicted has since been transported for horse stealing and that it was chiefly through his instrumentality that he was entrapped into the commission of the act for which he was imprisoned. We would also entreat of you to bring before Her Majesty's merciful consideration of the cases of Thomas Booker, William Brooke and Peter Foden who are now suffering imprisonment for political offences. Booker and Brooke have already suffered more than two years imprisonment under the silent system which in your memorialists judgement ought to be considered a sufficient atonement to the law.
Your memorial lists humbly submit that in the long and cruel imprisonment of these men and also considering that upon the health of poor men depends their sole means of support and independence we do therefore earnestly request that you will be pleased to submit this the memorial to the merciful consideration of her Majesty and thereby restore those men to their impoverished and heart broken wives and families

Letter published in Northern Star 18/9/41

Sept. 8th, 1841

DEAR MARTIN, -I received your kind and interesting letter, and have the pleasure to inform you that I have no pain on me at this time. Bad digestion and bad appetite is only part of the blessed effects of eighteen months close confinement. My breath, Sir, smells intolerable; an evident sign that my inside is not what it ought to be. What else can I expect, Sir, when I think of the quantity of medicine that I have taken since I have been here, (for I never had any doctor's bottles in my life before,) for my legs and back pains, that were brought on by nothing else but close confinement. I told the magistrate so, and I have told the surgeon so many times; and I think former letters are to the same purport. I have had an opportunity of putting it to the test since I have been in hospital these four weeks. I have had no medicine for them, but have had plenty of exercise, and the consequence is that my 1egs have not swelled. Neither have I had any pain my back.

Sir, I do not blame anyone here. The surgeon did his best, I believe, to keep them from swelling,. You may depend that I shall not be satisfied by being told that it is rheumatic, if they are bad again. It is known to no one but myself what I have suffered these last twelve months, with my legs swelling every day for want of exercise.

Sir, you ask for a glimpse of our dietary table. Such was the wretched state of my appetite for three months before I came into the hospital, that half of it was sufficient for me; and since I came up stairs I have had plenty of good wholesome food; so I think it would be unreasonable to complain of anything that I do not feel the direct effect of.

Sir, believe me after reading your letter that the rascally Whigs were out of office, I went to bed and I do not know that I ever slept so sound since I have been in prison, so well pleased was I that the Government of this country was no longer in the hands of so worthless and detestable a faction.

Sir, I am sorry to see by your letter, that there are so many as twenty-four of us left in prison yet. What! not release Ashton and Crabtree! Scandalous. How can I complain when they are in prison? From the tender mercies of such miserable wretches as Normanby and Co. good Lord deliver us. Sir, you say you hope my principles still remain firm to the Charter of our liberties. Can you doubt it? Rest assured, my friend, that I shall neither Flinch from, nor deny, my principles, if they keep me in prison till I rot. It would be an easy method of putting down Chartism if sending men to prison could make them forego their right of thinking for themselves.

Sir, your letter informs me of George Henry Ward not stopping to vote for Mr. Sharman Crawford's addition to the amendment on the address; what can you expect from such milk and water fellows ? He is neither a gentleman nor a conscientious man, or he would not have said what he did about me when I was in prison and could not answer for myself, (I mean, of course, what he said to the deputation,) which was as great a falsehood as ever was uttered, wholly without foundation, and I defy either him or any one also to give proofs of my making use of any such language.

Sir, I was highly pleased with the account you gave me of Mr. O'Connor's liberation and reception in York; and from what you say in your letter, I conclude you intend seeing him when he visits Sheffield, if so, tell him that I am alive and should be glad to see him when he comes into the North. The time of visiting is from twelve to one every day. The railway runs close by, so that it will not detain him long. I can then talk to him freely about prison discipline. You can say that I have seen no one these sixteen months. Should he be in the North when you receive this, have the kindness to write a note in my name with the foregoing request.

I was not surprised at your account of Harrison, the Bradford spy. In my opinion, he is not so much to blame as the villains who first taught him to get money by such knavish tricks; but I think he will not find his speculation in horse-flesh to be so profitable as being fugleman for the Bradford Chartists. No, no, Sir, he will not have the Government to back him; but it is a pity to see a man lost for the want of a friend, and I think my old friend, Harrison, could not do better than memorialise his late employers, the Whigs, and remind them of the inestimable service he rendered to them when they were attempting to immortalize their names' by putting down Chartism. Stealing horses, Sir, is only a slight offence when compared to sedition, or attending what the Attorney-General calls illegal meetings; and, surely, when a man has rendered such important services to his country as Mr. Harrison, it ought not to be forgotten.

Sir, I shall petition the Home Secretary in a short time, I think of waiting a short time to see if anything will be done for me.

Having to make one sheet of paper do for you and my beloved wife, I must conclude ere I scribble it all over. I have not room to say all I could wish. Give my respects to Mrs. Martin, and all Chartist friends. Let me have a long letter; write it close. Let me know all Chartist news, what places O'Connor visits, and if O'Brien is coming to the Sheffield meeting. I look for, your letters as regular, and with as much anxiety, as the Whigs did for quarter day.

I am,

Yours truly,

SAMUEL HOLBERRY

CPR2

September 12, 1841

William Cooper Castleford pottery

Dear Father and Mother hi send my kind love to you hoping to find you well as it leaves me at present thank god for it hi am working on the railway keeping the road in repear for the Company and William Farmer is working with me and to hi am varrey clad to hear such Good news from Sam and hi hope he will soon bee out of prifson Daved Pears is Working on Methley Common on the Northmedlon [18] realway and he wants to know

---

18 North Midlands

wear Thomas is and what he is doing you must tell Thomas that is Dear Feabey Harthus his soon to be Married at Castleford Curch With a Glafsblower We shod of Com to the feast but we was then at work but if aney of you can come to se hus we shall be clad to se you wen you Com William Farmer and the Tho Horn and Mrs Horn James Horn sends thear bests respects to you all Mrs Dorter his got ha bed of the fine girl and is doing whel
So no more at present from your affection
Son William Cooper

Letter published in Northern Star 30/7/42 : Obtained in response to their request for all communications that had passed between the Secretary of State for the Home Office and the authorities of York Castle regarding the health of Holberry

The visiting magistrates of York Castle

Whitehall 16th of September 1841

Gentleman – Secretary Sir James Graham having deemed it expedient to give directions for the removal of Samuel Holberry from Northallerton gaol to the York Castle, there to undergo the remaining term of his imprisonment, I am directed to request you to call upon the surgeon of the latter prison to pay constant and particular attention to the prisoner's health, and to report thereon to Sir James Graham from time to time.
I am &c
(signed) S.M. Phillips

Letter published in *The English Chartist Circular and Temperance Advocate*, Vol 2, no. 119

York Castle 22nd of September 1841

My Dear Wife,
I have now the pleasure to communicate to you that I was removed yesterday from Northallerton to this gaol, where I shall be more comfortable both in body and mind. I am much better in health than I was the last time I wrote to you, and trust I shall gradually regain the strength which I lost in the horrible place I left. I shall be at liberty to use my speech and exercise at leisure. I trust you will keep up your spirits, and I hope the day will soon dawn when I shall be set at large altogether. I wish you to go to Sheffield, and to inform Mr Harney that I have got removed to this gaol by the Secretary of Ste, upon the surgeon's certificate of my ill health,

I am, my dear wife, yours very affectionately,
Samuel Holberry

Letter published in Northern Star 30/7/42 : Obtained in response to their request for all communications that had passed between the Secretary of State for the Home Office and the authorities of York Castle regarding the health of Holberry

York Castle 28th of September 1841
Samuel Holberry, a prisoner, brought to York Castle on the 22nd instant, is suffering from the effects of a bilious attack. He is weak; his skin and eyes are still suffused with bile; his pulse is quick, and his appetite bad. I offered to place him in the hospital, which he declined, stating, he was very comfortable, and could more easily take exercise where he was. His diet was altered to suit his appetite; and I have every reason to hope his health will gradually improve.
(signed) George Champney,
Surgeon to York Castle

HS/1/2 29 Sept

My Dear Holbery

I feel proud to have an opportunity of communicating to you at so short distance, and in a less barbarous situation than you have of late been subjected, by your Cruel Persecutors, the purpose of this is to inquire of you if you now, and if prison rules do not prevent you from making known how many of the Bradford Chartists there is confined in Northallerton, and what are their names, Likewise, how many there is in Beverley + Wakefield their Names also, as we are meeting Mr Skivington here this week when I intend to bring forward A Memorial in their behalf showing up the Characture of the Villain Harrison the witnefs against them
Dear Holbery I would be proud to be the means of adding to your comforts in any way that I can whilst you are in your present situation which the prison rules many allow if you will let me know what can be done for you if you are want any Books or Writing paper that I can get you, and your Governor will allow let me know and you shall have them immediately. I do sincerely rejoice that you have been brought back to York as what I have seen of the Governor and officers of the prison they

are Men possed of Humane + Kind hearts + tho the rules may be strict yet it is pleasant when you have such men to Enforce them. I hope you will be allowed to answer this and state all particulars that time will allow as it is of great consequence that I should know to night I will send on at ½ past 4 o'clock for your answer if you can furnish it by that time in the meantime I remain sincerely yours on the cause of humanity + truth,
Edward Burley
Septr 29th 1841
19 Bilton Street
Layerthorpe
York

HBY1/3

Mansfield Octr 8 /41

My Dr Holbery
I am happy to inform you that your letter has arrived same, bringing us the joyful tidings of the increase in your health and strength. I do afsure you the friends of Mansf.d are allways happy to render our suffering Brothers all the afsistance that is in our power. I have likewise to state to you that we had commenced with a memorial on your behalf but your removall has caused us to then memoralise on behalf of R. Peddie which took place last night in the market-place and a Glorious meeting we had. I only wish yourself had been there to witnefs it, we had collected some money for you which will be forwarded to your friend Martin as soon as the collection is closed. O how the how it gladdens my heart to think that the more our tyrants persecute us the more determined we seem to persevere in the good cause of truth and righteousnefs.
When you have the opportunity of writing to us again we shall be glad to hear from you and likewise hear of your enjoying good health. I have sent you 3 postage stamps they will be usefull to you, we shall take every lawfull means to gain you a remifsion of your unnatural sentence We had a Nottingham friend here at the meeting, and he will acquaint our sterling friend Sweet of your respects, Oconner his expected at Nottm. Soon, I will send you all particulars in my next, but I hope you will be amongst us before that time, If not I shall not forget you, you are wellcome to all our pafsd services for you, and for all the future ones that is to come, which I hope you will soon receive the benefit of by being once more set at Liberty from the fangs of a cruel Whig government and restored to the bosom of your Wife and family, and for the sufferings that you have

endured may you for ever be blefsed by divine providence on this earth and in the World to come, Amen.
I remain your, Brother Chartist,
Thomas Dutton Ratcliffe Gate no. 901

HBY1/4

Mansfield October 11th /41

Dear friend
I am happy to be the bearer of the glad news that our Mansfield friends are alive to the interests of our incarcerated brother. I did not think the collection (mentioned in my last) would have closed so soon but when I read your letter last Sunday to our friends, they immediately requested me to transmit to you the sum of 6s the whole of the amount collected, which you will find in this post office order enclosed in this letter, so farewell for a while
Yours in the bonds of unity
Thos Dutton
Ratcliffe Gate no. 901

PS Please to write when you receive this.

HS1/3

Brampton Nov 7th 1841

My Dear Holberry

It is with feelings of pleasure I again sit down to addrefs a few lines to you I am very happy to find in your last that you are fast recovering your health which I doubt not will be a grate blefsing to you For I am sure the torturing punishment you endured in the infernal den (I mean the Hell of Northallerton) must according to my ideas have worked upon your system that if you had not been removed must shortly have ended in your death but thanks to an all wise being that case has been averted and I hope ere long you will afsume your wonted health and strength I will afsure you that your friends here have felt deeply for your Sufferings and Sympathise with me for your future health and prosperity believe me my dear friend that your <u>Pretended Friends</u> in Sheffield are about coming to their senses tho old Bookers proceedings for his goings on since he has been liberated attempting to injure you in the Estimation of your real Friends in Sheffield (and I am happy to say they are increasing) thinking to enoble himself at your Expense his friends (if he had any and no doubt he had) has turned their backs upon him Enough about him My letter was inserted in Last weeks Star and by the side of it was a very pretty letter in your behalf wrote by Edward Burley 19 Bilton St, Layerthorpe York, it breaths the Spirit of Great Liberty throughout it is an appeal to the Sympathising Chartists of Great Britain I perceive by the Star this week that my letter (a Copy of it I would forward to you if you would be allowed to receive it and I believe you would) has been taken up at the public meeting on monday Evening Last week in Figtree Lance on Monday Eveng, last week. It is brief I will give you the whole of it – Mr Needham (Henry) brought on the subject of Certain charges made against Mr Holberry at the present time in York Castle referring to a letter on the Subject which appeared in Last weeks Star from Mr Wm Martin of Brampton after a lengthy discuſsion in which Meſsrs Harney, Gill, Needham (Henry) Mc Ketterick, Buxton, Wells & March took part each speaker Highly eulogising the Character of Mr Holberry as an unflinching patriot and an honest man The following Resolution was moved by Mr Gill and was adopted by the meeting – That this meeting expreſs their perfect Confidence in Mr Holberry and treat as idle calumny all mis-statements to the contrary regard him as a man of integrity and a Patriot of Stirling worth. So you will perceive that what that old renegade did has ended in smoke. Enough about him I think , no more about it than if you had never heard of it and when the time arrives you get your Liberty then call him to account for his misdeeds. I shall write a letter to Mr Harney this next week thanking him for taking the subject up O Conner is still in Scotland Yet the work goes bravely on there. I will aſsure you such Demonstrations as I never before read of the cause goes bravely on in England but Poverty stalks abroad More than Ever the Bastiles are getting full and Thousands of our artizans and Mechanics are starving which the Great Majority that are in work are barely getting a Subsistence what will the be the End no one can forsee and the newspapers tell us things will be worse the Tower of London has been on fire the week about 400,000 pounds damage done the Duke of Rutland had the produce of 200 acres of corn destroyed Last week but one by fire the Derby Town Hall his burnt down and all the Municipal Records destroyed I see by the Chesterfield Chronicle that more cornstacks have been attempted to be fired on Tuesday last and was discovered before any serious damage was done. It is a Great pity to see good corn destroyed in that manner But misery & poverty stalks through the land and is really alarming the Middle Claſses more begin to cry out that something must be done to avert a Revolution which some of the Whig papers say is almost at hand our British Government in Canada gave orders for the seizure a a Colonel Grogan an American who they say was actively Engaged in the Canadian Rebellion they the constables or authorities seized him on American Ground in the Dead of the night in his Bed at his Brothers House and Maltreated him most unmercifully the American authorities demanded his release as soon as they thot it convenient and our bold adventurers were obliged to release him or the consequence might of perhaps reverted upon their own heads McLeod is acquitted after seven days Trial so after all their will be No War with America the Continental Nations of Europe seem in a very difsafected state the Mexicans are struggling for a republic Louis Phillip does not sit very easy on his throne Spain has broken out again but i think it has closed I see By some Large placards upon the walls and inducement for people to emigrate with a free passage to South Australia but Mind you not to return under 10 years. <u>Humbug</u> By a Private letter I have seen from an Individual that if an Emigrant works upon Government works there (and he has had a free passage) 5 shillings per week his stoppd out of his Earnings so you see when they Transport him there he cannot return untill he has served 10 years what do you think of such chicanery and Fraud as that I have Enclosed an order for fifteen shillings for you on the Post office in York in Your name the Person who Receives it for you will need to give in my name occupation (Hatter) &c and I have enclosed 12 Letter Stamps and in my next a friend has promised to send you six more say in your next if all is right I have just received a letter from Brighton Respecting Poor Peddie & Brooks which I shall attend to You May Expect one from Brighton this week as Morling has been so busy My Wife Desire her best respects to you likewise does your friends I would have you write to Sutton in Ashfield I have got the secretarys name this week it is Mr Wm Parker Framework Knitter Pringle Green Sutton in Ashfield write to him first opportunity and remember me to them I will conclude for the present By submitting myself yours as Ever Wm Martin

HBY 8

Attercliff Nov 14 1841

Deare Husband i reseved your kind Letter you in formed me that you had a pain in your side and i am very sorey for it but i hope you are not so bad as you whas in Northallerton my Deare you must excuse me not riting to you to inform you that I reseved a Letter from Mr Cleave for it sliped my memorey but Deare Husband i Got a Letter from him and the money two. Dear what Tomlinson is that at Sutton in Ashfield. my Dear Husband i think you had beeter rit to ower freands at Brighton for them to Get up a Petition in faver of you for your releace as tha sad tha whould Petition again and again so i think thare time can not bee better spent. Dear Husband i have a word or two to tell you a bout the Harrison the Bradford spyd he has Got Committed for two years to Lancaster Castle for horse stealen had it a been haney whon healce thay must a Gone to sum hother House of correction a hole like Wakfield or Bevelley Robert Peddie in Bevelley Hell informes the Publeck that tha have removed him from hard Laber bee cose he is so poreley that he can not stande it aney longer. Dear Husband i Got to inform you that ower preshes Qeen has Got safely Delivered of a Prince but tha ar to throng firen the Gons and ringing the Bells to a tend to you. I Farther and mother and hole the Fameley sends their kind love and respect you hoping to find you the same as this leaves us hole at present. So no more at present from your affectionate Wife Mary Holbery

Petition in possession of Holberry Society (see page 54)

To the Right Honourable Sir James Graham
Secretary of State

The Humble Petition of Samuel Holberry a Prisoner in the Castle of York
Sheweth your Petitioner was tried for Sedition and Conspiracy at the Yorkshire Spring Assizes 1840 and Sentenced to four years Imprisonment with hard Labour n the House of Correction in Northallerton
That Your Petitioner having served about a year and a half under such severe Discipline that his bodily energies were debilitated and his life endangered that although considerably better he is still in a weakly state and fears that much longer imprisonment will undermine his Constitution so as to render him unable to support his Wife and Family by his Bodily labour
That your Petitioner most humbly solicits your intercession with her most Gracious Majesty, that now when all her Majestys subjects are rejoicing at the happy event of her giving birth to an heir to the British Dominions, the Royal Mercy may be extended o your Petitioner that he may be a partaker of the general joy and your Petitioner will as in duty bound ever pray for blessings on Her Majesty and her Royal offspring,

Samuel Holbery

HBY/5

Retford Dec 5 1841

Dear Son
I am sorry to hear that you are not likely to get youre liberty at present that I ham glad to hear that you are better in health than you have beene for some time, it in the Doncaster paper that thear is one ovm {*of them*} out from York that was in from bradford but I have forgot is name youre Mother is very porly at this time she has been so for several weeks but the rest of us in good health at this time & hope this will find you the same, there his a little fresh news in gamston but not much Mrs Baileys farmer has got Married to the hous keeper + Wm Blonk has his houskeeper in the famileyway and James wright is ded and is son George is taken up for Steeling Led from Worksop Manner he is Bound over to the Secions for trial it will go har with him and I think I should like youre wife to com over to Gamston to be with youre mother a wile for she is not abel to do aney thin at all in the house So we shall be glad if she can com over to Gamston to be with her alittel time so no more from your Loving farther and Mother at this time.

Dear brother I hope thes few lines will find you in good health and good spirits as they leave us at this time I should have sent for youre loving Wife sum time since. But she wrought to me to say that She could not com till crismas becaus they had an increse in thare family, and She was abliged to stay with them but we shal be glad to se her when she comes over I will do hall that lise in my pour to give you both content in your mindes for I have my liberty if I be not doing very well but she Shall have such has have in my house and welkham to it, I have much respects for you Both I have left Worksop & got down to Retford to live, I have took a Shop in Retford on the Spittel hill to try my luck there, so if she will com to see us she Shal have a share with us such as whe have in hour house Brother Wm & sister Lucy says that they should like her to go to them but thay think Mr Walker would be angry with them if thay kep compeney, but wether it be because thay do not want or no I do not now If I was as well of as them I should not care what no one says about keeping compeney for I would have what compeney I liked to keep for ath{?} Mr Walker or aney body hels.
So no more from youres affectionatly Wm and Hannah Rhodes
this is my addreſs Wm Rhodes Grocer Spittel hill, Retford

HBY/6[19]

Sheffield dec 5 1841

Dear Holberry
I received your letter on the 25 of last month, and am extremely sorry, to hear that Sir James has Refused to advise her Majesty to Grant its prayer. I am sorry to hear that my last letter but one was stoped, I am glad to hear of your health been on the improvment, the prospects of trade has for being on the improvment, this last Week but the grinders have Struck for an anvance of 35 per cent, Mr William Martin last late prison at Northallerton goal {sic} is on the Road to America. I will let you Know all peticulars in my Next, We have had a horrid murder in the town, this last week, the case is the murder of Mary Nall by her husband to whom she had been married about 8 years though from domestic differences she had scarcely lived with him half that time and had on several occasions brought him before the magistrates on charges of ill-usage. After living separate a considerable time they met on saturday week at a beerhouse in the Wicker, they met again on saturday last and slept together at another beerhouse in the same part of the town; and on the following day (sunday) went to his sisters (a house ill fame) beehive lane Glofsop Rd where they returned to bed at about nine o'clock in the evening, the sister then went out, and locked the door; and on returning, after eleven o'clock, found Nall on the hearth, putting on his boots, upon asking him where Mary was he replied they had been having words together, in consequence of wich he had murdered her, she told him he should not go away until she had fetched some one in, and again locking the door she proceeded to her mothers in Wicker owing to some delay in getting her mothers in the Wicker the sister did not get back till one o'clock. On going up stairs with a watchman they found Mary Nall quite dead on the bed and her husband (the murderer) lying by her side,
Hoping these few lines will find you in Good Health,
I am my dear Friend, your kind and sincere
friend and well Wisher
HW Needham

PS I have been down to Attercliffe this morning all was in Good Health

---

19 Henry William Needham was a penknife cutler. He was born in 1820. He lived at Broomhall Street with his parents and younger siblings. He was on the Sheffield General Council for the National Chartist Convention

HBY/7[20]

Rockingham works, December 7th /41

My Dear Holbary
It was with much surprise and regret that I heard from Mr Needham you have not received my last letter which I sent according to promise soon after I heard from you, with surprise because as I put the letter in the post myself. I cannot concieve how it is that have never received it, and with regret because I am aware that in your present circumstances it would be a source of great grief it to you if you thought I had not answered your letter. I speak according to my own feelings when placed in the same position as yourself.
You will perceive from this that there has been no neglect on my part and I should feel very sorry indeed if I thought you entertained of such an idea the fact is I have all along been wondering why you did not write.
I saw Mrs Holbary last week and was exceedingly sorry to hear from her your severe indisposition. I was also in company with a Lady yesterday (a friend of mine) who was at the Castle a few days since, made many enquiries about you and to add to my grief confirmed what I had heard from your beloved wife, I hope you will write as soon as you can and let me know particularly how you are in health, and if I can be of service to you any way let me know for nothing in the world would give me greater pleasure than to elevate your misery or if we cannot get a mitigation of your punishment to make it pafs over as easy as possable
I am happy to inform you that the staple trade of sheffield is beginning to revive, hundereds and thousands of the working clafses who have long been starving are now a little better in their circumstances, and I am in hopes that the day is not distant when happiness and plenty will take the place of misery and destitution. Waiting your immediate reply and wishing you every happiness possable in your present situation believe me ever to remain Yours affectionatly W Wells
I am too late for post as usual

Direct for me Messrs Wostenholm and son
Rockingham Street Sheffield

---

20 This is the William Wells who was imprisoned at the same time as Holberry. Some sources suggest he was a cousin – there is no evidence for this.

HBY /9

Attercliff Dec 26 1841

Dear husband i receved youre kind and interestn letter i and hole the famely sends thare kind love and respect to you and we are hole very Glad to hear that your health as so much improoved Dear i reseved the in close you sent in Henery Needam Letter and you must excuse me not ritin to anser it for the reson whos that we thought we whod wate to see if he got a oder he whent on Tuesday to the Town Hall he so Mr Parker and he sad he had no abjeckshon but he wanted to inform is Brother Majestrats of it so he can not geve im a ancer the Thursday next Mr Brownhill is not at home but i hope he whill get whon as he is a Good Frend to me and if he coms i shall send youre things with im Dear Husband you informed me tha had stopd you from the priveleg of ritin so ofend and for haven nedfull things whis you whant and i am very sory to heare of that as tha whos the only priveleg you had we have been thinkin the best way whod bee for Mr Bernley at York to sopline you with the things you wanted but if Henery coms he whill see about it. Dear we have had a letter from my Brother William and he sends is best respect to you he has not come hover but my Brother Charles and Thom has gon to see him. Thom liks is trade very whell my Dear we have had a letter from William Rhodes and he sends us whord that youre Mother is something better if she keeps beter you must excuse me not Goin for if i whos to go my Mother whod have to geve up her washen as my sister as hapend her misfortin and as for goin to see them you must be aware that i have not had any money from Manchester wek before Books came home so i can not travel mush a bout my Dear if i cod i shod like very whell as i am aware that tha ar geten old but i hope i shall bee able to go and see them with you this somer. We wish you a happy new yeare as we can not wish you a mery Christmas we have kild oure peg and we wish you whos hear to help us to heat it it weaght 18 stone 6 pound. Frends in the park send thare best repect to you my Dear i wish you whod send them few lines in your next. Farther and Mother and hole the famely sends thare kind love to you and hopes this to find you in good health as this leaves us hole at present do no more at present from you affectinate long hart rendren wife Mary Holberry

HBY 10

1841 December 28 Retford

Dear Brother
this comes with that kinde love to you and I hope it will find you in good health as it leavs us at this time I have sent over for youre Dear wife twice since I have been Retford and she wil not come over to see as nor yet give us satisfaction wether she will come or not, you wish her to come into Nottinghamshire for the good of her helth and I have sent for her twice and I think it strange she will not com to se me I do not no now that I have don aney thing amis that she will not com to se me I have promised to Bear her exspences Back when she thinks proper to go Back I cold do with her for two or three months if she cold com now for we are Bussey I have wrout twice to you and I have never recived any answer from you I think you have forgot us I hope you will wright to your Loving Wife to now the reason that she will not come to us and then give us an answer Back as soon as you can what whe have done amiſs that she will not com to see us I wish to looke on her and I hallus have don before time and if she will not com let us now if you ples for we want to now wether she will com or not Your mother is a deal better than she has for she as been very porley your farther is in work at this time, but not very abel to do it.
So no more from your well wishers
till whe hear from you again
Wm & Hannah Rhodes
Grocer Spittel hill Retford

HBY 11

Bradford 15 of January 1842

My Dear Holberry
It is some two Long years since last we met and you will doubtless have thought Ere this that I had Entirely Forgot you But Believe me my dear Fellow such is not Nor Ever can be the case For I allways make it a point of duty never To allow neglect to prevail over The better part of Man Especially When an old and A Boſsom Friend Forms or aught To Form the subject For Consideration I have Long had a desire To Write you and was only prevented From doing so By not Knowing By What means or through what medium a Letter might Reach you in Fact so anxious Was I To communicate with you and Let you know that I was still in the Land of

the Living that I wrote to my Friend Harney of Sheffield some Time ago Requesting him To send me the necefsary Information upon that subject But as yet have Received no answer however your Late Fellow prisoner hanson called at my house this morning and informed me that you were fast recovering from the effects of the scanty diet and Rigid Discipline of Northallerton house of Correction Which for a moment made me Forget I was Lame the Cause of which I shall explain Before I conclude this humble Epistle For Beleive me Nothing Will give me so much pleasure as To hear of your Wellfare my Dear Fellow out of the 2 years that have Elapsed since I last had the honour and pleasure of your Company I have Been Eighteen months of Wandering Mendicant During Which Time I Traveled through England Ireland and Wales and over part of the Boundlefs Tract of a Fathomless sea upon my Return I Found my domestic Circle in a state of Disorganisation and to ad To the Chapter of my accidents I was Emediately arrested and safely Lodged in Durance vile where I was detained For the space of Ten Days at the expiration of which I was Liberated at the Request of the Lord Normanby afster Entering into My own Recognizance of 50 pounds and procuring in sureties in the same sum of 100 pounds To answer For my appearance when called upon I left the Confines of the prison on the 5th July and on 24 of October Following Namely Last October was sent To sent to Leeds on a delegation of Course I Went per Coach and when about a Mile From the place of my destination my hat Blew of and in Endeavouring To secure it My Foot slipped and I Fell when My Left Leg got Entangled Between the spokes of The Whell and Was Emediately Broken in 2 places Below the Knee and the thigh Bone severely Injured. Two humane persons Entire strangers To me who were pafsing at the time very kindly Carried me to the Becket arms inn where I wrote a letter and addressed it to the parties with whom I was to Transact Businefs requesting them to wait upon me at the Infirmary I then sent to Leeds For a hackney Coach Which soon arrived and Conveyed me To the above Institution where I was placed upon My Back and in that position Remained For six weeks daring To Turn Neither to Right or To the Left and only allowed to Raise myself up in a perpendicular position when necessity Required For a temporary purpose at the expiration of the above period I could Lift My Leg the surgeons then Bound it Tightly up and discharged me aye and without a pension Too – up To the prefsent Time I Canot Walk Without the aid of crutches Nevertheless I hope To Be able to Resume my employment in the Course of A month hence that is if There Be any For me Trade is in A diprefsed state throughout The Entire of these kingdoms thousands are starving for want of a sufficiency of the Necessarys of Life

and it is the opinion of Many that it is not Likely to Improve For the
Commercial Influence of this Country is Entirely Lost Mr Joseph Brook
Brother to William Brook now of Northallerton went over to se him at
Christmas and he Informs me that William has Been Very Ill But is in a
fair Way of Recovery that he is in Good Spirits But To all apearance the
mere shadow of his former self he Desires his Compliments to you Mr
William Martin has Left Bradford and I think Removed to London Bussey
is New York and keeps an Eating house or Rather the Eating house Keeps
him I should like to say something Respecting the political World But I
suspect that Introduction of political Matters are not in acordance With
the Rules of your prison and therefore I Forbear Mrs Flinn Desires To Be
Remembered to you I hope you Will Write Me per the very Next post
Give Me all particulars allso How Far the Rules of Your prison will admit
of political matter and in the meantime My Brave Fellow I Remain Ever
Yours in The Fraternal Bond of Indosulable and Never Dying Friendship

George Flinn
Nelson Court
Bradford Yorkshire
PS in describing the distreſs which Exists throughout the Country I Forgot
to mention that Four years ago there was scarcely A house in Bradford
unocupied and all though Building has Not Increased more than the
population there are at the present upwards of 2000 houses unocupied in
this Borough hundreds of Familys have had their homes Broken up their
means of comfort anhilated and their Numbers {?} or they are Crowded
Together 20 or 30 persons in A house To save Rents While the Rates are
heavily augmented so all Who are so Fortunate as To Remain
householders this is a heartrending But A True picture

George Flinn

HBY 12

Brampton January 16, 1842

My Dear Holberry
You no doubt will think that I have entirely forgot you I have been waiting
all this time waiting to hear from Sutton but have not as yet heard from
them I have wrote to Brighton Nottingham and in my next you may
expect something I was rather surprised at receiving your last thro my
friend H Needham and you say you cannot write me Direct Let me know

the reason I have high forfeited your confidences you may depend upon this that any thing I can do shall not go undone I have appealed to the Chartist Public in your behalf through the Star this week I see they have inserted it I tell you what My Friend I perceived By your last that you have not received my letter of 21 Novm nor that of Dec 5th I cannot tell the reason for I don't know that there is anything in there offensive to the Powers that be Perhaps you will be permitted to receive this you must Excuse this half sheet as I forgot to get a Supply of paper last night in my last I wished when you wrote to your Dear Wife that he would tell her to Let me have a Letter from her as I have never heard from her since she was at York the Great national is getting numerously signed thro the Country I perceive Parliament Meets on the 3rd Day of February and the Convention on the 28th Let me know if you are still under Restrictions to your Correspondence my dear My Wife as been very ill but is fast recovering has not been out of a fortnight I hope you continue in good health I have not as yet wrote to Mr Burley in fact I have had no time work is very slack expected having a turn out that it has Pafsd over for the Present the country is in a Deplorable condition through Deprefsion of Trade thousands upon thousands having nothing to do and what the end of these things will be I cannot foresee My wife desires to be remembered to you the Great Walsingham has never been amongst us since October 4th there is a Chartist & Republican for you His brother Bill has done them brown at Bradford and Decamped with the money to America and I suppose Walsingham is to follow him in May next Pendleton & friends Desire to be remembered to you Let me hear from you as soon as Convenient Direct as before
I shall conclude for the present and remain with my Best Respects Your sincere Friend & Wellwisher Wm Martin

HBY 13

Sheffield Jan 23 1842
My Dear Holbery
I received your kind letter of the 18. in your last you say you must trouble me to forward the two other parts of that letter, Now Dear Sir do not Call it trouble, the anything that I Can do for you, or any of your friends I will have the Greatest of Pleasure,
Your last letter leaves me to say something of Real friendship in General, Real friendship is not confined to any situation in life, it is Common in the meanest Cottage, and has sometimes even been found in the palace, simplicity of manners, and integrity in all our actions naturally lead us to

expect sincerity in the Conduct of those With Whom we are in any way Connected, the imperfections incident to human nature are so numerous, that we are Solicitous of finding some persons to Whom we Can unbosom our minds, and lay open the inmost recefses of our hearts, A real friend, in order to preserve the Character he has assumed, will endeavour to discharge every duty incumbent upon him to all his fellow Creatures Dear Sir I Never said or thought that ingratitude did form part of your Catulogue, No far from that, you say that you are Determined not to trespafs any more on me, do <u>not</u> say that you do any such a thing, For you do <u>not</u>

I cannot inform you at Present who will preasents the Petition for the Executive Council have not Name the M.P. But I think it will be Mr Duncombe, your Brother William Will be in York on the 23 or 30, I asked for an Order to see the Felons side of the Castle, and he told me that it Would Do for both But if you do not get your liberty, I shall try for an order to see through the Castle this spring I have not seen Mr Wells But he show me A letter to your Affectionate and loving Wife last sunday in the Room, I Beg to inform you that one Pound for each of the Wife here Came last Week, I have wrote to Manchester about Mrs Brook, family and I will not forget the others, there has been A General Subscription for Mrs Frost to save her Property from being lost, £196 Was Got A Memorial Will be Brought Before the Meeting to morrow evening for you and your friend Brook and Peddie, there will be two Concerts and Balls held at Bradford for the Benefit of the Mefsrs Brook Peddie Naylor and Walker, Price of admifsion on each occasion twopence each Your friend Flinn Will lecture at Halifax to Day, I have to him and Mr Martin to Day, there will be 1.000 loaves given away on the 25, it been the Day that the Prince of Wales is to be Christened the following extract from a letter received from Mrs Peddie, he has no prospect of being relived of any portion of the term of his sentence, but Wishes much that he might be removed to York Castle Dear Sir to Give you some idea of the horrors of a Winters evening spent Beverley house of Correction, I shall make the following extract from his letter, I exprefsed a wish to be to the inspector Who lately visited me that I might be favoured with afire in my Cell during the dead of the Winter Where I am locked up at six o'clock at night without fire or light, Sleeplefs Nights are one of the Consequences of my Complaints, indeed it is Generally in the night that I suffer most acutely, the window of my Cell fronts the east, the iron frame of Which either its nature or Clumsy Construction does not fit the wall Closely, so that it admits the air very freely it is moreover placed immediately at the foot of the Bed in A direct line with it, at the top of Bed is a large hole in the Wall, above a foot square meant as A ventilation I presume But which acting upon the window Keeps up during the night A Constant draught or Current of air upon the face of the sleeper Which during the late strong east winds became powerfull as on some occasions to move the Bed Clothes above me; and I have not once but often found tracts or small Book left by me upon my Bedstead at night strewed over the floor in the morning By the strenth of the Breeze in addition to this sorry accommodation my husband has suffered so much from his dietary system, that he has been frequently under the necefsity of starving himself for a few days to get rid of it

My Dear Holberry after much petitioning he has been allowed the Great Boon of one herring two days in the Week, he has also been allowed an additional Blanket for Which he is thankfull, and which he Considers a Real blefsing the only hope in Which it appears his friends Can serve him is, if pofsible to get his Removal to York Castle

At present my Dear friend let my purse being at your service, but let it never be more open than my heart. Conceal nothing from me and all I have is yours. We Were once friends let us Remain so, Let the sincerity of my friendship be estimated only according to my actions and if it shall appear that I have acted inconsistent with the sacred name of friendship, let me be for ever blotted out of your memory hoping this will find you in good health and a speedy Liberation
HW Needham
I am your sincere Well-Wisher

HS4

19 Bilton Street Layerthorpe
My Dear Friend
I received your note of yesterday and hasten to comply with your request, I feel proud that I can serve you in any way, I am glad to hear you are better in health, but sorry that the authoritys are so deaf to the prayers of Humanity, as not to grant you that boon, which they are about to grant to convicted felons, but my Friend I hope for better, I do think that the Commons if properly appealed to will recommend you that favour which the prejudice of an Individual will not submit to do, I will promise you + fulfill it, that the scheme shall be tried, Parliament meets on the 3rd and will have a petition adopted in York in your behalf week after, Mr Yorke the Liberal Member of York has promised to support the national petition, and to him, shall I entrust the petition in your behalf, I think he will do justice to it he is a new member never having had a seat in Parliament

before the last general election, but he is a persevering man and one who promises fair to be of service to the peoples cause he having during parliamentary holliday taken a tour through a great part of the country, to inquire into the circumstances; and wishes of the people, he has gone from house, to house, in many places and declares it beyond the power of mortal tongue, to describe the sufferings of the people generally; he is the son of the late Henry Redhead Yorke who was tried at York in 1795 for conspiring and sedition at Sheffield + sentenced to 18 months Imprisonment. Sir I mention these facts that you may form an idea as to his being a proper person to communicate your wishes to, Dear Sir, I am glad to hear that your wife is well, I hope the kind hearted men of Sheffield will see to her support, I am very sorry that the familys of those who have borne prosecution for their countrys good, are not better supported, but my Friend I can assure you it is not the ingratitude of the people but their poverty, I have now before me a letter from London, which states that the poor are becoming so numerous their, that they in many parts of the Metropolis last week have gone in numbers of 10,+14, to Bakers + provision shops and helped themselves, not running away, but allowing themselves, to be taken into custody; + the Public Prefs of to days arival prove it to be too true; I know not what will be the End of it, but I pray that something may shortly be done to aleviate their sufferings I shall be proud to serve you in any way you can suggest, and I hope you will be allowed to communicate with me upon the subject, I do not think that the Authorities, that you are more immediately under, can, or will object, to you endeavouring to obtain that liberty, which they themselves enjoy, (viz) to be restored to the bosom of your family and friends, all must admit that the evils for which you are convicted are fully served their is now no excitement, all is peaceable, and orderly and many very many of the men, who composed the Juries, are no joined to our ranks being convinced of the justnefs of our demands, we are progressing rapidly, I am glad to hear that you are going to have a visit from Mrs Hs Brother I hope if he has not been when you receive this you will desire him to call upon me; in the mein time I remain dear Friend
Yours most affectionatly
Edw Burley

York Jan, 30th 1842

PS If your Brother comes on Monday or any weekday he will find me at the Workshops, Mr Henry Cobbs, Paper Stainer, Monk Bar, York

Extract of letter by Holberry to Mr Burley, published in *The English Chartist Circular and Temperance Advocate*, Vol 2, no. 119 (only this part of letter exists)

10th February 1842

"I am of the opinion that a staunch adherence to principles has closed up all the avenues of mercy against me; but, my friend, the same love of Liberty which first taught me to detest tyrants and tyranny, will still (as it has done) support me under privations, and all the miseries which the law has prepared for felons, or what perhaps is still worse in the eyes of the Aristocracy, convicted Chartists; but I must not give vent to my feelings, or this will not pass the Castle Toll Bar."

He also writes in the letter that he is suffering from swelling in the legs, which is prevented him walking and taking exercise, and is otherwise very unwell.

HBY 14

Feb 10 1842

Dear brother I received your kind letter today and I am going to retford to the post office wee received a letter from your wife last week she was in good health wee have just killed a pig and we shauld like to send you some porkrind but we are affraid you could not get them and wee have inclosed a dozen of stamps for you in this letter William is better and we are all in good health Dear Brother we think it would be better for you to not to write letters in the northern star paper by what wee hear wee are in great hast and we will send you another letter soon so no more a present from your affectionate Brother and sister
William and Lucy Holberry
Danes Hill
Excuse hast

494/1

Attercliffe Jan 30th/42
Dear Husband
I again take up my pen to adres thes few lines to you hoping this to find you in good health as this leaves us hole {*all*} at present thank god for it. Dear Husband ireseved your kind and interestin letter and i did as you reqiested me in forwarden that letter to Mr Martin on the same afternoon and a note to them hoping they whould Excuse me not ritin to them

sooner and i tould them it whos not bee cose i had for got them but it was oure neglect.

My Dear i sopose you now the {?} Christineng is hover and i dout it whill be no better for you as them sort of Gentry holways looks at home and forgetes them a broad we ma hope it whill not bee the same with you but i dout it whill as we now them so whell i hope we ma bee disepointed and see you at home bee fore long

My Dear iashure you there whos so much rejoicen in our Country of distress if tha did not now it whos the day of Christineng there whos so much rejoicin tha whod not a nown. Dear Husband you reqiested me to send you whord if i had took that note to Mr Ludlum i have and tha tould me last Monday tha had sent a letter to William in York and Mr Ludlum tokes of comemine to York sizes if God spares him and if you continey in the Castle he shall Get to see you if he can the Fig Tree Lane Chartis has got up amoral {*a memorial*} in faver of you Marshill and Brook and Pedey tha sent it to her Majesty last Monday. Dear Husband you wanted to now if you heald {*owed?*} any one anything i had/pad {*paid*} not Shaw {....} in my confinement but my {....} is pad and it has not lade in my powre to pay Mr Shaw as i should but i have sent the bill as you desired and my Brother Thomas sas whot you ar in is ded he whill freely for Give you and he whod it whos twice as mush my Dear i have rote to Retford and your request i shall rite Gamston. I Farther and Mother and hole the famely sends theare kind Love and respect to you hoping this to find you in Good Health as this finds us hole at present yours frends in the Park sends there best respect to you and Uncle is a deale beeter and he hopes you ar the same.

So no more at present from your long and constant hart rendren wife
Mary S Holbary

HBY15

Sheffield Feb 20 1842

My Dear Bloved Holberry

I received your welcome letter on the 19th inst, Sir I thank you for the maner I which you opening your mind to me, But let me Tell you Sir that you took my last letter in the wrong Light. For let me tell you Dear Sir that I would sooner suffer my Right Arm to Be Cut from off my Body than insult you in the maner you think I have.

the letter that was for your Sister you appear to think I though was an hint for me, Ho Holberry I though No such A thing upon my Honnor, you say that I impute unworthy motives, By you sending your sister letter through my hands, O God forbid such A though should henter my mind, I had spoke to your truly Affectionate Wife two or three weeks since about some Stocking, I Did Not Read your Sister letter, only that part to the Shoemaker,

you appear in my Eyes to be a Brave Gallant Sincere True Patriot and Not the Selfish sordid wretch you Dream I not think you are, I agrea with you that Nothing hurts A mans mind so Bad has to know that his wife and family is in Want While he is in Prison for Advocaten the Rights of man Dear Sir I am Extremely sorry my last letter Compels you to mention family affairs, although A Working man I have some Money to Spare I am Both Glad to heare you Can give the Castle authorities such A Good Word, In Reply to that part of your letter about the Star, I Beg to inform you that No Part or Parts of your letters have appeared in the Star since you Came to the Castle, Mr Burley has had one in the Star, and Mr Wm Martin has had one in, about Old Booker, I have seen Mr Ludlam, I have Just Received A Letter from Mr Peter Shorrock, Secretary to National victim fund informing me he sent £1 0s 0d on 27 Sep 1841 to Dear Brooks Wife, and another on Jan 25 1842. they have an Appeal in this Weeks Star, I have been to Attercliff to Day all Was in good health,
PS A Reply to the memorial has Come, Sir James his regret that there is no sufficient Grounds to Justify him to Comply With the prayer thereof hoping this find you in good health your affecionate admirer and sincere friend HW Needham

HBY 2

Gamston Feb 20th

My dear sun I am glad to heare from you onse more and Glad to heare that you are Better in helth than you have been for sum time but I should be more glad once more to se the fase of my daling Son if it plese god to spare oure lives til that day whe can see thy lovely fase, whe are in good helth and in good spirits for that day When god thinks fit to call us to is bar for us to give an account of our past years wether they be good or bad, my dear son I would have you to get fuly prepared for that time, and then we shal meet fase to fase in that plase where theare is no oppession no trobel no prison no torment and only one master to Please I think thear is nothing fresh in Gamston in worldly affairs but we still keep looking to the

Lord for help and for marcy so no more from youre loving Farther + mother at this time John and Martha Holberry

Dear brother I have received youre youre letter on the 11 of this month and I went to se about your Shoose and they have don them and sent them by Mr Smith on the 17th whe went to Mr Foggs to see about sum bookes for you and he sed that is Mrs should look some hout for you and whe sent up for them three times and Mrs Fogg sed that she cold not find them so whe got 2 books from Mr Osticks for you, and there is 1 dozen of stamps for you in this letter and there has been a good few stamps sent to you before and we think you have got all of them I have beene out ever since youre letter com so you must exquse me not writeing to you sooner youre farther + Mother says that you must not think much at them for they cannot write themselves or els they ofen write to you I have to write for them or els they never would not get Aney to write for them I have Bot you one pare of stockings and sent them with the others things I have not time to write any more this time but I will write to you again in a short time and I will send you hall petikerlers so no more from your Brother + sister Wm + Hannah Rhodes. I remain your well wisher till Deth Part us

HS5

Dear Holberry
I take this opportunity of writing these few lines to you hoping they will find you as well as can be expected you can be whilst you are resident in the gloomy dungeon. I have sent your shoes and the association will pay for the Leather and I will give my labour and I only wish I had it in my power to do more for you but I am happy to inform you that our cause is progreſsing very fast and I hope you will keep your spirits up and I hope we shall get the charter yet so I remain your since friend and brother chartist Robert Cooper.
Bradley Buildings, Hungate, York February 20 1842

494/3

Sheffield Park Feb 27th 1842

Dear Holberry
Your kind letter of the 8th inst. I duly received and am happy to hear that you keep well pray do mind what you are about as regards your health, for depend upon it, that when ever the time comes when you will have to

leave your dungeon (and I hope to god it is not far off) you will find you are not so "Dungeon Proof" as you may think. had all the World told me that confinement would have effected me as it has done I could not have believed it. I should think that for three or four months I almost lived on Pills and Physic and my body was covered with Plasters &c whilst I was so weak that a child might have thrown me as the Shevield chap says "in a position to court the stars." I believe the best thing you can do is to take as much exercise as possible.

You say that the "authorities appear no way disposed to mitigate your unmerciful sentence" and am sorry to hear this further borne out by the Home Secretaries reply to the memorial sent from this place, in your behalf, some time since however I cannot but indulge the hope that we shall soon have you at home. Another petition shall be sent either to Her Majesty or the Secretary of State very shortly and I can pledge my word that your Sheffield friends will leave no stone unturned for the attainment of that desirable object, the principals which you advocated and for which you are now suffering are every day gaining ground those prejudices which have long existed in the mind of the Middle Clafses are now to a great extent laid aside – The Masters have shook hands with men, and the men with their masters and I believe there is scarcely a town in the Whole Kingdom where the united voices of bothe parties are not crying out to the Legislature for Commercial and Political reform. The Ibbotsons, The Bramleys, the Palfremans (Mr Luke Palfreyman) the Rev. R.S Bailey &c. of our Town have now seen the necefsity of joining the people and are advocating the cause. And only a few days ago at one of the largest meetings ever held in the Town of Nottingham over which the Lord Rawcliffe presided that Nobleman said that he "demanded the Charter" which when obtained would make the nation prosperous and the people happy – with regards to trade I am sorry to say that never was it known to be so bad as at present you may form some idea of its depressed state when I tell you that at our own place we formerly employed between six or seven hundred hands, we have had to reduce them to about one hundred, and twenty more last week received notice to quit.

My Dear Holbary I have now got to the end of my sheet. I am sorry I have not room to say more but wishing you every happinefs in possable in present circumstances and hoping you will soon be restored to your family and friends. Allow me as an old friend of mine says to shake hands with you in my heart . and for the present bid you farewell. I am respectfully yours W Wells

HS6 (from HW Needham)

Sheffield March 6th 1842
My Dear Holberry
I received your kind and welcome letter on the 30th Dear Sir, I beg you to except my sincere and heart felt thanks for your Kind and Well Wishes for my further Wellfare and may you be speedly in Company With your Affectionate Wife, and Rewarded by the Enactment of those great and Glorious principles, for which you are so unjustly suffering. Dear Sir, I thank you for the pocket. I shall say more then now, in my Next. Sir, I have the honour of been an Odd Fellow, they will be very useful to attend the Alter, But Not till you Come home. Dear Sir, I am extremely sorry that thay Would Not allow you to Read it for it his A Good Book, I am sorry that Mr Flinn has Not Answer you letter, Dear Sir, you are Wrong in supposing that you have Wrote to plain, No, No, I have Received A letter from him Dated the 12th Feb, O What A letter it his. I would have sent it to you But you Would Not Be Allowed to see it, he is one of the Noble and up Right orniments of the working clafs, I have wrote to him this last Week, Poor Old Marshall has got home, O What A book it his it to see him, I will send you a full account Next Week Pleas to inform Me if Mr Martin Writes to you for he has Not Worte to me this 3 mt

HBY 30

Sheffield March 6 1842

My Dear Holberry
I have been down to Attercliffe today, your Kind and Affectionate Wife was in good health and Spirits your Brother in law was there, he Came from Northallerton By the Railway With poor old Marshall and two others, he left Sheffield this morning By the ten o'clock train
Whilst I was there the Post man Brough your Wife A letter from you, Dated the 25th Feb the York post mark was March 4th
Dear Sir if the letter that you Name in Your last Kind letter, has anything in about me I hope you will send it me and I will send it Back for there his some Demons that our tring to stab me in the in the Dark
Sir Mr O Connor is going to present the Memorial to the Queen in person, the Drefs will cost him £200
Dear Sir O What A shame it is that he Can not see her with out that Drefs, Sir trade his very Bad in the Country, it is estamated that there his 900,000 out of work, the Petition to our Dear Burley Was sent this Week

Dear Sir I find that your kind Wife has Not Sent the Sheos, I shall send a parcel in the Cours of two or three Weeks and they shall Come in it or any thing els that you may Want pleas to send Word if you want anything, hoping this Will find you in Good health
I am Dear Sir your affectionate friend
HW Needham
PS in haste

HB Y 16

Retford March 7th 1842

Dear Brother
the Reason I write to you is that you sed in your Last Letter too me that when I had read the inclosed I was not to Leave no time in forwarding it, theare was nothing to forward in it, you say in youre that you will not trobel me for aney moore stamps when I wrout to you about the stamps I thout it no trobel to send you sum more but I thout Perraps you had recived all you had had sent you, when you write to your Lovin wife tell her that whe she we shal be glad to see her at the fair if she can Com over to see us tel her she is welcom to such as whe have in our house you say sumthing about sum shirts but if yore wife Comes over whe shal understand her about them if you tell her in youre Letter
So no more from youre well wishers
Wm and hannah Rhodes
writ again as soon as you can

HBY 17

March 7th 42

Dear Brother
Wee received your kind Letter wee are glad you are in good Health as it leaves us at present thank God of that. I would have sent you two shirts but I did not know how you maid them so we have inclosed a post office order of five shillings to your wife to get them with there is a man being killed near Doncaster and our younger Master William Walker we think he will be ther for a witnefs at York and will Go to the Castle and if you have any thing to say perticular say to him we cannot all ways answer your Letters Directly as ther is only post come here twice a week wee have hered nothing from Gamstone since wee rote to you but William is going

on sunday we remain your affectionate Brother and Sister William and Lucy Holberry

We hope you have got your stamps

HS7

Dear Holberry
I herewith send you the petition which I have got drawn up in your in your behalf and which will be adopted tomorrow (Thursday) Evening at A Public meeting, I stated in my last to you that I had applyed to Harney for information + he had had the kindnefs to draw me the Petition as you see it. I intend to send it to Dunscombe, + apply to Yorke to support it, I have to send word to Harney at the time it is Presented and he will write to Ward and several others I am desired by Harney to say that you will receive A Letter from him in A few days if their is anything in the Petition objectionable say and it shall be done to your will, I will send you word this Exact time I shall send it so that you may write to the M.P. I had your friend Leedham at my House on Thursday Last he was at our council meeting on Sunday Morning also, I have not seen him since, I have been very bussy we have had an outdoor meeting this Nite a very large one to hear our District Lecturers farewell addrefs I hope you are enjoying good health and that we may soon meet unfettered is the Earnest Prayer of yours affectionately
Edward Burley
York March 8, 1842
wrote in great haste as I have nine letters to write before I see bed it is now near 1 o'clock.
EB
PS I will call that the office for the Petition tomorrow at noon if you will send it in for me as I shall be at the Court.
Many thanks to you for the Hansome Pockets.
I did not get them this Nite you sent them very unkind of them with whom they were left

HS9

To the Honourable the Commons of Great Britain and Ireland in Parliament Assembled
The Petition of a Public Meeting of the Inhabitants of the City of York held this day of March 1842. Sheweth,

That Samuel Holberry Operative late resident of the borough of Sheffield, was convicted at the York Spring Assizes of 1840 of Conspiracy and Sedition, and sentenced to Four years imprisonment in Northallerton House of Correction.

That the said Samuel Holbery when sentenced to imprisonment for the above term was not sentenced to hard labour, yet, at the commencement of his confinement he was placed on the treadmill; a punishment (in the opinion of your petitioners) when the sentence of the judge is considered – clearly illegal

That though subsequently the said Samuel Holbery was removed from the degrading (and in his case unlawful) punishment of the treadmill, yet, during the whole time he remained at Northallerton, he was subjected to the regulations and restrictions of the "silent system" which in the opinion of your petitioners is none other than a system of torture, opposed to every dictate of Christianity and every principle of the constitution of these realms.

That in the month of last the said Samuel Holbery was by order of the of her Majesty's Secretary of State for the Home Department removed from Northallerton House of Correction, to the County gaol of York, where he is at present confined.

That while confined in Northallerton House of Correction the said Samuel Holberry suffered grievous with swellings in his legs, pain in his back and general debility and though in York Castle his treatment has been considerably improved still the above symptoms of a broken constitution are not removed. And your petitioners cannot help expressing their fears, that if he shall be doomed to suffer another two years imprisonment the remainder of the term to which he was sentenced premature death will be his melancholy fate, or, at the best of the life of disease his unhappy lot.

That the said Samuel Holbery has in private life, borne always a the character of industry sobriety, honesty and trust worthiness unimpeachable, as such has earned for himself the undiminished confidence of his employers, and the esteem of all who knew him – Further during his imprisonment in his demeanour has been blameless and his conduct unexceptionable

That your petitioners feel confident that an act of clemency on the part of the Sovereign advised thereto by the members of your Honourable House, and Her Majesty's present administration, could not fail to be properly appreciated by all classes of the community. And would in this instance (as in many of the similar cases) not only save from disease – probably death the prisoner; but would also impart joy to the bereaved and sorrowing wife, and peace to the affected family of the captive.

That your petitioners submitting the foregoing to your consideration – particularly reminding your view that the said Samuel Holberry has already suffered two years Imprisonment in expiation of the offence of which he was convicted – do respectfully and urgently intreat the interception of your Honourable House in behalf of the said to Samuel Holberry in order to obtain his discharge from further imprisonment.
And your petitioners will ever pray.
Signed in behalf of the meeting

Chairman.

HS 8

19 Bilton Street Layerthorpe York
My Dear Friend
I take the opportunity of informing you that the petition was adopted on Thursday Evening by A numerous and enthusiastic Meeting I moved the adoption of the petition which being seconded was ably supported by Mr Maw from Middlesbrough and carried unanimously I have requested an immediate answer from them and for Duncome and to H R Yorke Esq Soliciting them to give the petition all the support they possibly can, I have requested an immediate answer from them and from Duncome to say when he will present the Petition I shall let you know the answer I receive as soon as it arrives, if you think it advisable to write to them you can do so, I think you should, I have just wrote to my Friend Harney stating the course I have taken and intended to take and recommending him to get your late Employers to write to Duncombe also, I hope that the course I am, and intend to pursue will have the desired effect, at all counts my Friend you may depend upon it, that no stone shall be left unturned to serve you, I am sorry to hear of the coldhearted and unchristian attack made upon you by Ward, but we must not expect much better from men whose hearts are so callous to the interests and well being of "our order", men who have party interests to preserve, + who profit by the present state of things are not the men to sympathise with those who strugle to effect A change, but my Friend I am glad to hear that the justnefs of our principles have the effect of bearing you up under your affliction, and I trust that the time is not far distant, when you will be at Liberty and enjoying those great and sacred principles for which you are so unjustly suffering believe me, the present are most critical times and A shadow overs o'er the Political orizon which indicates to me, that A crisis is fast aproaching, Godspeed it, and direct it, that it may prove a blefsing to all

classefs of Society, it is my painful duty to inform you that A ferocious and Bloodthirsty attack has this week been made by a set of hired ruffians paid by the Corn Law repealers, upon Feargus O'Conner and A meeting which he was about to addrefs in the Hall of science at Manchester they were armed with atchettess pokers and other weapons several are dangerously wounded some with arms and one with ribs broken + some with both, Feargus was knocked down by a blow from Astone over one of his Eyes some ruffian made a stroke at him with some sharp Instrument which cut through his hat, he has been very lucky to Escape with his life, he knocked one fellow down Just as he was aiming A blow at the Rev Mr Schofield with the leg of A table, some of the Party have quarrelled amongst themselves on account of some of the ruffians having been allowed more blood money than themselves it is proved that 5£ was offered to one of the party to throw Feargus from the Hustings beneath which were a number of men with bludgeons were placed great has been the excitement Feargus was not to be intimidated he determined upon Delivering the Lecture the night following, upon which announcement Bills were put out by the repealers calling upon the Irish to assemble in their thousands to meet the enemies of Daniel O'Connell, the Chartists mustered strong but the assassins were not to be seen and the meeting passed off as though nothing had been to do; the above was instigated + paid for by men who have filled the dungeons of England with men, under the pretence of preserving the Peace,

In hoping this will find you in good health and our humble efforts crowned with success in your behalf, I remain affectionately
Your Friend + Well Wisher
Edwd Burley
March 13, 1842
I have directed the letters to the House of Commons as I did know their residence I am informed they will get them

HBY 19

Attercliffe March 13
Dear Brother i again tak up my pen to adres theas fue lines to you hoping to find you in Good health and strangh as this leaves us hole at present Except Myself and i have got a veary bad could Deare Brother has you whanted to know if youre Wife my Sister rote her hone letters she is sory to inform you she can not but she can reed yours herselfe – Brother my sister was veary sory when she receved youre letter Feb 25 it whos March 6 when she receved it she took the note to Mr Banes and he tould her he

whod do what he cod in faver of you he whent to the Townhall to see Mr Holdrson but he whos Gon to York so he cod not see him. we receved a Letter last week from youre Brother William and he sent a post office 5 shilling for youre shirts Dear Brother we can not blame you for wanting some shirts as prison shirts is in the state as you say tha ar in Dear she whill make you them Brother Knight colled and and spent one knight with us he rod with Thos Marshall from Northallerton and he sends is best respects to you she sent that knot to Martin it is about six weeks since i receved a Letter from Martin we receved hole of the things you sent and thanks i cannot describe to you to brother as I am soperly you must excuse me not saying more Farther and mother sisters and brother hole sends thare kind love and respects to you hoping this to find you in Good health as this leves us hole at present
So no more a present from your fafull Brother and wife Mare Holbary

Pleas Brother if that young man is not got out Pleas to get ant in the Park a Pare of Gloves or a poket as she as knitted you youre Stockins and i Dare say she whod think as much of them as aney one

HBY/18

Sheffield March 14 /42

My Dear Holberry

I write these few lines to you hoping they will find you in good health as it leves me, thank god for it, I have been Down to Attercliffe to day your affectionate Wife was in good health and Spirits, your Brother in Law, Thomas was very ill with the pain in his side, I Received your kind presents, Truly sensible of the honour Conferred upon me, and the politeneſs with which it was attended, I accept your handsome presents With My heart felt Pleasure and shall always prize them as the gift of friendship,
Dear Sir the news from India is of A most Disastrous Character, the British Army in Cabool being reduced to Great extremities for want of succours, a treaty was entered upon, When in a conference With the chiefs of the insurrections Sir Wm Mac,Naghten, the envoy from England, was shot and his attendants Were aſsaſsinated, the army then atempted to force its way through the Koord Cabool paſs wich his almost perpendicular ascent of 1.100 feet, the pas itself is six miles long, and not exceeding two hundred yards in the broadest place, a river runs through in wich crofses

the road 23 times and through official accounts have not been received, there is much reason from accounts to belive that the Army has Been Distroyed, it consisted of the 44th British and five Natives regiments, to the number of 6,507, the insurgent Army amounts to 25,000 a squadrod of Irregular Cavalry of Light Company, and artillery With three 9 pounders and A 24 pounder howitzer, Lady McNaghten and the other ladies were sent to grind corn, they intend to Keep them as an exchange for Dost Mohammed,
State of Trade
a Statistical table, Shewing the Condition of the working clafses of Carlisle, Jan 3, 1842,
grand total 11,945 coverage per head 1s1¼d, here We have 7.000 out of employ,
Cost of the army £9.060, 000
ordance 2 075 807
the navy 6 614 159
Hoping this finds you in Good Health HWN

A letter of the 17th March quoted in *The English Chartist Circular and Temperance Advocate*, Vol 2, no. 119, states: "he complains of an attack of Influenza, and painfully predicts that the result of his treatment will be death."

Letter published in Northern Star 2/7/42

York Castle, April 1 1842

Dear Burley, I have received no answer to my last and I am afraid you never received it. I am anxious to know if you have heard from Mr Duncombe. When he mentions my case in the house, cut the extract out of the newspapers and forward it to me. I am rather better than I have been. I have been looking for some news from you all the week; write on Sunday. Sir, I wish you would send me a stick of Spanish juice[21] for my cough it troubles me so at nights that I cannot sleep. I am sorry to inform you that my dear wife is very poorly. Give my respects to all friends, accept the same yourself, from your well wisher
Samuel Holberry

---

21 Spanish juice = liquorice

HBY 20

Birmingham April 2nd 1842
My Dear Holberry

I hardly know how to express my sympathy towards you and your brave and noble hearted wife. It would appear as if our accursed system of misrule had doomed the best and kindest portion of Gods creation to suffer "All the slings and arrows of outrageous fortune," My dear fellow you have no conception of the numerous things which are hourly pressing themselves on the attention of those who are engaged in the present struggle for the deliverance of mankind from the unnatural and heartrending Situation into which the folly and selfishness of a few ignorantly bigotted mortals have driven them – I dont blame you for considering yourself deeply injured and neglected. I know what my own feelings were when placed in a similar situation and consequently much appreciate the bitter pangs which you endure when reflecting on "mans ingratitude." I must confess that I have not done as much as I ought to have done to comfort and assist you, but I shall endeavour to make amends for my neglect. You say in the letter now before me that 18 months Silence on my part was not keeping my promise, Certainly, as far as you were concerned, As far as not writing to you, your observation is Correct But in the other case it was not so, for I have done as much as any man in England to explore the infernal system of torture and slow murder practiced in the Houses of Correction in Yorkshire, but all that is of little consequence to you who is suffering the bitterness of separation from the society of your wife and all the Joys of life, and for what? Because you done what you considered necefsary to the welfare and happiness of your fellow creatures – Politicians may differ. But it is the extreme of cruelty to subject a fine kind hearted fellow to a worse treatment than the most abandoned wretches. I must press upon you therefore the necessity of bearing your suffering with fortitude, and hope for the best as I believe you will stand a better chance of deliverance under a Tory, then a hypocritical Whig administration – the damnable Whigs! We have got rid of them for ever, thanks to the denunciations of the Chartist victims – Holberry, we have annihilated the accursed cold hearted faction and rather than see them reinstated I would vote for an <u>Absolute Monarchy</u> – I hate the name of the villains who doomed hundreds of good husbands, fathers, and brothers to worse than death for advocating that which they pretended to favour……

It grieves me to hear that your health is giving away from long imprisonment, and as you think every body will forget you because Duffy has – <u>you shall not be forgot</u>, I will take care of that, and as you ask me when the next Convention meets – I have to inform you that it will be assembled in London on the 12th of this month, I am elected for the Counties of Warwick and Worcester and shall endeavour to procure your release whilst there – I am intimately acquainted with a person who is a bosom friend of Lord Ashley, a very feeling and kind hearted man although a Tory – Lord Ashley might have been a member of the present Government were it not for his determination to advocate for a <u>Ten Hours Factory Bill</u> to which I have devoted a great part of my time and I think through his influence on being made acquainted with your real character that something may be done towards getting you home as four years imprisonment is a horrible punishment.

I dont wonder at your disquiet of the bad language made use of by the felons with whom you have been forced to associate and think that a another strong reason why you should be released from their company. You mentioned Browne in your letter. He has left this country for America a month since and thousands of the steadiest and best workmen in the country are following his example. Martin has gone also.

I am sorry to hear of your wife's illness and shall comply with your request by writing to her.

You say that you were not supplied with drawers but I am confident that the very best drawers &c that were made were marked with your name and forwarded to you.

My paper is nearly done I shall therefore conclude by requesting you to write and Jog my memory in case you think I am likely to forget you whilst in London I will endeavour to raise something to help you on the first opportunity and in the meantime

believe me to be your

sincere friend

George White

39 Bromsgrove Street Birmingham

Please to give my requests to Mr Noble the Governor of the Castle He is a worthy man

HBY 21

10th of Aprill 1842

Dear friend
I rite you the foliwing linese to you Hoping to find you better i a very sory to hear of you being so very bad i went to Peter Cokings and e inform me that you was better wich i was very glad to hear ah you being better dont think i was very neglicting not riting to you soner as my health as been so very bad since i left Northalton i am a deal better you will incruire of the schoolmaster yat money e sent to Northalton to me you will be so good as to tell me now when you rite to wife all paticlar i was very glad to heare of removall back to Yorck I will rite to you all peticler wen i have receved answer to this letter so no more att prefsent and well wisher
John Marshall

HBY/22

Sheffield April 14 1842

My dear Holberry,
I received your Kind and Welcome letter of the 6th and the 12th. I Wrote you on the first But Strange to see By yours that of the 12th that you have Not Received It.
Dear Sir With Plesuer I hear that your Health is Better, I hope your Cough is Better, Mr Duncombs took a Wise policy and if the Members hav any humanity abought them you Would have been At Liberty Now But Keep up your Spirits Sir I hope you Will be at home Soon, Mr Wells his Writing A Petition in your Behalf it Will be Adopted Next Week
Dear Sir I posted the letter for Mr White as Soon has I got it, I Beg to inform you that the Executive Wrote out the Petition, also that to Redford, Mr Watkin his A great Deal better in health he has Wrote A Legacy in the Star to the Chartist, Dear Sir I am glad to See that Mr Martin has wrote you I Did not Want you to violat the Laws of true Friendship, Dear Sir You have Received a parcel from your Kind Affectionate and loving Wife, Sir the Reason I did not send anything in it his Bixton{?} had Not his things Ready but he will send his week, I have been Down to Attercliffe to Day your Wife was in Good health, hoping his Will find you in Good health, I shall Write you on the 19 for I have got a bad pen and Ink and All of {?} tremble

Affectionatly

HWN

Letter in Northern Star 23/4/42

York Castle, April 15th 1842
Dear Martin, I received your letter of April 3rd, and intended answering it sooner, but I have been very unwell; I find my constitution is gone, and that without an alteration I shall soon be in my grave. I do, Sir, find myself going by inches. I saw Mr Shepherd last week from Northallerton, and he told me I was looking full as bad as when I left Northallerton. I can assure you, Sir, that I am very far from being as I ought to be. I am attacked with such violent pains in my legs, and also in my limbs, that I can get no rest at nights.
I hope you will excuse my not answering sooner, as it is not because I would not, but the reason is I could not. Remember me to Mr Goodlad and all friends, and accept my kind respects to yourself.
And I remain,
Yours sincerely,
Samuel Holberry

A letter of the 17th April quoted in *The English Chartist Circular and Temperance Advocate*, Vol 2, no. 119, states: "he is very ill – very ill – and scarcely able to hold a pen; he has lost the little strength he gained on first leaving Northalleton.

HS 10

April 19th 1842
My dear Friend
Should it be ordained that you and I should never be allowed to enjoy it such each other's company again allow me to tell you that you will always occupy a place in my remembrance, I have found great comfort in your presence, & believe my dear friend, that I am sorry in having to endure a Separation but as I've already perceive, that your Health is in such a precarious state, as not allow me to spend our time together, otherwise, nothing would have given me greater pleasure than to have spent the remainder of my time in your company, believe me dear Friend I shall at all times be most happy to receive a few lines from you, and more so to hear tell of your Health recruiting and your being restored to your Wife

and relations, hoping that you will accept of the few simple lines I have
herein penned as a token of my respect for you.
Samuel! this day thou and I shall be parted,
And God only Knows, wether for ever or not;
May his Mercy one Moment never desert thee;
Until that by me, thy name is forgot.
Even by me will they name be cherished and dearly.
Lest I should forget it, I write Sam Holberry
Health be thy portion when I'm gone from here,
O, may God defend thee from all the trouble of fear,
Let this on thy mind (long or short be thy stay)
Be impress'd "I shall think on thee when far away.
Even now I am loath to bid thee Farewell!
Remember although in my Heart thou dost dwell
Right glad shall I be, either to hear or to see,
York Castle no longer, confining Sam Holberry
And believe me to be yours sincerely
W Batty

You will always find me, by directing
Wm Batty,
Messrs Otters, Gascoigne and sons
Ch Garforth
Leeds
Don't forget to let me know how you come on in the hospital and when you leave here send me word

A letter of the 21st April quoted in *The English Chartist Circular and Temperance Advocate*, Vol 2, no. 119, states: " he is worse – suffering sever pains in his limbs – his stomach is shockingly disordered, and all appetite for food of any kind gone from him.

Letter published in Northern Star 30/7/42 : Obtained in response to their request for all communications that had passed between the Secretary of State for the Home Office and the authorities of York Castle regarding the health of Holberry

York Castle April 22nd 1842

The health of Samuel Holberry, a Chartist prisoner in York Castle, has not been so good as usual during the last two months. His appetite, is at

present, bad, and the functions of the stomach and liver are disordered, and I have thought it right to place him, for a time, in the hospital.
(signed) George Champney,
Surgeon to the York Castle York Castle 22nd of April 1842

HS 11
Sheffield No. 11 Hartshead April 22, 1842

My Dear Sir
The writer of this is to you personally unknown, but perhaps not altogether unknown by name, I have no interest in flattering you, but permit me to say though I have never saw you – I have long admired you for your unflinching honesty and sterling courage.
I have not hitherto written to you, because I was not personally acquainted with you, but you must not suppose that I have been indifferent to your situation; on the contrary (as Mrs Holberry can testify) I have been instrumental in getting adopted at public meetings, several petitions and memorials in your behalf since I became a resident in Sheffield – I extremely regret that my poor efforts have been productive of little good A few weeks back I wrote a memorial in your behalf which was adopted at – and send from York to Mr Duncombe for presentation. I wrote to Mr Parker and Mr Ward "our <u>Liberal</u> members" to support the prayer of the petition when presented – Parker replied refusing to support it – it was only yesterday I got a letter from Ward – I give you the following extract from his letter – "I have so often stated, both publicly and privately, at Sheffield, the reasons that compel me to decline my interference in this case, that it is hardly necefsary for me to repeat them here – I will only add, therefore, that I have never yet met with a Sheffield Chartist, except you only (and you are not a Sheffielder I believe) who did not admit, in arguing the matter with me, that if a man play the game, which Holberry tried to play, he must take the chances of it; and that upon the whole, he may think himself very well off. I have the honour to be Sir, your very obed.t sert Mr G Ward
After such a letter I think it would almost amount to insult to <u>you</u> – to appeal any more to the tender sympathies of this <u>liberal</u> gentleman
Mrs Holberry called on me today and informed me, what I was extremely sorry to hear – that you were much worse in health (I was previously unaware that you was in bad health) – I hardly know what to do to serve you – our tyrants have no bowells of compafsion – only this week, the Attorney-General and Sir Jas Graham have refused to see deputation from the Convention in behalf of Frost Williams and Jones – however we'll try

again – I will get a petition or memorial by Monday and Mrs Holberry will try and get the signatures of sone of the magistrates to it – let us hope it may do some good.

We shall send I suspect twenty-five thousand signatures to the national petition from Sheffield – on Monday I shall write again to Messrs Parker and Ward requesting them to support it. Also to the two county members. It is to be presented the 2nd May when there will be a grand procefsion in London – on the 3rd May Mr Duncombe brings forward his motion on the National Petition – I would have written an account of Chartism in Sheffield and the Country at large, but was afraid it might prevent my letter reaching you.

I shall be glad to hear from you – and if you can point out anyway in which I can serve you I will be happy to do so. Sincerely hoping this will find you better.

I am fraternally yours – George Julian Harney

HBY 23

Retford Apr 22

Dear Brother I sent you a post office order for 5 shillings last monday I should like to now if you have received it I should of rote when I sent it but I could not both the Children as been very Ill we did not expect the baby living it as been so ill I sent it the order to York I thought you would soon get it

We are all well and is glad to hear that you are better I will rite as soon as I can and say more

I remain your efficnate and Loving sister

E Tallants

HBY 24

Sheffield Apr 24/42

My Dear Holberry

I received your Kind and Welcome letter of the 20th

It is with feelings the most painful that I have read your letter.

It is with extreme sorry that I now addrefs you, when I think of your present melancholy situation but I hope the same same providence which supported you during your trial, will support you in the hour of trouble, Dear Sir, I hope by the time you receive this, you will have Recovered from your Illnefs and your appitite Will have Returned and that your Stomach

Will have Recovered to A proper State, so that it will not refuse the food that you Eat

Oh! Sir! I hope that your Constitution is not Broken Nor A ruined Man, and I hope that you Will have Much pleasure when you get your Liberty and before Long. more so then if you had been the along side poor old Claton.

We shall send A petition in favour of your Liberation to the House of Commons Next Week, it will be sent to Mr T. S. Doncombe Esq M. P. his A Addrefs is Albany London

Dear Sir I have wrote to Mr Campbell and to Mr OConnor and to My Much Esteemed friend Mr James Moir Esq, from Glasgow Dear Sir Do Keep up your Spirits, for What ever you Can think off send me Word and I will do it, and what ever I Can think of Will do, With out puting unaffected modesty to the blush,

Sir, Mr George White has moved that A committee be appointed to wait on the Secretary for the Home Affairs, and take other steps to procure the releas of Holberry, Peddie, Brook and all the others political prisoners, Mr OConnor Seconded the resolution in an energetic addrefs, Various other delegates expressed their opinion, and A Committee Consisting of Messrs Bairstow White and Moir Were elected.

I shall write them this Afternoon, I Shall Get a friend to Write Me A memorial to Sir James.

Dear Sir your kind loving and Affectionate Wife Was to Wait on Mr Albert Smith Cleark to the town Hall lot to know if any thing Can be Done for you

Dear Sir I hope your Wishes will be fully Bore out aboute your Health and all things else I was down at Attercliffe on thursday Night Where your wife was in Good health but extremely sorry to hear that you are Not better.

Dear Sir I should have sent sooner But I have Not any Money When I receive your Kind and Welcome letter, or I Could Not have hesitated one moment in answering your letter, and had I known that my Worthy friend had been in Want of the sum mentioned, I should never have put his unaffected Modesty to the Blush by suffering him to Ask it. No Sir, the offer should have Came from myself

However the sum I had not by me But I will send it about the 28, the Reason is that I had I have had to Settle Law sute Concerning A Newspaper that was sent through the Post office, and My friend had wrote in it, the Cost £1 18s 16d, Now My Dear Sir Do not think that I Name this for to Refuse letting you have it Oh No 1000 times No! But let me beg, that if you Consider me really as your friend that You Will suit the payment to your own circumstances Without being confined to any

particular time, and Not only so but that you will likewise Command my humble assistance in every thing else, Wherein I can serve you
Sir I have to inform you that the National Petition will be presented on Monday the 2sn of May, By Mr T.S. Doncombe. Nearly 4, 000, 000 the period of Sitting of the National Convention is Limited to three Weeks and that no alteration can take place, the 2nd May will become memorable in the annals of Chartism
I am Sir, yours with the
greatest sincerity
Henry William Needham

Letter in Northern Star: Extract of Letter to Mr G J Harney, Sheffield combined with missing pieces contained in an extract from *The English Chartist Circular and Temperance Advocate*, Vol 2, no. 119:

Hospital, York Castle, April 24th 1842

Dear Sir – I this morning received your very welcome letter. I am not at all surprised at Mr Ward's conduct – it is just like him: but why did they not hang or transport me, if they thought I deserved it? They would then have put an end to my sufferings at once; instead of which they have destroyed my constitution by unjust treatment at Northallerton; they have brought me to that state I cannot eat, and thought I have been allowed half a pound of mutton every day, and tea night and morning, since I came to the Castle; although I am allowed all this, I am reduced to such a state of bodily debility that I can hardly crawl – I am only a shadow of my former self. There is a poor convict lying beside me in the last stage of consumption; he is wasted very little more than I am. And, dear friend, you may rest assured that I shall never serve two more years in prison; no, before half that time is expired I shall be in my grave. Perhaps that will give Messrs Ward and Co. great pleasure, they may then think I have satisfied the demands of the Law. The punishment inflicted on me is worse than if they had put an end to my sufferings at once. Believe me, Sir, I would rather leave this place a corpse, than remain here till my health is so far gone as to leave me a burden to my friends. I have not the least fear of death, and never felt more calm in my life. * * * * I think if you were to write to Brighton, and get them to send the memorial to Captain Puchell, it might have some effect, as a report went to the surgeon here, last week, to the Home office, on the state of my health. It is with difficulty I have wrote, the pain in my side is so distressing.
I am yours truly,
Samuel Holberry

HS 12 York April 1842

Dear Holberry
I have last night rec.d a letter from our friend H W Needham from Sheffield inclosing 2/ one of which is from your Dear Wife and the other from himself with a request I would purchase you some oranges + confectionery in compliance with which as far as the first is concerned I have acted but do not know what confectionery would be admitted or what you would like, I have sent you 1/ worth of oranges thirteen in number and have kept the Shilling until I receive your orders, I hope this will find you better than when I last heard from you your Wife + all Friends send their affectionate regards to you the memorial left Sheffield yesterday Needham is sanguine of succefs, he promised to write to me again on Sunday when I will write to you the particulars which he may send write to me soon Excuse this short letter I will send you more news next week
I am in great haste just now
praying for your speedy release
I remain Dear Friend
Yours affectionately
Edw Burley
PS can you spare the "Book," Robins ancient History it has been applied for, if so do send me the dirty Handkerchief, the oranges have come in. Excuse it

Letter to Burley in Northern Star 2/7/42

York Castle, April 30th 1842

My Dear Friend – I am sorry to inform you that I am no better: I am reduced to a skeleton, and if no alteration takes place for the better, I shall soon not be able to crawl. My appetite is very bad, and the little food I take I cannot digest without the assistance of medicine, and then only with pain and difficulty. You perhaps will be surprised to hear that the Castle is a worse place for a man in sickness than the House of Correction at Northallerton. When I was ill there, I had such food as I could eat, but here the case is different, and if a man's stomach cannot take the food allowed, he must go without. You will not wonder at me being so debilitated, when I tell you I can take no portion of the food allowed for dinner excepting a few potatoes; and you are perhaps aware, that it is not every day we get them. A bit of bread and a sup of what in the Castle is

called tea, is the only (except a potato occasionally, food I have taken for the last three weeks. My eyes are sunken in my head, and could you see me you would think I had the jaundice. My friend, I feel too weak to say more. I shall be glad to hear from you when convenient. Sir, I write nothing but facts, and you have no occasion to be afraid of making use of my words; when they have said all they can of me, they can neither call me a liar or a felon. Give my respects to all friends, accept the same yourself, from yours truly,
Samuel Holberry

HBY 25

1842 Retford May 12th

Dear Brother
I hope these few lines wil find you in better health than you was when you wrote to Sister Tallants whe was in formed that you had beene very hill you Could hardley write to her, the Reason I have not wroute to you sooner my Wife has beene very hill and I thouht I would wait A alteration tooke plase befor I wrout to you, and I Could give you An answer how we we hall was
Whe are hall in a midelin way at this time youre Deare Farther + Loving Mother sends thare best Love to you and feeles very ansues of seeing the face of thare darlin Son Once More, thay hope the time is not fare Distant When they will himbrace a Lovin kifs from their darlin son for thare time is growin Short in this wald
Brother William wishes to be remembered to you he has waited of me writin to you for he says that he his a very bad writer so he hopes that you will exshuse him not writin, I now he wishes you wel the same as if he wrout himself, I saw A frend this nite and he says that youre petishen has gon up to London and I wish its suckces, he says that a grate maney in Stockport sined thare names for youre Relise, when you wrout to Retford for that trifeling of money you should have wrout to me, for they Com to me, I have send you 12 stamps in this Letter For I think you seeme afraid to write to me for aney thing, Dear Brother be not afraid of sendin to me for aney thin for I am willing to do aney thing to give you comfort in youre mind Mr Lightfoot has had a very bad misfortun his Mill is Bornt downe to the ground I think it will Reuin him
Whe sent for youre wife to com to the faire but She never Com nor whe have not hard from her since, give hour Best love to her when you write to her and to hall the family

So no more from your well wishes, Wm and Hannah Rhodes
Retford

Extract from letter of the 17th May to Mary, quoted in *The English Chartist Circular and Temperance Advocate*, Vol 2, no. 119

"I believe it would give satisfaction to certain parties to hear that I had 'gone the way of all flesh,' Well, the certainty of such an event would trouble me less than my enemies imagine; but, my dear I think of you, and the thought distracts me; but I will not say more, for fear I should hurt your feelings."

Letter in Northern Star 2/7/42

To E Burley, 19 Bilton Street, Layerthorpe, York
Hospital, Castle, May 19th 1842

My Dear Friend – I did not receive yours of the 10th until the 16th. I should have answered it sooner, but the surgeons had been raising an eruption on my side which was so painful and run such quantities of corruption, that I have been for for three days and could not stoop, but neither the eruption, the blisters, not anything else that I could have taken inwardly or applied outwardly has done me any good. The fact is, I believe my lungs are affected. I am worse now than ever I was at Northallerton, and far more reduced. I am so badly troubled with dispepsy that I cannot digest the little food I eat without the assistance of medicines; but it is no use troubling you with complaints, or I could fill this letter with them. When you see Mr Crowther give my compliments to him, and tell him I am obliged to him for the stamps he sent me. You can tell him the reason I did not answer his note. Dear friend, I want to borrow a feather pillow (if any of our friends has one to spare) till I get better. I would have sent for one from home, but the carriage costs so much, but I hope the Convention has made some arrangement for the wives and families, and not left them destitute, as they have been for months past. Sir, I am almost lost for want of something, when the fever is on me so strong I drink such a quantity of water that I feel it does me harm. I wish you would be so kind as to send me sixpennyworth of oranges. I will repay you as soon as I get some money. I cannot write more at present. Let me hear from you when convenient. Give my respects to all friends, accept the same for yourself, from
Yours, truly, Samuel Holberry

HBY 26

Sheffield May 22. 1842
My Dear Holberry
I received your Kind and Welcome of the 18th and it is with a heart feltsorry that I now addreſs you seeing that it is Not of your own writing my heart sickneſs when I think of What you have suffered both in Northallerton and since you Came to the Castle and for that But the honest expreſsion of your sentements, and Condmed for the Acts of others. But Never mind that I have strong very strong hopes that you will shortley leave your Gloomy Retreat and return to the bosom of your Kind Affectionate and loving Wife it is with extreme regret that I see according to your letter you are got worse and that troublesome pain in your side is no better I should have Wrote to you on the 18 inst but I whanted to see the Star so that I might send you all the information that I Could In hopes that it it will Cheer you up your Spirits.

I Beg to inform you that Brighton as sent a Memorial to the Home office but have not received an answer to it they will send another Next Week if they Do Not get answer, and there is several other Memorials been sent to the Homes Office for your Liberation But there is no answer Comed Concerning them and with regard to our Memorial I Beg to inform you that I have got 25 signatures of sum Note. I had an interview with Mr Albert Smith on tuesday last when he informed me he had Named your Case to some of the other Magistrates but an account of it been the Seſsions that Week We had better take the Memorial and get sum others signatures I waited on Mr Howes firm and they Both Promised to sighn the Memorial When We had Got Mr Wards Mr Holland MD said the same.

Mr Ward one of our members Wives Waited on Mr Aslin Ward yesterday With the Memorial and he has sighned it and she Waited on the vicar and he in formed her that he Would the Chaplain of the Castle and hear What he had to say of you I waited on Mr Charles Congreve Merchant With Memorial and he Will sighn it if the Chaplain gives you a good Charicter Sir Arnol James Knigh will sighn to morrow there is 33 promesed to sighn When Mr Ward had sighned Which We shall get to morrow
in haste for Post
your affectionate
Henry W Needham

PS Dear Holbery I have seen your loving Wife to Day she Was in good health But Sorry to hear that you are No better

I will write you on the 24 Pleas lett me hear from you as soon has you Can With regard to your Health
hoping this Will find your health much Better then Went I heard from you

HS 13

19 Bilton Street Layerthropre York

My dear Holberry
I rec.d your letter, am sorry that I have not had an opportunity of answering it sooner the reason was I did not get the pillow untill last night from Mr Pulleyn silk dyer North Street, I could not possibly spare one myself as I should have been proud to have sent it you immediately, I rec.d A letter from Your wife on Sunday Night inclosing one for you and 1/ to buy you sixpenny worth of oranges and the rest in confectionery, my Dear Friend I am sorry you have taken the shilling from her, I do not know what sort of confectionery she means but I have sent you 6d worth of oranges + my Wife has sent you 2 oz of acid drops, which I hope will be of some service to you, + I have sent you the shilling to do as you think proper with, I am sorry to say that nothing has been done by the convention for the Wifes + Families, but Mr O Conner will be in York in the Course of 2 or 3 week when I will get him to make an appeal in their behalf, I hope you are mistaken in regard to your lungs been affected, + that before you are so far injured as that, Sympathy will have Entered the Iron Hearts of your oppressors, I have just rec.d an answer sent to Duncome by the Secretary of State to the last memorial I sent + Duncome says it is just such a one as he expected from that quarter Sir J Graham says he cannot see sympathy in your case or situation to justify him consistently with his public duty to advise her Majesty to comply with the prayer theirof so <u>much for Sir J Graham</u> the people must and will treat with him in <u>due time</u>
my Friend we are going on well in York their is nothing more I can say at present than my assuring you of my deep sympathy for you, + my determination to do all I can for you.
I remain Sir Most Affectionately
Yours Edw Burley
May 24th 1842

Excuse the struggle scribble I am in Haste

Letter published in *The English Chartist Circular and Temperance Advocate*, Vol 2, no. 119

York Castle, May 24 1842

My Dear Harney

I received yours of the 22nd, and am sorry to inform you that I get worse every day; I cannot digest sufficient food to support my body, and all the medicine I have taken has not in the least benefitted me; my side is very bad, and all the blisterings &c., seems to do me no good. I hope you will look after my petition, and get as many signatures as possible, and I hope it will have effect. I return my sincere thanks for your kindness, and hope your endeavours will be crowned with success. Your affectionate friend
Samuel Holberry
P.S. My reason for not writing before is, I did not feel able.

Letter published in *The English Chartist Circular and Temperance Advocate*, Vol 2, no. 120

York Castle, May 27, 1842

My Dear Mary

I received your kind letter, and Mr Burley brought me some oranges. I feel rather easier this morning, but you may depend I am a poor object. My dear, you say you should like to come to York to see me; to that I cannot give my consent. In the first place we should have to look the through the odious bars, and it would only make you more unhappy, to say nothing of myself; besides I have no complaint on me at present that is likely to terminate my existence; that my illness should bring me into consumption is all that I am afraid of, but I believe they will not let me die here, except it be by a sudden visitation. Keep your spirits, remember you have the satisfaction of knowing you have done your duty. … That God may bless you, and restore me to your arms is the sincere prayer of your devoted husband.
Samuel Holberry.

Letter in Northern Star 2/7/42

To E Burley, 19 Bilton Street, Layerthorpe, York

Hospital, Castle, May 28th 1842

My Dear Burley – I have received your kind letter, and the one from my dear wife; likewise the oranges and pillow. Tell the gentleman who lent it me I am very much obliged to him. Accept my thanks for the oranges, and give my respects to Mrs. Burley and tell her I am obliged to her for the

acid drops, though I have not got leave to have them yet. York Castle is a queer place for a sick man. I wish I was back in Northallerton hospital (hospital mind) til I get better. There I had everything that a reasonable man could require cooked by females, and done as it ought to be. Dear Sir, you rather blame me for telling my wife to send you a trifle of money for to get me a few oranges. I might add that I had wrote to two friends (I had perhaps as well say places) for a trifle for the same purposes, but to no use, and that is not the worst. But I am aware this is not a proper place for me to make complaints of that nature. What I have said above, I hope and trust you will not mention to any one. You should not have sent the shilling to me, no one will buy me oranges or anything else with it; it is contrary to the rules for any one belonging to the Castle to buy a prisoner anything, or I should not have given you the trouble, but I will ask Mr Pearse, the schoolmaster to try and get the shilling, and return it to you for the purpose it was intended for, but you had better buy me nothing but oranges. I am as frugal as possible with them: one of a night is all I use. You have just received an answer as I expected from Sir James; he has sent the same answer to a poor unfortunate convict that lays beside me in the last stage of a consumption who was recommended by the magistrates, backed by the surgeon's certificate. Give my respects to all my friends; accept the same for yourself,
Your well wisher
Samuel Holberry
P.S. Be careful how you word your letters; they draw the pen across different words that are strong

HBY 27

Sheffield May 29, 1842
My Dear Holberry
I received your Kind Welcome letter and should have answered it sooner but I Wanted to be able to give you some information relating to the memorial. I beg to inform you that onacount of it been the fair last Week only a few Signatures. but to morrow We Go to Waite on the friends. So that I hope that the Delay Will only be short, I so Mr Albert Smith on thursday he inquired after your health and he though that you ought to be Liberated he Inquried how many signatures was got. I informed him that We Could have got as many Signatures as Would have filed the Memorial if the Magistrates would have Signed it first he said he would use is influence with them. I thought I had informed you that Mr Parker informed Me that they will transmit the Memorial Homes office and they

Will State there opinion has regards your Case. but It his the first Case that they have interfere with and I Can assure you that they will Do their best for you When We have got aboute 30 more Names. Which I think Can be got to morrow or the Day following

My Dear Sir I wrote to the Governor of Northallerton gaol for a faithful Character of you while you was in it. He as sent has good A Character as I expected, I laid it before the Magistrates,

Dear Sir in my last last Week I for got to inform you that the Convention appointed A deputation to Wait on Sir James three times but the Old answer came in reply.

Sir, Mr Joseph Brooks as been on a second pilgrimage to Northallerton for the purpose of seeing is brother. the following is an extract from is letter in this Week Star.

I saw him on Whit Tuesday. Alas! What a strange alteration; the bloom that used to adore his manly Cheek had nearly all fled, his Countenance was pale and sallow, and marked With scorbutic eruptions I told him he looked much Worse then When I last visited him. I asked him how he felt? his answer Was, that his Constitution Was Completely broken. He attributed it to his long confinement. But though his Constitution is injured and his health impaired, his love for liberty is still unconquered; his spirits still remains the same Determined to battle with tyranny and oppreſsion to the Last moment of his Life, he has got nine months and A few Days, there his and appeal now made for him to find his own provisions, and that Will Cost from eight or nine shillings Weekly.

My Dear Holberry moste heartely Do I wish that the Memorial will have the proper succeſs and When therefore you are Released from your Gloomy Retreat and Return here be aſsured My Dear, that no one here Will feel greater satisfaction at seeing you than,

your truly affectionate and sincere friend,
HWN

HBY 28

Sheffield June 3th /42

My Dear Holberry

I have Received your Kind and Welcome letter of the 31^{ist} and it is with deep felt sory that I have Read it. But am in haste the Memorial as been taken to the Magistrates and they Will Give an answer to morrow

I have seen your Kind Wife to Day she was in good health But sorry she had you not at home

I have sent you 5 stamps all they have at the post office
I shall write to morrow When we get an Answer
in haste
HWN
hoping this Will find you a great Deal Better and A speed Liberation
Yours was ever faithfull
HWN

Letter published in Northern Star 30/7/42 : Obtained in response to their request for all communications that had passed between the Secretary of State for the Home Office and the authorities of York Castle regarding the health of Holberry

7th of June 1842

Samuel Holberry, the Chartist prisoner in York Castle, is suffering from severe pain in the left side, the effect of chronic inflammation of the left lobe of the liver, extending to the stomach, and perhaps the colon, which, from his having had former attacks, I believe to be organic disease. His digestion is very bad, and he is very weak; and I consider him to be in great danger. I am of the opinion that his symptoms have increased, and his health has been impaired, of late, by the length of confinement, and the great anxiety of mind he appears to have suffered since his imprisonment.
(signed) George Champney
Surgeon to the York Castle

HBY 29

Sheffield Jun 10/ 42
My Dear Holberry
I write these few lines to hoping you will have Rose from your Bed of Affliction never to Suffer again for I am sure that you have Suffered in the extreme. But I hope these few lines will find you intirley Recovered from your Illnefs Dear Sir I should have wrote you before now but your Kind loving faithful and Affectionate Devoted Wife thought that you Would think if the Memorial was not Named in the Letter you that there was no hope of you getting out of the Castle so thought I and this his the Reason that I have Not Wrote Before Now Sir your Wife as seen the magistrates to Day. When they agread that Mr Albert Smith Shall write to the Surgeon this afternoon for an account of your health and for the Surgeon to

answer By Return of Post, Mr Hugh Barker Esq and J.P. has promised to Do all that he can to obtain your Liberation, your Kind Wife Received A letter last night from you and it was With extreme Sorry that I heard you was no better in health.

I have wrote Mr E Burley and have sent him 2 shillins for him to Buy you Oranges and a little Confectionery hoping they may Do you Good is the earnest Wish of your Well Wisher H.W.N.

one of the Shillines Was from your Wife and I have sent you the other. Sir I wrote you on friday last and Sent 3 postage stamps When you Write Pleas to say Where you Got them or not I have sent 12 more which you are Welcome to, hoping that you may not stay in the Castle to use them.

I remain yours most sincerely,

HW Needham

PS I have been Down to Attercliffe tonight When your Wife was in good health But sorry she has not got you at home yet

I will Write you on sunday Good night God Blefs you

HWN ½ past 11

My Dear Holberry Keep up your spirits, for I hope that you Will be at home very soon

Letter published in Northern Star 30/7/42 : Obtained in response to their request for all communications that had passed between the Secretary of State for the Home Office and the authorities of York Castle regarding the health of Holberry

York Castle 11th June 1842

Sir, the Visiting Magistrates desire me to enclose you the certificate of the surgeon of the York County Gaol, respecting the state of health of Samuel Holberry, a Chartist prison in York Castle.

The visiting magistrates can bear testimony to Holberry's good conduct during his confinement in this prison; and in his present state of health recommend his release from gaol, considering it the only means of affording a hope of his ultimate recovery.

I have &c.

(signed)

Barnard Hague,

Chairman of the Visiting Magistrates of York Castle

Barnard Hague Esq.

Whitehall 17th of June 1842

Sir, I am directed by the Secretary Sir James Graham to acknowledge the receipt of your letter of the 11th instant, with its enclosed medical certificate, respecting Samuel Holberry, a prisoner in York Castle; and to acquaint you that, under the circumstances therein stated, Sir James Graham has felt warranted in advising Her Majesty to grant the prisoner a pardon, on condition of entering into a recognizance, himself in £200, with two sureties, to be approved of by the Visiting Justices of the York Castle in £100 each, for his good behaviour for five years from this date. I am, therefore, to request that such recognizance, when entered into, may be transmitted to me, and upon receipt thereof, Her Majesty's warrant will be forwarded for the prisoners and liberation.
I am, &c. (signed) S.M. Phillipps
Samuel Holberry
Conditional Pardon

Victoria R

Whereas Samuel Holberry was at a Gaol Delivery holden in and for the County of York on the 5th day of March 1840, convicted of Sedition and Sentenced to be Imprisoned Four Years for the Same and to find Sureties himself in £50 and two Sureties of £10 each for his good behaviour for the further term of Three Years, We in consideration of some circumstances humbly represented unto us, are Graciously pleased to extend Our Grace and Mercy unto him and to grant him Our Pardon for his Said crime on Condition of his giving Security himself in £200 and two Sureties who Shall be approved of by the Visiting Justices of the Gaol for the Said County in £100 each for his good Behaviour for Five Years from the date hereof. Our Will and Pleasure therefore is that upon giving Such Security as aforesaid you cause him the said Samuel Holberry to be discharged out of Custody and for doing this Shall be you Warrant. Given at Our Court at St James's the Seventeenth day of June 1842 in the Fifth Year of Our Reign

494/2

Attercliffe Jun 19 1842[22]
Dear Husband
i agen take the plesher of riting thes few lines to you hoping this to find you beter than when you rote last my Dear Husband you must Excus me not ancser youre letter before now the reson whos i wanted to see whot i cood do with the Petition i have been time after time in youre last you stated that the surgeon whod send statin youre health i whent to them and tould them whot you sad {*said*} Parker oared {*ordered?*} Albert Smith to rite to the Surgeon at York Castle he did so and tha reseved a ancer {*answer*} Last Tuesday and i made my self shoure of Geting the Petition sined by what tha said but as tha can torn and say what tha think proper tha have torned from that tha have been considren tha ar fore week an i have left them considren of it yet and i beeleve myselfe tha whill not sine it at hole but i mean going to see them agen tha shall not say tha have been considren till tha have forgotten it for i whill remind them of it by goying to see them but i hope you whill deseve both them and me by coming home and in a short time that Five Shillings as whos for you i got My Harney to rite to the star office about it but tha have not Acknowledge it yet but he is going to rite agean. theare is 13 Shillings this week from Sutton in Ashfield it is forwed to Mr Martin so i expect you will reseve it if you have not ples to answer this as i am Desires to now and I hopes you ar something better
T Farther and Mother and hole the family sends thare kind Love and respect to you hoping this to find you better and shot of the pain in your side
So no more at present from youre devoted and loving wife Mary Holbary

Letters published in Northern Star 30/7/42 : Obtained in response to their request for all communications that had passed between the Secretary of State for the Home Office and the authorities of York Castle regarding the health of Holberry

York Castle 21st of June 1842
Sir, as the gaoler of this prison is unavoidably absent at the Insolvent Sessions at Wakefield, I have to report the death of Samuel Holberry, the Chartist, who died this morning rather suddenly. On receipt of your

---

22 This letter is postmarked in Sheffield on the 20th June and York on the 21st, so would not have been seen by Holberry

instructions, received last Saturday, I saw Holberry, in the presence of the gaoler, and read to him the letter, and gave him a copy of the amount of bail required. I immediately, on Holberry's request, sent the schoolmaster to write a letter to such person or persons as he wished, telling him, at the same time, to desire his bail to bring a note from a magistrate at Sheffield that they were responsible persons, as far as the amount of bail required (£100), and that he should return with them, which was done; and I also requested that they would be here to-day, as I was obliged to leave for London in the morning, on particular business; and I will call at the Home Office, if you require further information. The inquest will be held as soon as the coroner can come.
I have &c.
(signed) Barnard Hague
Chairman of the Visiting Magistrates of York Castle
P.S. No reply to Holberry's letter of Saturday's date has been received.

To the Right Hon. Sir James Graham, Bart
York Castle 21st of June 1842
Samuel Holberry died this morning, at half-past four, of chronic inflammation of the liver, which implicated some of the other abdominal viscera.
(signed)
William Anderson
Deputy Surgeon to York Castle

Dates Unknown:

HS14 *(presumably 1842 given the reference to "Spanish juice")*

Dear Husband
Pleas to say
in your next
if you reseved
hole that is down
hear, and if thear
is hole that you
want at present
and if not pleas to say
your two shirts is

hole mos to strong
but tha whill be
better when tha have
been washt whonce or
twice and i hope tha
whill sut you tha
whill bee wharnce
2 shirts
1 pare wosted stockings
som Black Cotton for your waistcoate
whon stick of Spanish juce
2 Bales wite wosted
Come and brush
2 stockings needles
12 stamps whon Mrs Jackson in the
Park wishes to bee rembed to you and
she has bout you thes stamps she keep the scresby taven {*Shrewsbury Tavern? - there was such a tavern on South St, Park*}

HS15 *(presumably late 41 / early 42 given that the reference to spring and that he is "better")*

Dear Brother
I have sent your shoes and two pairs of stockings and your Brother William tould me to send you some riting paper I have sent you 2 Books the weekly visiter and the ank is {*?*} inqurer Dear Brother I am sory to here that you are not litley to get out this spring but I hope you are mis took surely thay have not got harts of stone I think it is better for Farther and mother not to now it will only had to their troubles Brother William sent you a letter last week and 12 stamps in it I was glad to here that you wass better I hope and please god that you will continue so till you get out I was suprised to hear that Ant and Cousn never come nere you I am sure that I was never shall notice them if thay don't Looks on you I hope there will be a time when we shall meet again I have sent you a 3rd pair of stockings and 3 Books Mr Ostick as sent you 2 Books and sister of one Dear Brother you must excuse me saing more for I am very busy we are going to remove in to Carrilgate but I shall rite again before long so no more at present from your ever affecnat and loving sister E Tallent
I have sent apare of cauled stockings of B and 5 books and sixpence

CPR5
To Mr John Cooper
Hattercliffe
near Sheffield
Halifax

My Dear Brother
I wrote these few lines hoping to find you all in good health as they leave all of us at present thank God for it I am quite surprised that you not sending an answer to our last I am rather afraid there is too little of that brotherly love amongst us which we out to profeſs or I think you would have wrote before this but I will aſsure you it will hurt my feelings very much if you have that hardneſs of heart to forget that I am your Sister though I were at the end of the world I have the same Claim according to what there is amongst us as if I lived the next door to you and that there is now more than 18 months expired and yet I have recieved no information which gives me A little uneasyneſss Dear Brother if you have made A settlement I hope you will please to Answer this and let me know what it is and by what means I must come at it as I could send my son Francis over indeed he talks of coming at the races. please give my best respects to all my brothers and Sisters and accept the same yourself and let me know if my Brother Richard is on the same farm yet or not you must know we are still living in the Maltshovel yard will you please to send me word what the sign of this public house was that we putup at in Sheffield and I want to know likewise if you made anything of the Cow hoofs we brought and we have A quantity more so you must please to send me word about them and please to answer this as soon as poſsible so no more at present from Affectionate Sister and Brother,
Betsy and Charles Marchand

***

Samuel Holberry's army recruitment record from: WO 12/4821

	Date recruited (March 1832)	Age	Height in feet inches		Remuneration £ s	
Samuel Holberry		24	15	6 6½	2	10

Biographical Sketch of the Late Samuel Holberry taken from: *The English Chartist Circular and Temperance Advocate*, Vol 2, nos. 118 – 122 May-June 1843

(Communicated by a friend at Sheffield)

> Had I a thousand, thousand lives,
> Oh! I would give the whole.
> I die, as men should proudly do,
> For home and liberty,
> I sow the seed that yet shall grow,
> And make my country free.
>
> Robert Nicol.

Samuel Holberry was born November 18th, 1814 at Gamston, a small village in Nottinghamshire, and situate three miles to the south of East Retford. His parents, John and Martha Holberry, are natives of the same county, as have been the progenitors for periods extending as far back as their respective "lineages" can be traced. John, the father of Samuel, has pursued throughout life the occupation of a farm labourer, and has lived for forty-eight years in a cottage under the Duke of Newcastle. Samuel was the youngest of a family of nine children. At the time we write (1843) four sisters and two brothers are residing in the neighbourhood of Gamston; one sister died many years ago at the age of eighteen, and one brother, a soldier, is supposed to be in America, but has not been heard of for some years. Samuel acquired the first rudiments of education at the church school of his native village, and subsequently attended a day school under the superintendence of a Mr Blincorn. At what age his school training terminated we have not been able to learn. Our knowledge indeed of the earlier years of his toil for bread are very scanty. We believe, however, that when a comparative child he worked for a short time at a cotton factory in Gamston, and that his boyhood and youth were passed as a farmer's servant. His last situation in this capacity was with Mr Solomon Waterhouse, of Clayworth, about five miles north of Retford. But the monotony of a farm labourer's existence had no attractions for the subject of this sketch; of an ardent temperament, he was anxious to "see the world," and push his fortune amid scenes more distant and exciting than those of his native home. In fact, a *soldier's* life was the one which charmed young Holberry; nor can this be wondered at, seeing that he had an elder brother in the army, and that three of his maternal and two or three of his paternal uncles had also worn the scarlet uniform. Accordingly, when little more than seventeen years of age, Samuel enlisted in the 33rd regiment of foot; his discharge states that he was enlisted at Doncaster, on 24 March, 1832, at the age of eighteen years; the reason of this is, that he had previously been refused admission into the army on account of his youth, and now stated himself to be older by a year than he really was to overcome that objection. From Doncaster he was immediately marched to Gosport. We have no materials whatever for any description of his life while in the army, he having, unfortunately, when on a visit to his parents some years later, burnt the letters he had addressed to them while wearing the red coat. It is known, however, that he was never out of the United Kingdom: he was in Ireland a short time and also stationed at Woolwich, and, for a longer period, at Northampton. During his military sojourn in the latter town, he attended an evening school, and availed himself of the too few opportunities allowed by his then position, to acquire really useful knowledge. As his mind improved, he began to see through the false glare of military "glory" which had so much enchanted him when a boy; and this, aided by the slavish discipline to which he was a matter of course subjected, speedily inspired him with disgust for the "life of a soldier." He accordingly now acceded to the before frequently expressed solicitations of his parents, to quit the army. His discharge was purchased, and he pronounced his farewell to the "ranks of glory" after a service of three years and twenty-five days. His discharge is honourable testimony to his character; and though the praise of military officers is not of any great importance in Chartist eyes, yet it must be admitted that even such testimony is evidence in support of the morality and probity of the subject of this memoir.

After rusticating in his native village – and enjoying the hearty congratulations of his affectionate parents and other relatives – for a few weeks he proceeded to Sheffield, and obtained employment at Mr How's cooperage, where he remained about twelve months. He was then engaged by Messrs Baines and Co, distillers, with whom he remained about eighteen months. Some differences in the firm itself having induced them to discharge Holberry and some other of their workmen, he visited London, where he procured employment at a distillery in Upper Thames Street. After sojourning in the great metropolis about ten months, Holberry returned to Sheffield at the request of his former employers, in whose service he was retained until within three months of his arrest, when certain arrangements between Mr Baines and his partner resulted in again depriving Holberry of his means of subsistence; over and over again has a Mr Baines expressed regret that he had ever parted with so valuable a servant. We may add that poor Holberry filled a situation of great trust and confidence.

As some proof of his frugality and sterling honour, it may be stated that in less than three years after his discharge from the army, he paid back in full the sum of twenty pounds to his parents, advanced by them to purchase his discharge. What better evidence than this simple fact can be required to prove the existence of an independent spirit and virtuous heart, in one filling but an humble situation in society, and as a matter of course, but indifferently remunerated for his labour?

Some few months have after leaving the army, and settling in Sheffield, Holberry made the acquaintance of his future wife, Mary Cooper, to whom he was united on the 22nd October, 1838.

Mrs. Holberry, at the period we write, after three years of heart-corroding anxiety and mental anguish, is still a truly fine woman, tall in stature, of graceful deportment, handsome and expressive features, possessing an excellent temper, and, considering the defects of education, a mind of no mean order. Here as we shall presently show when we come to describe Holberry's person, were two beings pre-eminently fitted for the enjoyment of all the happiness their situation in society would admit of, torn asunder by a cruel tyranny: the one to die a miserable death in a felon's cell – the other to spend months and years of hopeless sorrow.

In all probability Holberry first acquired a taste for politics during the period that he was in the army, as Mrs Holberry states that he had adopted the principles of Radicalism before she became acquainted with him. Towards the end of 1838, he became a member of the "Sheffield Working Man's Association," at that time assembling in George Street, but shortly afterwards removed to Fig Tree Lane; and in which body Holberry speedily became remarkable for his indomitable zeal. The stirring events of the ensuing year, 1839, are two well known to require more than a brief recapitulation. The Convention of Chartist delegates assembled in London, charged with the presentation of the National Petition. That document was presented, and, as a matter of course, was rejected by the usurping legislature to whom it was addressed; that is to say though ordered to "lie on the table," its statements were insolently denied and scoffed at; one gentleman characterising it as "a piece of ridiculous machinery." The simultaneous meetings followed; then the re-assembling of the delegates at Birmingham, and the Bull-ring outrage, at which the unarmed people were brutally assaulted by bludgeon men of the London police.

As might be anticipated, the just indignation and disgust of the people, throughout the country, was excited to the utmost, by this out atrocious outrage. In Sheffield and its neighbourhood – as at most other towns – large meetings were held, at all of which Holberry took a conspicuous part. As winter approached, torch-light meetings were held in the suburbs of the town, and excited considerable sensation. We now come to that unfortunate event in Holberry's career which decided his fate, and ended in consigning him to the grave, in the flower of youth and the pride of manhood.

In November 1839, occurred in the ever-to-be-lamented outbreak at Newport, in Wales, the origin of which is still shrouded in mystery – but we will not dilate upon that, in every respect, unfortunate event – our readers know the fate of that estimable man, and noble patriot, John Frost, and his unfortunate companions. The first week in January 1840, or last week in December 1839, Frost, Williams, Jones, and the other persons charged with being concerned in the Newport "outbreak" were brought to trial before the Special Commission, at Monmouth, and while the trial was proceeding, the lamentable affair which involved poor Holberry in the meshes of the law took place at Sheffield. In the ranks of the Sheffield Charter Association, at that time, were too many thoughtless and unreflecting men, the greater portion of them honest hearted, but devoid of judgment and discretion; such men are always easily duped by the rascally agents of unprincipled rulers. Holberry, brave, generous, confiding and frank, was easily induced to take part in certain movements over which prudence dictates that the veil should be drawn; the these prudential considerations prevent us stating many acts of Holberry's life at this particular period, which could they be stated, would testify his patriotism and devotion to the cause he had embraced. Mouthing fools, who afterwards cowered before the power they had provoked, and traitors who urged men to acts they took care not to participate in, and who no doubt were well rewarded for their villainy, soon brought things to a crisis. At midnight, on Saturday, January 11, 1840, Holberry was arrested at his own house, by Rayner the chief police officer, assisted by a body of constables. Holberry was in bed when the officers entered, and startled by the tread of the officers upon the stairs, he had partly risen, when the latter entered the room and secured him; there was no opportunity for resistance, and the betrayed patriot, compelled to yield, was completed to the Town Hall. About ten minutes after the arrest of her husband, the officers returned and arrested Mrs Holberry, conveying her also to the Town Hall. Here she was thrust into a dark and filthy hole, and there kept without food for eighteen hours, with a wretched woman brought into the cell in a state of beastly drunkenness. On Sunday eve, Mrs H. was brought before a number of magistrates sitting in the Town Hall, and there questioned, and again and again advised, and urged to give evidence against the persons in custody; promises, as plentiful as blackberries, were held out to her that if she would give evidence she should be handsomely rewarded, and her husband set at liberty; if she refused, she was told she would be tried for high treason, and at the very least her husband would be transported for life. Promises and threats were all in vain, and the magistrates ordered her to be taken back to prison. She was removed to another part of the "Lock up," and was then incarcerated until the Tuesday morning with a woman charged with attempting to drown her infant child. On that day she was discharged, her "inquisitors" finding her invulnerable to threats and promises. The detention of this noble-minded woman was altogether illegal; but what matter? "might makes right" and "rich men rule the law."

***

On Monday, January 13, the persons arrested – viz. Samuel Holberry, Thomas of Booker, William Booker, and Samuel Foxall (the last named subsequently betrayed the confidence of his associates) – were brought up before a full bench of magistrates and were remanded until the following day for final examination. The chief witness against the accused was a miserable caitiff named Samuel Powell Thomson, a Chartist class leader. The miscreant admitted, on cross-examination, that he had been one of the principle concocters of the "plot," and had, moreover, taken a prominent part in inveigling poor Holberry into a participation in it. On the evidence of this thoroughly base being, Holberry and John Booker were committed to take their trial for high treason, and the same day were removed to York Castle, under an escort of dragoons.

On the ensuing Monday, James Duffy, John Clayton, William Booker, John Marshall, Thomas Penthorpe, Joseph Benison, and Wm. Wells were committed to York on a charge of conspiracy on the evidence of Foxall, who previously had been arraigned along with Holberry and the elder Booker.

The Spring Assizes commenced at York on the 5th March, 1840. The judges were Mr. Justice Erskine, and Mr. Justice Coleridge. At the opening of the court, on Monday, the 16th, Samuel Holberry, James Duffy, Thomas Booker, William Booker, and William Wells, were tried on an indictment which charged them with having "unlawfully conspired and confederated with other persons at Sheffield, on 12th January, 1840, to create a breach of the public peace, and with obtaining arms and other instruments for the purpose more effectually of accomplishing their object."

The Attorney-General (Sir John, now Lord Campbell), Sergeant Atcherly, and Mr Wightman, appeared as the prosecuting counsel; Holberry was defended by Mr Watson, Duffy by Sir Gregory Lewin, and the tow Bookers by Mr Murphy; Wells pleaded guilty.

The Attorney-General, in stating the case against the accused, sounded his own "trumpet of praise" for clemency, in not pressing the charge of "high treason" against Holberry and Booker. Exhibiting a dagger found on Holberry at the time of his arrest, the Attorney-General, *a la* Edmund Burke, flourished the "awful weapon" before the eyes of the terror-stricken jury; and that nothing might be wanting to produce *effect*, the counsellors' tables covered with hand-grenades, bullets, ball cartridges, and shells, found, or said to have been found, in the ransacked houses of the several defendants. It should be added, that none of these things were manufactured at Holberry's house, but were brought there a few days before his arrest, by parties who, if not hired knaves, did as much mischief by their folly, as they could have done had they been employed to do the work of the despotism. The principal witnesses for the prosecution were the traitors Thomson and Foxall.

Mr. Watson and delivered a lengthy, argumentative and eloquent address in defence of Holberry. At nearly 10 o'clock at night the jury retired, and after a short absence returned intercourse with a verdict of GUILTY against all the defendants.

On Saturday, March 21, the defendants were brought up for judgement; when Holberry was sentenced to be imprisoned in the House of Correction, Northallerton, for *four years*, and that the expiration of that time, t*o enter into recognizances himself £50, and two sureties in £10 each, to keep the peace for three years, and to be imprisoned until the the sureties were entered into.*

Duffy and the elder Booker, were sentenced to *three* years imprisonment, and the others to shorter periods.

On the 20th of the same month, Holberry was removed different Northallerton and immediately subjected to the inhumane and *regulations* of that "hell-hole" of English prisons. The accursed "silent system" is there established in all its rigour, the diet is coarse and scanty, prisoners are allowed to be visited only once in three months, and, in fact the regulations are generally are of the most degrading, annoying and vexatious character. Added to all this, Holberry and his unfortunate associates, on reaching Northallerton, were placed on the *treadmill*, to which iniquitous treatment they were subjected every day for four or five weeks, when Holberry was removed. It must never be forgotten that this torture was altogether illegal and gratuitous on part of the petty authorities of the gaol; the sentence pronounced by the judges having simply been one of imprisonment without reference to labour of any kind, much less that of the treadmill.

A few months was sufficient under the murderous discipline of Northallerton Hell-hole to destroy the health, and to utterly ruin the naturally stronger constitution of poor Holberry. On the 30th January, John Clayton died in this prison after little more than ten months confinement. For six weeks poor Clayton had been in a dying condition, it was not until 28th January, two days before his death, Clayton's family received any intelligence of his illness, too late to afford wife or child the opportunity of soothing the last of moments, or closing the eyes of the murdered victim of Class Legislation.

The death of Clayton roused the friends of the other prisoners to active exertions in their behalf, and petitions, praying for the pardon of Holberry and the others, or at least their removal to the County Gaol, were sent to the Queen; and about midsummer of the same year, the two Bookers and Duffy were liberated, the latter having been first reduced by his prison treatment to a state bordering on death. From that condition it took months to restore him to anything like a moderate share of health, but he never fully recovered from the effects of his treatment, and at the present time (May 1843), is, we grieve to hear, in extreme ill-health. But no mitigation of *Holberry's* punishment could be obtained. At length he became so seriously ill, as to induce a *Surgeon* of Northallerton, to make application for his *immediate* removal to York. This was acceded to by the Home Secretary, Sir James Graham, and on the 21st September 1841, he was agaim taken to York Castle, from which he never came out alive! The following letter addressed to Mrs. Holberry announced his removal.

"York Castle, except 22 1841

"My dear wife,

I now have the pleasure to communicated to you that I was removed yesterday from Northallerton to this gaol, where I shall be more comfortable both in body and mind. I am much better in health than I was the last time I wrote to you, and I trust I shall gradually regain the strength which I lost in the horrible place I have left. I shall be at liberty to use my speech and exercise myself at leisure. I trust you will keep your spirits, and I hope the day will soon dawn when I shall be set at large altogether. I wish you to go to Sheffield, and informed Mr. Harney that I have got removed to this gaol by the present Secretary of State, upon the surgeon's certificate of my ill-health,

I am, my dear wife, yours is very affectionately,
Samuel Holberry."

Poor fellow! these anticipations of a brighter future with fated never to be realised. The state of his health on removal to York is thus described in the report of the surgeon, printed in the copy of correspondence between the Home Secretary and the Authorities of York Castle.

"York Castle, 20th of September, 1841.
"Samuel Holberry, a prisoner brought to York Castle, on the 22nd instant, is suffering from the effects of a bilious attack: He is weak; his skin and eyes are still suffused with bile; his pulse is quick and his appetite bad. I offered to place him in the hospital, which he declined, stating he was very comfortable, and could more easily take exercise where he was. His diet is altered to suit his appetite, and I have every reason to hope his health will gradually improve.
(Signed) George Champney.

Surgeon to the York Castle."

We have no further report from the surgeon, until the 22nd of April, 1842, when the surgeon states he has placed him in the hospital; but the letters to his friends testify to the steady progress of his disease.

In a letter addressed to Mr Burley, of York, dated the 10th February, he states that he is suffering from swelling in his legs, which prevented him walking, and taking exercise, and is otherwise very unwell. We give the following extract.

"I am of the opinion that a staunch adherence to principle has closed all the avenues of mercy against me; but my friend, the same love of Liberty which first taught me to detest tyrants and tyranny, will still (as it has done) support me under privations, and all the miseries which the law has prepared for felons, or what perhaps is still worse in the eyes of the Aristocracy, Convicted Chartists: but I must not give in to my feelings, or this will not pass the Castle Toll Bar."

In a letter dated the 17th of March he complains of suffering under an attack of Influenza, and painfully predicts that is the result of this treatment will be death. In another, of the 17th April, he states he is ill – very ill – and scarcely able to hold a pen; he had lost the little strength that he had gained on first leaving Northallerton. On the 21st of the same month, he writes that he is worse – suffering severe pains in his limbs – his stomach shockingly disordered, and all appetite for food of any kind gone from him. Petitioning in his behalf was renewed by his friends, but without success: the two self-professing *liberal* and *humane* Sheffield Members, Ward and Parker, were appealed to, to use their influence to procure his release, but *both* refused! It was principally in allusion to this application to the local Members, that the letter from which we give the following extracts, has written to Mr Harney.

"York Castle, 24th of April, 1842.

My Dear Sir

I this morning received your welcome letter. I am not at all surprised at Mr Ward's conduct – it's just like him: but why did not they hang or transport me, if they thought I deserved it? They would then have to put an end to my sufferings at once; instead of which they have destroyed by constitution until I am in such a state of bodily debility that I can hardly crawl, and, dear friend you may rest assured that I shall never serve *Two years more in prison. No! Be happy for half of that time is expired, I shall be in my grave*. Perhaps that may give Messrs Ward and Co, great pleasure; they may then think I have satisfied the demands of the Law. Believe me, sir, I would rather leave this place a corpse, than stay here until I am removed only to be a burden to my friends. I have not the least fear of death, and never felt more calm in my life. It is with difficulty I have written this, the pain in my side is so distressing.

I am yours truly
Samuel Holberry.

In a letter addressed to Mrs Holberry dated the 17th May, he intimates he is getting worse, and adds "I believe it would give satisfaction to certain parties to hear I had 'gone the way of all flesh.' Well, the certainty of such an event would trouble me less than my enemies imagine; but, my dear I think of you, and the thought distracts me; but I will not say more, for fear I should hurt your feelings."

About his time memorials in behalf of the sufferer were forwarded to the Home Office, from Sheffield, Barnsley, York, Brighton and other places; to all which applications the like answer was returned by Sir James Graham, who coolly stated that there was no sufficient grounds to justify him, consistently with his public (?) duty in advising the Queen to comply with the prayer of the memorials. The sufferings of a dying man were no "sufficient grounds" in the eyes of Sir James Graham to warrant him performing an act of mercy! But we will not – nay, scarcely dare – venture any comment upon this conduct of "Secretary, Sir James Graham." Certain are we, however, none will envy his power to inflict suffering, and death – aye death – who call to mind the promise of that Eternal, whose worked never fails; and who has declared that He will not have mercy on those who deny that mercy to others.

Another course was now adopted; a petition was drawn up by Mr. Harney, in which the state of poor Holberry was forcibly depicted, and his speedy death affirmed to be certain, unless immediately released. This petition was intended to have been signed by the magistrates, clergy, and other influential persons resident in Sheffield, and it was hoped would succeed where other measures had failed. The Rev. Thomas Sutton, Vicar of Sheffield, and several others, readily affixed their signatures, but the magistrates delayed under one pretence or other, until the influence could be of no avail; the petition was never presented, Holberry's released being ordered by the Home Secretary without it, but too late to save him from a dungeon death.

It is in allusion to the above petition that the following extract from a letter to Mr. Harney, the last received by him, refer.

"York Castle, May 24, 1842

My Dear Harney

I received yours of the 22nd, and am sorry to inform you that I get worse every day; I cannot digest sufficient food to support my body, and all the medicine I have taken has not in the least benefitted me; my side is very bad, and all the blisterings, &c, seem to do me no good. I hope you will look after my petition, and get as many signatures as possible, and I hope it will have effect. I return my sincere thanks for your kindness, and hope your endeavours will be crowned with success.

Your affectionate friend
Samuel Holberry.
P.S. My reason for not writing before is, I did not feel able.

*

"The simmer e'enin's setting sun
Into my dungeon throws
Ae single ray, a holy flower
That, 'mid the darkness, grows:
O' freedom's happiness;
And thought the joy I cannot taste,
I love it not the less

It whispers what the free enjoy

On mountain and in glen,
Things holy, fresh, and beautiful,
That I maun never ken,
O! stay awhile, thou simmer ray,
Nor leave me thus alane;
O! dim and dimmer, now it grows;
An' now the light is gane!"
Robert Nichol

The hapless victim of that fatal disease, consumption, is generally unconscious of the seeds of death sown in his breast. A dreadful – dreadful to those who watch by the stricken one's bedside, and know the import of the sign – calm, presages of the coming wreck of life. The patient is no longer tormented by nervous irritability, and gloomy thoughts which marked the incipient stages of his malady. The chill hand of the destroyer is upon him, but a delusive hope buoys up the patient; previous suffering has left him worn and exhausted, but he fancies that all will yet go well with him. Alas! the departure of pain is but the harbinger of approaching death. Such evidently were the feelings, and such the hopes – fated never to be realised – of poor Holberry when he penned the following letter, the last addressed by him to that wife whom he loved so greatly, and whose heart was all his own:

York Castle, May 27, 1842

My Dear Mary,
I received your kind letter and Mr Burley[1] brought me some oranges. I feel rather easier this morning, but you may depend I am a poor object. My dear, you see you should like to come to York to see me; to that I cannot give my consent. In the first place we should have to look through the odious bars,[2] and it would only make you more unhappy, to say nothing of myself; besides I have no complaint on me at present that is likely to terminate my existence; that my illness should bring me into consumption is all I am afraid of, but I believe they will not let me die here, accepted by a sudden visitation. Keep up your spirits, remember you have the satisfaction of knowing you have done your duty.

That God may bless you, and restore me to your arms is this sincere prayer of your devoted husband. Samuel Holberry"

1 Mr Burley, of York, a true-hearted Chartist, who was a constant and unwearied friend of Holberry during the his incarceration in the Castle. Several letters received by Mr Burley were read at the inquest, and published in the Northern Star; but as their contents are similar to those from which we have given extracts, they are omitted here.
2 This refers to an interview, the only one during his act incarceration, which Mrs. Holberry had

Poor fellow, in less than one month from the time he wrote the above, he was a cold – cold corpse!

Early in June, the following certificate, from the Surgeon at York Castle, was forwarded to the Home Office:

"Samuel Holberry, the Chartist prisoner, in York Castle is suffering from its severe pain in the left side, the effect of chronic inflammation of the left lobe of the liver, extending to the stomach and perhaps the colon, which, from his having had former attacks, I believe to be organic disease. His digestion is very bad, and he is very weak; and I consider him to be in great danger. I am of the opinion that his symptoms have increased, and his health has been impaired of late by the length of confinement, and the great anxiety of mind he appears to have suffered since his imprisonment.

(Signed) George Champney

June 7, 1842 Surgeon to the York Castle.

This is backed by the recommendation of the York Magistrates, procured a communication from the Home Secretary, stating that he at length, "felt warranted in advising her Majesty to grant the prisoner a pardon, on condition of his entering into recognizance, himself in £200, with two sureties in £100 each for his good behaviour for five years." This order was dated the 17th of June. What was this but an affectation of the mercy – a cold-blooded insult offered to perishing poverty? Does it not seem as if "Secretary Sir James Graham" reasoned with himself somewhat after this fashion – "I cannot endure to be longer pestered by these repeated applications – nor will I relax my grasp on this Chartist traitor; I will, therefore, extend 'her most gracious Majesty's' 'most gracious pardon' to him, but clogged with such conditions as I know he cannot perform. If these feelings did not influence "Secretary Sir James Graham" to annex such monstrous – such cruel conditions to the 'royal act of clemency,' then must he have been – but this is scarcely probable – *criminally ignorant* of Holberry's actual position in society. But whichever supposition we adopt, it is yet certain that the Home Secretary's conduct in this matter, was such as to render his name execrable

The two sureties in £100 each were sufficient obstacles to render

sometime previous, with her husband, when they were separated by the iron bars, and only permitted to converse with each other in the presence, and of course, within the hearing of a turnkey. About a month before his death, Mrs. H. applied to the Sheffield magistrates for an order to see her husband without being compelled to look through the bars of his den, but even this poor boon, was refused, though it was well known he was dying!

Holberry's immediate release possible. None of his Chartist friends in Sheffield were of sufficient *respectability* to be taken as sureties, and other persons were not willing to run the risk of being bound for the lengthy period of five years. Alas, poor Holberry! he had not five days to live, when the order in question was dispatched from the Home Office. His wife was anxiously employed seeking the required sureties, when this victim of "man's humanity to man," breathed his last, at the hour of half-past four on the morning of the 21st June 1842. The report of the surgeon is as follows:

"York Castle, June 21, 1842.

"Samuel Holberry died this morning at half-past four, of chronic inflammation of the liver, which implicated some of the other abdominal viscera.

(Signed) William Anderson.
Deputy surgeon to York Castle.

***

The official announcement of the termination of Holberry's existence reached Sheffield on the morning of the 22nd; but as "evil news ever travels quickest," the mournful intelligence was made known to his friends the previous evening. The Chartists of Sheffield were that evening assembled in their well-known Hall in Fig Tree Lane, to hear a lecture from Mr. Bairstow, whose address was suddenly interrupted by the melancholy intimation that tyranny had added another name to its long list of victims – "Holberry was dead." We cannot describe, as the scene deserves, the effect which this announcement produced upon the densely crowded audience. For awhile all held down their heads – an expressive silence prevailed – then tears gushed forth from the eyes of "old men and young" and females sobbed aloud, but sympathy for the *destroyed* speedily gave place to indignation against his *destroyers*; and "curses both loud and deep" were uttered by all present.

But the widow, how can we depict her misery when informed that she had no longer a husband? Aye, *that* indeed is not to be portrayed. He must be "something *less* than a man" who having witnessed that scene can even at this distance of time, recall to mind, and coolly sit down to write even a sketch of it. We are not composed of such stern, say rather brutal, material, and cannot therefore, add more than that Mary Holberry, like Rachel mourning for her children, refused to be comforted.

The personal and political friends of Holberry immediately resolved upon still further evincing their sympathy for his fate by a public funeral and by appealing to the country on behalf of the widow; the former was nobly carried out; the latter has not yet realised such an amount of pecuniary aid for Mrs. Holberry, as was originally anticipated. This, no doubt, is to be ascribed to the great sacrifices required of the Chartist body, in their legal contest with the Government, consequent upon the recent prosecutions.

An inquest was held on the body, and a middle class jury returned their matter of course verdict, of "died by the visitation of God;" thus exonerating the authorities of York Castle from censure, notwithstanding it was admitted in evidence, that no report of the deceased's state of health had been made, between the 22nd of April and the 7th of June; although the same witness (the deputy surgeon) further acknowledged that as far back as April, Holberry's condition was such, as to render it extremely doubtful whether, even if he had been released in April, his existence would have been preserved! And yet, two months after the period in question, we find Sir James Graham, in the very mockery of humanity, requiring the expiring man to find sureties to keep the peace for *five years* – was not Holberry murdered?

We extract from the Northern Star of July 2nd, 1842, the following graphic account of the funeral:

"From the moment that the death of poor Holberry became known, the Fig Tree Lane Council determined upon bringing the body of the deceased to Sheffield and giving it a public funeral in testimony of the high esteem in which the deceased patriot was held by his brother Chartists of this this town. Mr Samuel Ludlam, a veteran in the cause and a personal friend of Holberry's was delegated on the Tuesday night to proceed to York to demand that the body. The following morning, Wednesday, Mr Ludlam and departed on his melancholy mission, and returned to Sheffield at midday on Thursday, with the body, in the company of Mr Robert Demaine, and Mr Peter McLaughlen of York, whose zealous services cannot be too much admired and applauded. The body was lodged at the house of Mrs Holberry's parents at Attercliffe, with whom she resided.

On Friday, green placards, edged with black, were posted through the town announcing the funeral, as follows:

"Funeral procession of Samuel Holberry, the Martyr to Liberty – "Peace to his Soul!" – The friends of freedom will assemble on Monday, June 27th, 1842, in Paradise Square at one o'clock, for the purpose of forming into procession, with band, banners, &c; and from thence will march to Attercliffe, to meet the body of the departed Samuel Holberry, previous to its internment in the Cemetery. Marshals are appointed to form the procession and direct the route – it is particularly requested that all parties attending the funeral will abstain from intoxicating drink, observing our Motto of "Peace, Law and Order," and all will observe that strict decorum which the solemnity of the occasion demands. Mr G.J. Harney and Mr S. Parkes, will deliver appropriate addresses after the burial service."

Monday, June 27th, a day that will long be remembered in Sheffield came, and, the sun rose bright and glorious to smile upon the efforts of the people to do honour to the remains of their martyred friend. A large placard, printed at Birmingham, was placed outside Mr Harney's residence in Hartshead, and attracted the attention of many hundreds in the course of the morning. Certain jackals from the Police Office had made themselves busy in copying the placards, notices, &c, in front of Mr Harney's house, (whether they were officially employed we cannot say) and in the course of the morning Mr Rayner, the superintendent of the Sheffield police, called upon Mr Harney, and requested that he would withdraw the above placard. Mr H. politely declined doing so, at the same time telling Mr Rayner that he had nothing to fear, if the peace of the town was left to the keeping of the Chartists, and that they were not interfered with. By twelve o'clock some hundreds of persons had assembled in Paradise Square; the numbers speedily augmented to thousands. About one o'clock the people in dense mass left the square and proceeded to Attercliffe. The body was enclosed in a splendid oak coffin, handsomely decorated, made at York under the direction of the Chartist body. The following was the inscription from upon the breast-plate:

"SAMUEL HOLBERRY
Died a martyr to the cause of Democracy,
June 21st, 1842,
Aged 27"

All the mournful preparations having been completed, the procession started in the following order:
The band, playing the solemn air of Pleyel's German Hymn
Two undertakers,
Two mutes.
The hearse, beautifully decorated, containing the body of the deceased patriotism.
Large and magnificent black banner of the National Charter Association (Fig Tree Lane) with the following inscription:
"Vengeance is mine, and I will repay it, saith the Lord"
Clayton and Holberry, the Martyrs to the People's Charter.

On the reverse side:
"Thou shalt do no murder"
Two mourning coaches, containing the female relatives of the deceased
An open carriage containing several female mourners.
The male relatives of the deceased on foot
Members of the Council of the National Charter Association (Fig Tree Lane)
Members of the Association
Females, two deep – Men four deep.
Members of the political Institute, two deep, bearing a white banner, with the following inscriptions:
"Political Institute.
Birks – Clayton – and Holberry, Martyrs to the Charter"
On the reverse:
"The Lord hateth the hands that shed innocent blood"

The procession commenced its solemn march about half-past two o'clock; of course it was not confined to the members of the Association, as some thousands accompanied it on either side. On reaching the town, the road, along the Wicker, from the Railway Station to the Bridge, was densely crowded, and immense numbers continued to swell the mass, as it moved on. The pavement on the side of the road, the doorways, the windows, and, in some instances, the roofs of the houses were crowded with anxious gazers – even some of the chambers appeared to be literally crammed with human beings; and in every nook and corner, where a view could be claimed, there were men and women watching with seemingly intense interest the melancholy sight. We observed many, very many, females, unable to control themselves, giving vent to their feelings in tears. The procession having passed through the Wicker, proceeded up Waingate, the Haymarket, High Street, Far Gate, Barker Pool, down Coalpit Lane to Sheffield Moor. Leaving the ranks for a moment, the writer had a view of the procession from Mr. Barraclough's chambers in Far Gate; the site was truly splendid; but it was on Sheffield Moor that the mighty multitude showed to the best advantage. By the time the procession had reached this quarter, many thousands of persons were in advance of the band, and whilst the vanguard (so to speak) of the procession had reached the bottom of the Moor, the rear had not yet left at the top of Coalpit Lane. We will not ourselves pretend to estimate the numbers. The *Sheffield Iris*, a Whig paper, and no friend to the Chartists, says 20,000; when a Whig paper says 20,000, some idea may be formed of the real number. Several persons, not Chartists, have told us they estimated the number at 50,000. Suffice it to say that no previous assemblage in Sheffield within the memory of living man, has at all approached in numbers that of June the 27th. Is Chartism dead? We may observe that along the line of the march the shops were closed. We are sorry we cannot give the middle-class credit for intending any respect thereby. From Sheffield Moor the procession proceeded along the New Road to the Cemetery, the fields on each side being lined with spectators. On coming within view of the Cemetery some hundreds of persons were seen already within the gates, who had obtained admission to the ground by a private road. As soon as the gates were opened a rush, fearful, but fortunately only momentary took place. There was nothing like tumult or disorder, the rush that was made being occasioned by the intense and natural desire to get as near to the grave as possible. The band remained at the gates; the hearse, cultures and people following, *en masse*, up the gravel walk to the chapel. The coffin having been removed from the hearse and taken within the chapel, where were admitted the mourners and a few select friends, the burial service was read by the Reverend Mr. Landells, Independent Minister of Lee Croft Chapel. The coffin was then removed, and having been lowered into the grave, scarcely a dry eye viewing the sad spectacle, the Rev. Gentleman offered up a solemn and impressive prayer, and having done so immediately retired.

The following hymn composed for the occasion by John Henry Bramwich of Leicester, was then given out by Mr Samuel Parkes, and sung to the air of the Old Hundredth Psalm:

"Great God! is this the Patriot's doom?
Shall they who dare defend the slave,
Be hurl'd within a prison's gloom.
To fit them for an early grave?

Shall victim after victim fall,
A prey to cruel class-made laws?
Forbid it, Lord, on Thee we call,
Protect us and defend our cause.

In vain we prayed the powers that be
To burst the drooping captive's chain.
But mercy, Lord, belongs to Thee,
For thou hast freed him from all pain.

> Is this the price of Liberty?
> Must Martyrs fall to gain the prize?
> Then be it so! We will be free,
> Or all become a sacrifice!
>
> Tho' Freedom mourns her murder'd son,
> And weeping friends surround his bier;
> Tho' tears like mountain torrents run,
> Our cause is water'd by each tear
>
> O! may his fate cement the bond
> That binds us to our glorious cause!
> Raise! raise the cry! let all respond;
> "Justice, and pure and equal laws".

Mr Julian Harney, standing on the edge of the grave then addressed the assembled people in nearly the following words:

Sisters and brethren – We have gathered together upon this mournful occasion to pay a last tribute of respect to a departed brother; one of the martyred victims of despotism; one endeared to us alike by his public virtues and private worth; one who was emphatically "an honest man – the noblest work of God." You within the compass of my voice, but few compared with the many thousands of whom you are a portion – you who knew him as a public man can bear witness to his sterling honesty, his unbounded integrity, his thorough incorruptibility, and dauntless courage. His afflicted partner – his sorrowing relatives – those who knew him as a neighbour, or a townsman; all who had the happiness to enjoy his friendship can testify to his moral greatness; and that presence and tears this day are evidences of his virtues, and that veneration for the possessor of them. Yet we have assembled here today to mourn over the grave of one so good, so brave, so noble of heart and soul. Why, O why is this? What was his crime? What his offence? – for which he has been sent to the cold grave? He saw his country enslaved, her sons in bondage, her daughters in misery – he heard the cry of distress, the wail of agony which rang through the land; and his heart was moved with pity for his fellow creatures, and beat high with stern resolve to break his country's fetters. Oppression hovered over England, and freedom had fled her shores; but –

> "She has sons that never! never!
> Whilst heaven has light or earth has graves,
> Will stoop to be the despots' slaves!"

and of these was the heroic patriot over whose inanimate remains we now mourn. Brave himself, he believed in the courage of all who applauded his generous sentiments; and in the hour of trial, left unsupported, he fell. Possessing a heart without guile, he believed in the truth of all men; and confided in miscreants who betrayed him into the hands of the enemies of his country. What language can be too strong in which to denounce their the incarnate fiends – the Iscariot traitors – to whom I allude? Those "catacombs of living death" – to speak of them in the language of Curran – "where the wretch that is buried a man, lies till his heart has time to fester and dissolve, and is dug up an informer!" O! for gold uncounted, for power unlimited, for the wealth of Croesus, or the sceptre of the Caesars, I would not have that man's blood upon my head. But why dwell upon the crimes of the rotten-hearted villains that for the sake of filthy lucre would betray the cause of freedom? They were but the despicable tools of their day's employers – the oppressors that have pursued him to his grave. If nothing short of his blood would satisfy them, why the mockery of sentencing the him to imprisonment? Four years of torture, two of which have been sufficient to consummate the horrid tragedy! O! possessed I the power to give utterance to the thoughts swelling within my breast; could I launch the thunders of eloquence against the heads of the destroyers of Holberry, I would rouse ye to be men of more than common mould; my words should make

"The very stones
To rise against the earth's tyrants,"

and the cry of "Holberry and justice," ringing through the land, should strike the death-knell of tyranny, and proclaim to the world the overthrow of despotism and oppression!

***

Our task is not to weep! We must leave tears to women. Our task is to act; to labour with heart and soul for the destruction of the horrible system under which Holberry has perished. His sufferings are over! He is where "the wicked cease from troubling and the weary are at rest." He sleeps well! He is numbered with the patriots who have died martyrs to the cause of liberty before him. His is the bloodless laurel awarded him by a grateful and admiring people! How different to the wreath which encircles the brow of the princely murderer and the conquering destroyer! Compared with the honest, virtuous fame of this son of toil, how poor, how contemptible appear the so-called glories that emblazon the name of an Alexander or Napoleon! Desolated empires, or slaughtered myriads have preserved their names from oblivion, but will not in a future and a better age save them from execration; whilst with the Tells and Tylers of the earth, the name of Holberry will be associated, venerated and adored:

> "Far dearer the grave for the prison,
> Illumed by one patriot's name,
> Than the trophies of all who have risen
> On liberty's ruins to fame."

Be ours the task to accomplish, by one glorious effort, the freedom of our country, and thereby prevent, for the future, the sacrifice of the sons of freedom. Tyrants have in all ages and all countries strove by persecution to crush liberty; and by torture, chains, and death, to prevent the assertion of the rights of man. It would appear that our haughty rulers are bent upon following the same course, and seeking by the same means to arrest the progress of democracy. We bid them defiance! we tell these puny Canutes that, despite their bidding, the ocean of intellect will move on! Here by the graveside of the patriot; here under the bright blue canopy of the skies, let us enter into a "solemn league and covenant" – let the honest and true embrace in fraternity, and swear with me – swear by the imperishable truth of our principles – by the dead relics of our murdered brother – swear, "whilst the spirit of Holberry hovers over us, and smiles approval of the vow" – swear, to unite in one countless moral phalanx, to put forth the giant strength which union will call into being, and aid, assist, and fraternise with each other to burst the bonds which bind ye. Swear, as I now swear that neither persecution, nor scorn, nor calumny – neither bolts, nor bars nor chains, nor racks, nor gibbets – neither the tortures of a prison death-bed, not the terrors of the scaffold, shall sever us from our principles, frighten us from our duty, or cause us to leave the onward path of freedom; but that, come weal, come woe, we swear, with hearts uplifted to the throne of eternal justice, to have retribution for the death of Holberry! swear to our to have our charter law! and to annihilate for ever the blood-stained despotism which has slain its thousands of martyrs and tens of thousands of patriots and immolated at its shrine the lovers of liberty and truth! If ye do this and act upon your vow, while we mourn the death of Holberry, our children will rejoice that he died not in vain! but that from his ashes rose, phoenix-like, his dauntless spirit, inspiring you with the love of freedom! and the stern resolve to set your country free!

The deepest silence prevailed during Mr Harney's address, interrupted only by the occasional half-suppressed responses of his hearers.

Mr Samuel Parkes followed – Friends and fellow countrymen. The circumstances that have called us together are the most solemn, important, and affecting that can possibly be contemplated. We are called upon to do honour, not to one who was seated on a throne of grandeur, swaying the sceptre of royalty over empires – nor to one who inhabited the gorgeous palace, or costly mansion – nor to one who sought to lay up gold as the dust, or silver as the balance – nor to one who wished to raise a splendid monument whereby to perpetuate his fame; but to one who, deeply imbued with the feelings of humanity, deeply sympathising with those suffering around him, was ready to use any and every means for the purpose of lessening their sorrows and mitigating their woes. Thence it was that he became an easy prey to those vile tools, men of his own order, who were employed by the powers that be, to entrap unsuspecting into the meshes of the law; thereby hoping to defeat, by such means, the glorious end which Holberry had in view, the freedom of his countrymen from that political bondage in which, for ages, they had been held. Let no one dare to insult his dead ashes now that they are laid in the silent tomb. Many have been the base calumnies that have been cast upon his character by his enemies. Some have branded him with the name of traitor, assassin, and spoliator; as one who desired to enrich himself at the expense of others; but ah! my friends, such motives as those did not exist in the breast of the departed martyr. Ah! no; rather let him refer back to the causes which were in existence, which led him to adopt the means he did for the overthrow of class-legislation, and the annihilation of bad laws, and to which he was incited by the hireling spies of a corrupt Government. My friends, I have stated already that the circumstances which have called us together are of the most solemn, painful, and impressive character. Remember that we now stand upon the tombs of the departed of all ages. Look at the vast assemblage that have congregated and followed, in mournful procession, to this consecrated spot; and then contemplate that, at a day not far distant, worlds upon world shall be congregated together, not by the mere sound of music, but the blast of the archangel's trumpet shall sound through the caverns of the dead "arise ye and come to judgement!" See the graves opening, tombs shivering, the earth quaking, and the rocks rending, mountains falling, planet after planet, comet after comet, constellation after constellation, the sun turned into darkness, and the moon into blood, and the whole universe kindled into one grand conflagration. Then shall later nature utter her final groan; after which shall be seen erected in the high heavens above, the great white throne – white, indicative of its purity, upon which shall be seated the great judge of all the earth, around whom shall be gathered the oppressed and the oppressor, the monarch and the subject, the tyrant and the slave, who shall each receive, without partiality, according to his works. Then we trust to meet our departed friend enshrined in an immortal and glorified body in the climes of bliss; where the chains of slavery never clanks, the tear of sorrow never falls, and the sigh of distresses is never heard. I call upon you by all that is great, and wise, and good, to prepare for that solemn and important event: and while you are so doing forget not to the great and glorious struggle in which you are engaged, and for which Holberry has suffered a martyr's fate. Rally round the standard of your Charter, and for the sake of a Shell, a Frost, a Clayton and a Holberry; for the sake of a widowed wives and fatherless children of those departed patriots; for the sake of all that are now suffering; and for the sake of posterity yet unborn, rest not, day nor night, until by every legal and constitutional means you have made the charter the law of the land, and hereby proclaimed the physical, moral, and political freedom of the universal family of man!

The parties then left the grave, and the mass of people forming the procession left the Cemetery, returning to the town by the same line of route taken in coming to the ground. The mourners returned to Attercliffe; the people to Paradise Square, where they almost immediately separated, returning quietly to their homes.

It was ten minutes to seven when the people reached the square, the proceedings having thus occupied close upon seven hours.

Holberry left no children; Mrs. Holberry gave birth to a male child shortly after her husband's trial, but it died when only a few weeks old. Murdered beyond doubt by the suffering to which the mother had been subjected; the destroyer of the father slew the child.

In person Holberry was a fine looking man; in height he measured six feet one or two inches, rather slender, but walked very erect, large eyes of greyish cast, jet black hair, ruddy complexion, and handsome features. Such is the portrait, though a very imperfect one, of this ill-fated patriot. In other days, he might have played the hero's part, and won on the red field of fight, a name which would have descended to posterity by the side of a Tell all and a Hoffer. He was undoubtedly a courageous and fearless man, one whose hand would have done what his tongue threatened. When asked by his captors whether he had really meant to take up arms to accomplish his ends – "Yes, I'd fight for the Charter, and die for the Charter," was his answer. His demeanour on examination before the Sheffield magistrates was brave and unflinching; his accusers and judges cowered under his scorching gaze, and quailed before his rude, yet eloquent, denunciation of their oppression. His letters testify to his unshaken adherence to his principles even when labouring under most acute sufferings, and surrounded by all the horrors of his prison deathbed. It is known that had he made a certain promises to the authorities, which they wish to extort from him – he would have been liberated nearly twelve months before the period that he died. But no persuasions could induce him to comply with their conditions; he therefore, remained in his dungeon, and died the martyr's death.

The writer of this sketch had no personal knowledge of the subject thereof – knew him only by name – and only from Mrs Holberry has any particulars of his life. Having never before attempted a similar task, the writer hopes that his "first attempt" will be leniently dealt with; he seeks neither profit more applause, but has his reward in the consciousness that he has performed a duty (however imperfectly) which the Chartist party had a right to expect to see performed, and which was due to the virtues and patriotism of the deceased. May the people never forget the name and fate of Holberry, and may the recollection of these, inspire them with courage and determination to burst the fetters that bind them, and make the CHARTER for which Holberry died, the law and constitution of their native land.

Sheffield from the East

Acknowledgments

Thanks to the staff, especially Rob, at Sheffield City Archives and Local Studies Libraries. They are ever-helpful and the work they do in the cultural life of the city is invaluable.

Also to the staff at York Archives, North Yorkshire County Records Office, the Wellcome Collection and the National Archives at Kew.

Thanks also to Clara at Sheffield Museums Trust for her help and for looking after the Holberry bust.

I am grateful to Jane for her (longer than 10 minute!) consultation over a patient from 185 years ago.

Edward Hardiman for being so kind as to read the draft and provide useful and insightful feedback to improve the readability and accuracy of the book – many thanks, Ed.

END NOTES

1. S and N Kay, *How Great a Crime – to Tell the Truth, The story of Joseph and Winifred Gales and the Sheffield Register* 1889 Books, 2017
2. A Aspinall, *The Early English Trade Unions*, Batchworth Press,1949
3. In series of articles in *English Chartist Circular* May–June 1843 vol 2 nos.118–122, there is a section on Holberry's early life. The writer was able to talk people close to Holberry: Mary Holberry and possibly Samuel Ludlam. A transcript is included in the Primary Sources.
4. W. White, *Gazetteer and Directory of Nottinghamshire* (Sheffield, 1832) pp371–2
5. https://www.baptisttimes.co.uk, accessed April 2025
6. Report of Captain Williams, prison inspector, 18 January 1840 in National Archives HO 20/10
7. J.Weiner, *War of the Unstamped* (Itharca, 1965)
8. White op.cit. 371–72
9. *ECC* 118–122 and *WO 25/3849 Register of Men Discharged at their own request by the King's warrant of 14th November, 1829: Infantry – 30th-99th Foot* The former says " his discharge states that he was enlisted at Doncaster" the latter that he was recruited in Liverpool.
10. *United Services Journal* 1832–36 contains quarterly reports of locations of regiments under the heading "Stations of the British Army." *WO 12/4821 Commissary General of Musters office and successors: General Muster Books and Pay Lists. Infantry 33rd Foot*, National Archives
11. G Barnsby, *The Working Class Movement in the Black Country 1750–1867*, pp 27-33 identifies clashes during the general election between supporters of rival candidates and with the local forces of law and order in November–December 1832 in Walsall and Wolverhampton. The Scots Greys and the 33rd Foot were called in to calm the former. See for example *Warwick and Warwickshire Advertiser – Saturday 15 December 1832*.
12. M.J. Haynes, *Class and Class Conflict in the early nineteenth century Northampton Shoemakers and the Grand National Consolidated Trades Union*, Literature and History, vol 5, 1977 pp73–94; J Pigot, Directory of Northamptonshire, 1841
13. *ECC* 118–122
14. *Spectator* 14 November 1835; *London and Westminster Review* vol 25(1836) pp181–223 covers the report of a House of Commons

Select Committee exposing this.
15   *ECC* 118–122
16   *ECC* 118–122
17   *United Services Journal*, March 1835
18   *ECC* 118–122 (The *ECC* piece says the £20 loan was from his parents, the prison inspector notes say "friends")
19   *United Services Journal*, June September editions 1835
20   *ECC* 118–119
21   W. White, *History and Directory of Sheffield*, 1837
22   S. Pollard, *History of Labour in Sheffield*, Liverpool 1959, p 90; J..L. Baxter, *Origins of the Social War in South Yorkshire, a study of capitalist evolution and labour class realisation 1750–1855*, unpublished PhD, Sheffield University 1977 pp425-426 utilises Pollard and adds more data to show hierarchy of wages.
23   *ECC* 118-122
24   *Sheffield Iris* 18 December 1832; J Baxter "Five dead for democracy," *Bulletin of the Holberry Society*, VII, Spring 1983 pp 7–10
25   Baxter, thesis pp 340-349 discusses role of STGU in 1832 election campaign
26   His early role highlighted in J.L.Baxter and F.K.Donnelly, Sheffield and the English Revolutionary tradition 1791–1820, *International Review of Social History*, Vol XX (1975), part 3 pp 405-401
27   Brocco described in detail in R.E. Leader *Reminiscences of Old Sheffield*, Sheffield, 1875, p. 206 "the Brocco consisted of a steep and very rugged bankside. It reached its steepness as far as Edward Street and then extended in a slope and a comparative flat as far as Allen Street. The ground was red earth and stones with a thin covering of grass on the flats." Trade union leadership in 1819 was testified to three decades later see *Sheffield Independent* 11 July 1846 which was a testimonial meeting for retiring trade union leaders.
28   Baxter thesis pp351-366
29   F.K.Donnelly, The Destruction of the Sheffield School of Anatomy, *Transactions of the Hunter Archaeological Society*, vol 10, part 3, 1975 p.p.167–172
30   *Sheffield Iris* 22 December 1835
31   *Sheffield Mercury* 13, 20, 27 August 1836; Baxter thesis 359-60
32   Baxter thesis 359-61
33   *Northern Star*, letter from James Wolstenholme (probably James snr), Dun Fields, identifying his links with Stephens. Public meeting to

support petition against New Poor Law held in May 1837 did not identify him as being on the platform – *Sheffield Mercury* 6 May 1837 and *Iris* 9 May 1837

34   *ECC* 118–122

35   Baxter thesis, Appendix 7:3 lists all Chartists identified in the region many with occupation identified p.p. 678–686

36   *Sheffield Mercury* 1 July 1837

37   *Sheffield Iris* 17 October 1837 and *Sheffield Independent,* 21 October 1837. Henry Hetherington and Feargus O'Connor were at the first meeting which amazingly (in relation to later events) was in the town hall

38   *ECC* only mentions Upper Thames Street. The Hour Glass brewery was only brewery located there. Another possibility is the firm of Holme, Wilson Sewell & Co Distillers of 28 Upper Thames St.

39   Captain Williams report NRA HO 20/10

40   A.R. Schoyen, *The Chartist Challenge*, London 1958, chapter 2 "The New Jacobins" pp 28–41 covers London from Harney's point of view; J. Bennett, *The London Democratic Association, 1837–41*, in D. Thompson and J. Epstein (eds), *The Chartist Experience: Studies in Working Class Radicalism and Culture 1830–60*, MacMillan 1982

41   *ECC* 118–122

42   *A Report on the Sanitary Condition of the Borough of Sheffield*, James Haywood & William Lee, John Bridgford, Iris Office, 1848

43   Baxter thesis 440–46

44   Baxter thesis 442 the first home was in George Street

45   *Sheffield Independent* 29 September 1838; *Northern Star* 29 September 1838; *Sheffield Iris* 25 September 1839

46   Most accessible account of this "popular phase" slightly expanded from thesis version is in J. Baxter, *Early Chartism and Labour Class struggle: South Yorkshire 1837–40* in S.Pollard and C Holmes, *Essays in the Economic and Social History of South Yorkshire*, South Yorkshire County Council, 1976 pp 135–158

47   *Sheffield Iris*, 26 February 1839 for an example of report on rent collection

48   *Sheffield Independent* 25 May 1839; *Northern Star* 25 May 1839; *Sheffield Mercury* 25 may 1839

49   James Wolstenholme (probably snr) letter as secretary of Stephens Defence Fund published in *NS* 27 April 1839; *Sheffield Independent* 25 May 1839; Bedchamber incident explained concisely in R Brown,

Church and State in Modern Britain 1700–1850, Routledge, 2002 pp 240–241; D Thompson, *The Early Chartists*, MacMillan, 1971 chronology on pp 39–40 captures the flow of national events.

50 *Sheffield Iris* 2 July 1839; *Northern Star* 29 June and 6 July 1839; *Sheffield Mercury* 31 June 1839; *Sheffield Independent* 29 June and 6 July 1839

51 Thompson, op cit p. 40; *Northern Star* 15, 22, 29 June, 6 and 13 July 1839

52 *Sheffield Iris* 16, 23 July 1839; *Northern Star* 20 July 1839

53 *Sheffield Iris* 23 and 30 July 1839; *Sheffield Mercury* 20 and 27 July 1839; *Sheffield Independent* 20 and 27 July 1839

54 *Sheffield Independent* 20 and 27 July 1839: *Northern Star* 20 and 27 July 1839

55 *Sheffield Independent* 27 July 1839; *Northern Star* 20 and 27 July 1839

56 *Sheffield Independent* 27 July 1839; various correspondence between town magistrates to Home Office in this period include J Parker and C Brownell to Lord John Russell 26 July 1839, H.B. Cooke to Russell 27 July 1839, J Thornelly to Major General Napier 20 July 1839, in HO 40/51 in National Archives

57 *Sheffield Independent* 27 July 1839

58 *Sheffield Independent* 27 July 1839

59 *Sheffield Iris* 30 July and 6 and 13 August 1839; *Sheffield Mercury* 27 July and 3 and 10 August 1839; *Northern Star* 27 July and 3 and 10 August 1839; *Leeds Times* 27 July and 3 and 10 August 1839

60 *Sheffield Iris* 20 August 1839; *Sheffield Mercury* 17 August 1839; *Northern Star* 17 August 1839. The memorial to the Queen with its demand for Ireland's freedom came from the North East's Northern Political Union, published in the *Northern Liberator*

61 Sheffield Iris 20 August 1839; Sheffield Mercury 17 August 1839 Sheffield Independent 17 August 1839

62 Blackwell's career documented in F.K. Donnelly and J.L. Baxter, *Sheffield and the English Revolutionary tradition* art. cit; Blackwell's death noted in *Sheffield Mercury* 20 April 1839 and this references the Spenceans.

63 *Sheffield Iris* 20 and 27 August 1839; *Sheffield Mercury* 17 and 24 August 1839; *Sheffield Independent* 17 and 24 August 1839 commented on numbers of youth and women. A brother of one of the 1832 victims was arrested.

64 Statement of Samuel Powell Thompson in TS11/816/2688 refers to seeing Holberry at the third churchgoing and to him becoming a

65 *Northern Star* 23 July 1839, cited in E Yeo, *Christianity and Chartist Struggle 1838–42*, Past and Present, vol 91,1981 pp123–24
66 *Northern Star* 17 August 1839, *Sheffield Independent* 17 August 1839, Yeo art. cit. 129–30
67 *Sheffield Independent* 24 and 31 August 1839, *Northern Star* 25 August 1839 reference to "three rostrums outside in the graveyard"
68 *Sheffield Independent* 14 September 1839; Yeo, art cit pp 133–36
69 *Sheffield Mercury* 7 September 1839; *Sheffield Independent* 7 September 1839; *Sheffield Iris* 10 September 1839. For discussion of the early use of the word "aristocratic" see J. L.Baxter *Bulletin of Society of Labour History*, Spring 1980 pp13–16
70 *Northern Star* 14 September 1839 letter of George Chatterton, nailmaker and briefly secretary of SWMA
71 Ivor Wilks, *South Wales and the Rising of 1839*, Croom Helm, London 1984, p. 98 cites Vincent's Newport speech on 19 April during a tour of South Wales which led to his prosecution.
72 *Sheffield Iris* 17 September 1839 On Martin's case see Lt Col Marten to General Napier, 13 September 1839, in HO 40/51, National Archives. Martin was sought out for a violent speech delivered in Fig Tree Lane meeting room
73 *Sheffield Mercury* 25 September and 5 October1839; *Sheffield Iris* 1 October 1839
74 *Sheffield Mercury* 25 September and 5 October 1839
75 *Sheffield Mercury* 21 September 1839
76 *Sheffield Mercury* 5 October 1839; *Sheffield Iris* 1st October. In leaving for America he was following in the footsteps of many before him, including the Gales, as well as others around the same time.
77 Report on Holberry by prison Inspector Captain W.J. Williams December 1840, TNA HO 20/10
78 His wife Mary had also become pregnant
79 The elder Booker had been at Waterloo and 1812 siege of Washington. Marshall had been a marine on a warship in the Greek War of Independence in the 1820s.
80 *Sheffield Iris* 27 August and 3 September 1839; *Sheffield Mercury* 28 September and 5 October 1839; *Northern Star* 28 September and 12 October 1839
81 *Sheffield Iris* 22 October 1839. Wat Tyler, revered for leading the 1381 Peasants' Revolt, William Tell, upheld as a symbol of rebellion against

tyranny throughout Europe, Emmett and Fitzgerald for their fight for Irish liberty (1798-1803) and George Washington, deemed a successful warrior in the fight for political freedom (1776-83).

82 *Sheffield Iris* 3 September 1839
83 Birmingham's Brown in Sheffield *Northern Star* 21 December 1839
84 Much biographical detail in prison inspector's interview in December 1840–January 1841 in HO 20/10, and in statements in witness summaries in TS 11 814/2679; also Parker to Normanby 7 December 1839, HO/40/51. Irish born population of Sheffield parish 2.68%, Barnsley 4.9%, in 1851. Multiply x2 or x3 for community size. Sheffield home was the Isle: river from Ladies Bridge. They were shifting to the Crofts, a mile north west but still close to the central districts where Duffy lived.
85 *Sheffield Iris* 12 November 1839; *Northern Star* 16 November 1839
86 Statements in TS 11/813, 11814/2679, 11/816/2688 and correspondence in TNA HO 40/57
87 Samuel Foxhall statement in TS 11/816/2688 details the changing structures
88 Possibly the weapon fired in August: a horse pistol. It features in the description of his arrest on January 11/12th 1840.
89 Samuel Powell Thompson statement in TS/11/816/2688; Baxter, *Early Chartism etc.* op. cit. fn98 pp157–8 has a table of classes leaders and membership totals
90 R.E. Leader, *Reminiscences etc*, Sheffield 1875 pp 278–7 lots of oral history remembrances from older citizens captures detail unavailable elsewhere. Issue of source of money never resolved. Turner was Sheffield treasurer. He had attended delegate meeting in Manchester of the Frost fund. Holberry claimed later he ran off with their funds before the rise.
91 *Sheffield Iris*, 3 December 1839; *Northern Star* 7 and 25 November and 7 December 1839; Holberry interview with Captain Williams December 1840 TNA HO 20/10
92 *Sheffield Iris* 26 November 1839; *Northern Star* 7 December
93 *Sheffield Iris* 26 November and 3 December 1839; *Sheffield Mercury* 30 November 1839; H. Parker to Normanby 7 December 1839, HO 40/51
94 *Northern Liberator* 7 and 21 December 1839; *Northern Star* 7 and 14 December 1839
95 Foxhall and Thompson and others statements in TS/11/813

96   *Northern Star* 14 December 1839. Wells and Foxhall in HO 20/10. Brown was at 'Sky Hill' as he called it for the meeting that elected Boardman to go to Newcastle.

97   *Northern Liberator* 21, 28 December 1839 and 8 January 1840. *The Charter* 29 December 1839, Northern Star 28 December 1839. For reports of Porter's indiscreet language see *Morning Post* 3 January and *Sheffield Mercury* 4 January 1840

98   Holberry and others in accounts in HO 20/10. The table knife hafters were significant among those associated with the rising. Its union secretary, Harvey, was involved in the Chartist leadership in October-November. Old Booker was present at the trades council in 1836 calling for publicity be sent to the local press about the Sheffield trades support for the Staffordshire Potteries strikers, *Sheffield Independent* 17 February 1836

99   Trial accounts, TS 11 depositions and HO 20/10 interviews with prisoners

100   Holberry's movements can be established using Foxhall and Powell's evidence in TS 11/813, TS 11/814/2607 and from Wells statement in December 1840 to prison inspector in HO 20/10. Later reports at trials show how hilariously the delegates at the Wellington were concealing their purpose by saying they were establishing a "co-operative society."

101   Boardman and Holberry's close collaboration was possibly grounded in a common view of Ireland's oppression

102   Law was a trusted envoy from the West Riding Chartist leadership meeting over the years 1838–39 in places like Heckmondwike, Liversedge then Dewsbury. I call them the ' Junta'… John Sanders' brilliant book *Workers of the their own emancipation*, Breviary, 2024, profiles them in great detail.

103   E.g. *Morning Post* 3rd January 1840, report on Chartism in Birmingham; Wells statement to prison inspector in HO20/10; *Northern Star* 4 and 11 January 1840, See also *Robert Lowery: Radical and Chartist*, eds. B.Harrison and P Hollis, Europa Publications 1979, pp.157-160 for Lowery's personal and sceptical testimony.

104   Holberry's itinerary revealed by witnesses at York trial in March 1840

105   HO 20/10 interview of prison inspector

106   HO 20/10 Ashton's interview with prison inspector

107   Various statements in TS 11/816/2688, particularly Foxhall's, the turncoat, statement

108 Holberry statement to prison inspector Capt Williams December 1840, TNA HO 20/10
109 Press accounts of January hearings and March 1840 trials contain much of the detail
110 Hearings and trial and turncoat accounts of Foxhall and Thompson in TS
111 Mail coach stoppages a feature of signalling the 1798 rebellion in Ireland
112 *Yorkshire Gazette* 18 January 1840; *Leeds Times* 18 January 1840; *York Herald* 18 January 1840 among many
113 Turncoats Foxhall and Thompson's accounts, TS11/816/2688
114 Military movements in Sheffield in *Sheffield Independent* 18 January 1840; R.E. Leader, *Reminiscences of Sheffield*
115 *Sheffield Independent* 3 May 1864. Letter from A lover of truth; R.E. Leader, *Reminiscences of Old Sheffield*, 1876, pulled it together twelve years later.
116 Some rather fanciful writing has tried to claim that all the evidence against Holberry was concocted and that he was an innocent moral force man who was set up. This seems rather naive, and a simple application of Occam's razor is needed. It is, however, it is clear that the system of justice was not exactly even-handed.
117 *Leeds Times* 18 January 1840. A typical wide-ranging account of the meeting in Fig Tree Lane and the exposure of the horse pistol.
118 Contained in "Mary Cooper – Her-Story" p. 23, appendix to 1986 second edition of Sheffield's Revolutionary Democrat published by the Holberry Society
119 HO 20/10 interview with Captain Williams
120 Others had this message but were less keen. Saunders was potentially another agent of the local state. The reference to "Moscow" is the burning of Moscow in 1812 to prevent Napoleon's satisfaction as he watched on from the Kremlin.
121 Steel Bank is still marked on maps. It was an upward slope from around Commonside up the slope of modern Springvale Road towards Crookes.
122 TS 11/816/2688 Foxhall's account, deals with group avoiding town centre and heading into the wilds of Crookesmoor and Broomhill
123 Boardman was a survivor: left Sheffield possibly returned to a new backstreet address with wife and children. Unlike others who re-engage with local Chartism in 1841 and 1842, Boardman, plying the

124 trade of shoemaking, went to Hull in 1842 and was sought out by Chartist branch official Roger Pinder. *Northern Star* 26 February 1842 Wells interview with Captain Williams HO 20/10
125 R.E. Leader, *Reminiscences of Sheffield* p. 278 on how Foden ended up in St Louis in the USA
126 Holberry, his wife Mary, Thomas and William Booker, Samuel Foxhall, Samuel Thompson. Others swiftly followed like Duffy and Wells
127 *Northern Star* 18 January 1840
128 See for example p.2 of the *Sheffield Independent* 18 January 1840
129 *The Times* 18 January 1840
130 *Sheffield Independent* 18 January 1840
131 *Leeds Mercury* 18 January 1840
132 *Sheffield Mercury* 18 January 1840
133 *The Times*, 7 January 1840
134 The rising outcome was to split Sheffield Chartists into the moral force Political Institute and O'Connorite branches of the new National Charter Organisation
135 A Peacock, *Bradford Chartism* (Borthwick Papers) provides the best detail on this
136 Holberry interviewed by prison Inspector Captain Williams in late 1840 HO 20/10
137 Reported widely in region's press
138 Bayley to Maule 21 March 1840
139 House of Lords Session Papers 1839–40 Prison Inspectors 6th Report for North and East district pp161–66
140 *ECC* 118–122 and letters published in the *Northern Star* 1841–2
141 J Duggelby, "A Mind of no Mean order," Undertakings (news letter of the friends of Sheffield General Cemetery, 14 December 1999, p2
142 *ECC* 118–122
143 *Northern Star* March 1841
144 Holberry's Letters from the hell Hole in *Northern Star* 3 and 14 July 1841 and 18 September 1841
145 Williams Report in HO 20/10
146 Appended to notes in HO 20/10
147 *Northern Star* 6 February 1841
148 *Northern Star* 30 July, 14 August and 18 September 1841
149 *Northern Star* 25 June 1842 cited in report on inquest after Holberry's death

150 *Northern Star* 25 June 1842 inquest report
151 Regular reports in *Northern Star* from Harney from July 1841
152 *Northern Star* 30 October 1841 Letter HS1/3 Sheffield Archives. This was largely a misunderstanding over some money sent.
153 *Northern Star* 30/101841 letter of William Martin, Brampton 17 Oct 1841 deals with Booker's doubtful claims. Holberry was now being given "patriot" status in the *Northern Star*.
154 Allowed to receive or send one letter in a three week period as reported by martin in his Voice from Hell hole letter published in *Northern Star* 14 August 1841
155 In a folder of Holberry Prison letters in the Holberry Collection in Sheffield Archives
156 Duncombe had a radical Whig background and spoke up for Chartism
157 Martin was released early in 1841. He featured as a key propagandist against the "silent system" and the unsanitary conditions of Holberry and others in Northallerton He spoke at a Bradford rally in March *NS* 20 March 1841
158 See letters HS6 and HS7, Holberry Collection in Sheffield Archives.
159 The pocket is in the hands of the Holberry Society Trust but previously has been displayed in Weston Park Museum.
160 Holberry to Burley 1 April 1842 in Holberry Letters file
161 Holberry to Burley 17 April 1842
162 *Northern Star* 30 July 1842
163 Holberry to Harney 22 April 1842
164 Harney to Holberry 24 April 1842
165 Holberry to Harney 22 April 1842
166 Holberry to Burley 30 April 1842
167 Burley to Holberry 14 May 1842
168 Holberry to Burley 24 May 1842
169 Holberry to Harney 28 May 1842
170 Holberry to Burley 28 May 1842 reply to Burley's of 24th 1842
171 Holberry 25 May cited in original 1978 pamphlet p18
172 Holberry to Mary full harrowing text in 1978 pamphlet p.18
173 Samuel Holberry 1814–42, Holberry Society 1978 p18
174 *Northern Star* 2 July 1842
175 Phillipps at Home Office 17 June 1842 cited in *Northern Star* 2 July
176 *Northern Star* 2 July 1842
177 *Northern Star* 2 July 1842

178. *Northern Star* 2 July 1842
179. *Northern Star* 15 April 1843 p.2 for a description of the assembly room in Fig Tree Lane decorated with the bust at the centre
180. Best study is by Schoyen
181. O'Connor had issued warnings in his paper on both the 4th and 11th January 1840
182. *Northern Star* 16, 23, 30 April, 7, 14, 21 May 1842
183. *Northern Star* 2, 9, 16 and 23 July 1842
184. *Northern Star* 2 and 9 July 1842
185. *Sheffield Iris* 5 July 1842, *Sheffield Independent* 2 and 9 July 1842, *Sheffield Mercury* 2 and 9th
186. *Sheffield Independent* 9 July 1842
187. T Laqueur, The Work of the Dead, 2015 has a chapter on Chartist funerals and profiles Holberry's "bourgeois funeral" but recognises its scale
188. *Northern Star* 9 July 1842
189. Original in Sheffield Local History Library
190. *Sheffield Independent* 9 and 16 July 1842
191. *Northern Star* 9 July 1842
192. MP for Finsbury, with Yorkshire roots. Consistently spoke out for radical causes.
193. *Northern Star* 2 July 1842
194. *Northern Star* 2 July 1842
195. The plug plot or general strike of 1842
196. *Northern Star* 24 July 1842
197. *Northern Star* July–October 1842
198. *Northern Star* 2, 9 July 1842
199. Listed below
200. Duffy was released early from Beverley House of Correction on health grounds 9 February 1842
201. *Northern Star* 9 July 1842
202. Ironically buried in a paupers' grave in Sheffield General Cemetery in contrast to the high profile Holberry grave site
203. Himself an advocate of armed resistance. Indexed in John Baxter's 1984 Our History pamphlet appendix
204. *Northern Star* 11 February 1843
205. *English Chartist Circular* 1843
206. *Northern Star* 23 July 1842

207 They briefly had a majority in late 1840s. A Chartist leadership of council led to the report of Haywood and Lee on sanitary conditions.
208 *Northern Star* 9 July 1842
209 *Northern Star* 9 July 1842
210 *Northern Star* 15 April 1843
211 *Northern Star* 23 July 1843
212 For survey of shifting pattern see Baxter thesis 1977 pp 506–546
213 CSU: the Complete Suffrage Union, a reformist middle class-led organisation.
214 Baxter thesis 1977 p.499 for summary of Harney's role in the town
215 *Northern Star* 10 Feb 1844
216 *Northern Star* 10 February 1844
217 John Baxter, *We'll be masters now – the story of the 1844 Miners' strike in South Yorkshire*, Gainsborough 1986 pp 17–18
218 Survived into 1850s
219 Never had an overall majority but a big influence on local affairs for a decade.
220 *Sheffield Independent* 11 September 1847
221 Baxter thesis pp. 545–555
222 *Sheffield Independent* 17 July 1848, *Sheffield Mercury* 1848, *Northern Star* 17 June 1848; Harney letter in *Northern Star* 27 April 1850
223 The Pearson family, descended from Holberry Pearson, a silversmith who lived in Banner Cross kindly invited me to view the bust and take it away to negotiate the restoration in the mid-1970s
224 Sheffield General cemetery includes this grave in their organised public guided walks
225 *Sheffield Telegraph* February 1864
226 *Sheffield and Rotherham Independent* July–August 1874
227 *Sheffield and Rotherham Independent*, August 1874
228 *Sheffield and Rotherham Independent*, August 1842
229 R.E. Leader, *Reminiscences of Old Sheffield* 1874
230 Holberry pamphlet 1978 edition section "A worker looks at Samuel Holberry" p. 3
231 Tom Mann had just turned 80 headed that march according to Bill Moore, *Sheffield Independent* 5 April 1937
232 Holberry pamphlet 1978 p.4
233 Our organisation's history has been recently summarised in *Co-operators, and Radical Workers* pp 3–6 Sheffield 2024 published by

Principle 5 Co-operative Resource centre.
[234] The Holberry bust in its original state was featured on the cover
[235] Held at Sheffield's Weston Park Museum
[236] It took a while but ultimately we were grateful for Councillor Enid Hattersley's genuine enthusiasm.
[237] Bill Moore, *History from Below* 2005 captures the man and his contribution to working class history
[238] R.G. Gammage, *History of the Chartist Movement*, 1854, later edition by Merlin Books, 1969
[239] Mark Hovell, *The Chartist Movement*, 1918; Malcolm Chase, *Chartism a New History* 2007 MUP
[240] Local historians have largely done little or no service to Holberry but I would make an exception for David Price's book *Sheffield Troublemakers*. He has returned to Holberry, writing drama: his play was publicly read at Upper Chapel in 2025 on the day of Holberry's cruel death, 21st June and followed an excellent, thoughtful examination of Holberry's trial in an article in the *Hunter Journal*.
[241] *Armed Resistance and Insurrection: the Early Chartist Experience*, John Baxter, Our History, 1984
[242] Chris Searle, radical educationalist and writer, wrote a play for his, then, school in Sheffield on the theme of the Holberrys' life and times. Decades later, after years of academic teaching on several continents he returned to the city to pursue his writing. He was a great friend to Bill Moore and the Holberry Society, and a role model for John Baxter to start writing again in retirement; for five years he lived a few doors away. He adapted the play to a Chartist drama project, linking young people's performance in Sheffield and South Wales schools. The book of the play *Holberrys* was published in 2023 by Culture Matters. He's back in London now where he started a life of making big waves.